Robin Noble is an environmental  spent most of his working life in of Scotland, especially in Assynt, Assynt Community Council for 10 *Mist, The Victorian Transformation c<sub></sub> ... Highlands* (Saraband: 2016) was shortlisted for the Saltire Society History Book of the Year Award

# Under the Radiant Hill

*Life and the Land in the Remotest Highlands*

Robin Noble

BIRLINN

First published in 2023 by
Birlinn Limited
West Newington House
10 Newington Road
Edinburgh
EH9 1QS

*www.birlinn.co.uk*

ISBN: 978 1 78027 826 1

*British Library Cataloguing-in-Publication Data*
A catalogue record for this book is available from the
British Library

Typeset by Initial Typesetting Services, Edinburgh

Papers used by Birlinn are from well-managed forests
and other responsible sources

Printed and bound by Clays Ltd, Elcograf S.p.A.

# IN MEMORIAM

Bob and Jean Noble
My parents, who loved the North, and whose
inspired choice of holiday-home shaped my life

# Contents

# Acknowledgements

I suppose it has been obvious for some years that I would write this book. I have known Assynt since I was nine, which surely could be fairly described as 'almost a lifetime', and the parish has always been close to my thoughts, even when I was living elsewhere. In fact, writing now in the early months of 2023, living in Sussex, lively issues in Assynt are again luring me back into some quiet involvement . . .

As ever, my writing has been supported and encouraged by relations and friends, to whom my thanks are due: my wife Martine, my brother Rhoderick and Andy Bluefield. Kirsty Macleod of Lochinver helped organise my chapters at an early stage. And special thanks go to Lesley McLaren who has very patiently read a number of drafts; her comments have been hugely helpful.

My thanks are also due to Isabella Tree who, along with her publishers, Picador, has very kindly given me permission to quote from her important book *Wilding*.

In Assynt, I must record my gratitude to Ian Evans who gave me permission to quote from the magnificent volume *Flora of Assynt*, which he wrote with his late wife, Pat. I remember with pleasure several evenings when their generous hospitality was combined with stimulating conversation . . . mostly about Assynt! Gordon and Lesley Sleight, who were living there when I was, treated me in the same kind manner, and I have benefitted a great deal from conversations and comment with Gordon.

In my years in Assynt, I worked with many of the local landowners, and was, however briefly, part of many local groups; of the latter I must mention the Community Council, which was for many years my main focus among these. These involvements were almost always a pleasure, I remember so much courtesy and friendship. My debt to the wider Assynt community, over so many decades, will be obvious to anyone who reads the book. So many of those special families and individuals are no longer with us; some are named in the text, others (for no particular reason) not, but, like the members of my own family who feature in these pages, they enriched my life. Among those long-term friends, I must thank Bill Ritchie for agreeing to write the Foreword. His contribution, as one who has made a special mark on Assynt and beyond, means a lot.

In my limited experience, working with a new publisher can be rather intimidating, but I am most grateful to the whole Birlinn team; especially to Hugh Andrew for the time and patience which he accorded my initial approaches, and his decision to go with this book.

Subsequently, my principal contacts on the editorial side have been Andrew Simmons and Tom Johnstone; it has been a pleasure to work with them.

As we head towards publication, my thoughts are again with this wonderful place, the years I spent there, and the folk I knew. To all the current residents, I can only say I know that living in Assynt is by no means always easy, and sometimes difficult issues, either personal or across the parish, can dominate in a way that is far from comfortable. I hope they will always find the patience to work around these problems, as in an isolated location you must, and that Assynt may, in the long run, flourish and sustain those who love the place.

# Foreword

Assynt: described by Norman MacCaig in his poem 'A Man in Assynt' as 'this most beautiful corner of the land'. And beautiful it is, whether the mountains gleaming white in winter, or its myriad lochs and lochans splashed in summer sunlight. But Assynt has its dramatic, dark side too. Perched on the very western edge of Europe, it can be a place of violent storms and driving rain. It is one of the most sparsely populated areas in Europe with around a thousand humans, mostly in small settlements hugging the coast. Many are indigenous to the area, others are lured here by its magic.

Robin is one of those lured here by that magic.

I first met Robin and his family in 1974. They were living in the crofting township of Elphin, attempting, as Robin puts it, to be 'fully signed-up members of the contemporary, back-to-the-land, practical self-sufficiency, do-it-yourself and grow-it-yourself movement'. In the ensuing years, Robin and I enjoyed many a lively discussion, ranging from woodland ecology to the impact of crofters putting a match to the heather in spring!

But Robin's links with Assynt started much earlier. We first see the parish through the eyes of a nine-year-old. Bright, excited, curious. And that bright, excited curiosity never left Robin, as over the years and in changing circumstances, he got to know the people of Assynt and explored the natural and cultural environment. Though I don't think that Robin would claim to be an expert in all that came to the attention of his inquiring mind, his exploration of the archaeology, history, geology and ecology (especially the woodland ecology) of Assynt led him to acquire a breadth and depth of knowledge and insights far greater than most.

In this book, Robin shares that exploration and knowledge with great skill and in rich detail, painting a picture of Assynt which is informative, enjoyable, and just occasionally controversial!

Bill Ritchie

Note: Bill Ritchie has global conservation concerns, but is best known as one of the leaders in the movement for land reform in Scotland. He was one of the trio who masterminded the successful purchase of the North Assynt Estate by the Assynt Crofters, which led, ultimately, to the formation of the Community Land Unit, and several successful ongoing Community Land Trusts. In places like remote Knoydart and the Isle of Eigg, these have transformed life on the very edge of Europe. Bill, through his long residence in Assynt as crofter and lobster-fisherman, has a very real acquaintance with the realities of that life.

# Author's Note

The fine mountain of Quinag has three miles of western cliffs, composed of dark-red Torridonian sandstone. At times, the rays of the setting sun light up these cliffs, and the mountain glows in a dramatic way that is reminiscent of Uluru, the sacred mountain of indigenous Australians. Under this radiant hill is a long, dark glen, and in that glen is a cottage; whatever it is that I am, that cottage and the folk around it made me.

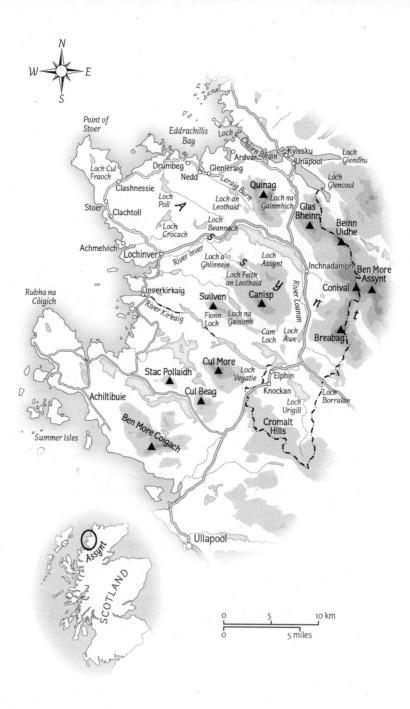

# Introduction

One fine day in July 1959, a heavily-laden, rotund old car drove down a short track in the far North-west Highlands of Scotland, and came to rest outside a low, whitewashed cottage. A rear door opened, a long-legged nine-year-old boy almost fell from the crowded back seat and ran for the front door. As it happened, this was unlocked, and he rushed inside, only to reappear shortly, grinning broadly. 'It's OK, Mum', he said, 'There is one!'

The 'one' referred to a functioning loo, and whether or not there actually was one had preoccupied the boy and his mother for a while. I was that boy, and for five years previously, our family – mother, father, Highland grandmother, two boys and assorted animals – had rented a wooden holiday-home on the quiet side of Loch Ness. This had no amenities and rotting floors; items of furniture were carefully placed to conceal holes in these, while my father had completely to rebuild the floor of what passed as a bathroom. The cottage had no electricity and running water only in the kitchen; there was no loo, and we utilised something called an 'Elsan', which might nowadays be called a chemical toilet. This was not a totally agreeable device, and it fell to my father to perform, at regular intervals, the duty of emptying it of its less-than-pleasant contents. To this end, he dug pits in one part of the steep garden and marked with a cross where each deposit had been made, to avoid digging again in the same place. Many years later, I passed the now much-refurbished cottage, and noting the luxuriance of the garden, wondered whether the proud owners had any idea as to what they owed its lush beauty!

We had all tired of the Elsan, my father of digging pits, and the limitations of living part-way along the shore of one of the longest lochs in the Highlands had begun to be felt and so, after five years, it was decided to look elsewhere for a base for our family holidays. We had seen an advertisement by the Assynt Estate, intimating that they had cottages to let in their much remoter northern parish, and we decided to investigate. On the appointed day my father had to be elsewhere for his work, and so the rest of us set out on this crucial and quite long journey. We eventually reached the small township of Inchnadamph, best known in those days for its traditional fishing-hotel, and there met the estate factor, who would in time become a family friend; he organised one or two very special days for us over the years. Outside Inchnadamph we inspected one cottage, and during the rest of the day we saw a few more: the sheep had been in residence in one, another was up a long, steep and rough track which could only have been negotiated by a Land Rover (which we did not have), and a third prompted a remark by the factor: 'If your husband were a do-it-yourself type of man . . .' which went down into family history. This was not because my father was not actually quite good at carpentry, for instance, as his bathroom floor had shown, but because he had made it totally clear that he did not wish to spend his short precious holidays in rebuilding some wreck.

That cottage was also, therefore, duly deleted from the list of possibles, and we toured right round the coast of Assynt before finding a solid, sensible, attractive cottage in a wooded glen, but close to the sea. It was, apparently, 'condemned' (which seemed not to imply any limitations on our possible use of it as a holiday-home), but appreciation of its attributes was made slightly more difficult by the fact that it was currently being used as a store by the shepherd, who, with his family, had lived there a few years before. (The estate had recently built for them a spacious and smart new house, up by the single-track road.) It was partly full of bales of hay and, although we could remember that it had the requisite number of rooms, when asked the crucial question by my father (who had now disposed of the Elsan): 'Has it got a loo?', neither my mother nor I could actually remember. We thought it had – we thought we would have noticed if it had not – but neither of us was totally sure. Despite this, the lease of the cottage was duly acquired, and the removal made in due course. All that day, my mother and I had been somewhat on tenterhooks, hence my hasty exit from the car and inspection of the plumbing.

And so, that day in July 1959, the cottage in Glenleraig became the holiday-home of the Noble family and animals, and would remain so until the very end of 1971. That spell of thirteen years would significantly alter the lives of us all, but of none more than me. It might not be too much to say that, in many ways, it became our spiritual home; certainly, that was to prove to be true for me.

In itself, there is nothing unusual in that. For many folk a particular holiday cottage, in a particular glen or bay, perhaps on a particular island, may assume a huge importance in their lives. For most of us, they give a sense of freedom, take us away from the cares of everyday life, and provide a safe location where we may truly 'be ourselves'. This quite rapidly became the case for me. At the age of thirteen, I was sent away to a boarding-school, which I hated, and thoughts of Glenleraig reminded me often that life actually was worth living, or would be again, soon. And when I was given holiday work from that school – books, perhaps, to read – I could never even open them while at the cottage. I could not let that outside world impinge. Eventually, I felt able to invite a couple of special friends from the school to visit Assynt and explore our wonderful hills, but it took a year or two before I could face doing it.

There are cottages like this up and down the land, and they often retain this special, 'safe' quality well into the adulthood of those who love them. Perhaps the most famous of all is the place which Gavin Maxwell called Camusfearna, 'The Bay of Alders', in his best-selling book *Ring of Bright Water*, which appeared one year after we arrived in our own haven, and which I have read and reread ever since. In his Foreword, written the October after we first entered Glenleraig, Gavin wrote:

> ... these places are symbols. Symbols, for me and for many, of freedom, whether it be from the prison of over-dense communities and the close confines of human relationships, from the less complex incarceration of office walls and hours, or simply freedom from the prison of adult life and an escape into the forgotten world of childhood, of the individual or the race. For I am convinced that man has suffered in his separation from the soil and from the other living creatures of the world.

Slowly, for the nine-year-old boy, this became true, and the cottage in the glen, in its wider, very special Assynt setting, established the vital connection between this individual and the soil which sustains all the living creatures of the planet. It shaped my world view, and subtly dictated the course of my life, with all its ups and downs. Long acquaintance with it and thoughtful study of it, in time revealed something of its geological, archaeological and historical significance; ecological lessons were learnt which are of relevance at least to the wider Highlands and, sometimes, far beyond.

Robin Noble,
Le Mas de St Paul, Pyrenees-Orientales

# 1

# Eden Defined

Quinag is a magnificent mountain, more a small range of contrasting peaks, which appears to sail over the bumpy Assynt hinterland like a fine ship. This description works best when it is seen from a westerly direction, from where the long cliffs appear as sheer as the sides of a liner. There is only one break in this western rampart, the deep 'V' of the Bealach a' Chornaidh, and although the descent from here is very steep, my father and I used it on occasion if we had climbed all the mountain from the cottage and were returning home in the early evening. As you climb down the rough, stony and heathery slope, you are in fact descending to a lesser bealach or col. That Gaelic word, relevant to so much of this Highland landscape, rapidly became part of our regular vocabulary, and has remained so. From here it is possible, in effect, to turn left and make a relatively short and easy descent to the main road at Tumore on the side of Loch Assynt, the major loch in the parish or, instead, to turn right and follow the infant stream on the much longer route down its own glen to the sea. This glen is Glenleraig, and shortly before eventually reaching the narrow inlet of Loch Nedd, we would regain our cottage.

This building itself was quite long and low, the original 'butt-and-ben' style cottage having had a spacious room (presumably a later addition but extremely well done) added to one gable, while there was a lean-to shed attached to the other. As you went in through the front door to a small, somewhat inadequate lobby, my parents' bedroom opened off to the right, and there was also a small boxroom off that, effectively behind the stairs. The boxroom was just 6 feet by 6 feet, and my father managed to construct quite a generous bunk bed in that space. He was only able to put it all together by the judicious use of a small hole in the wall-lining. This little room had a window to the back of the cottage, and my brother Rhoderick and I slept there for at least the first year or two.

To the left of the entrance lobby was the living room, and beyond, the (presumably) newer room, which became my grandmother's bedroom. The living room was in every way the heart of the house, partly because no fewer than four doors opened from it. It also housed the less-than-elegant, but extremely practical Nurex, a solid-fuel stove and cooker, which very visibly provided our hot water; pipes ran from it to an unconcealed combined water cylinder which perched on top of some corner shelves. This gurgled and talked to itself in a very encouraging way when the water was beginning to warm up, and, although perhaps rather basic, it made for a very cosy room if the weather was cool. One particularly attractive feature of the simple cottage architecture was that its windows were relatively large, had very wide internal ledges, and extended unusually low; my brother and I had a couple of small, almost dwarfish (but very comfortable) chairs by the living room window, from where we could keep our eyes on anything that might be happening outside. The broad ledges effectively gave us a handy play-space, out of the way of anyone else, where we could keep our toys, books and anything we were working on (like model cottages made of stone chips and Polyfilla, with cut rush for thatch). There was always at least one pair of binoculars at each of the main windows of the cottage.

One of the four doors opened on to steep wooden stairs which ascended to a long loft, provided with a decent skylight and tall enough for a grown-up to stand in. Initially, we simply used this for storage, but later on, once it had been, perhaps rather eccentrically, lined with sheets of glossy white cardboard my father had obtained from his works, my brother and I and any visiting boys slept up there on camp-beds.

The final door from the living room, where perhaps previously there had been only a window, gave access to the corrugated-iron extension, lined inside with pitch-pine planks, which housed the kitchen, and beyond that, the bathroom – with, of course, the fully-functioning WC.

The cottage had no electricity, and relied on paraffin lamps for portable lighting, for instance in bedrooms, and a Tilley lamp for general illumination of the living room. Lighting the Tilley was a complex ritual, and I can still recall the prolonged pumping to get up the required pressure, and the gentle hiss once the glowing mantle was properly lit. In addition to the Nurex for heating, the two main bedrooms still retained their cast-iron fireplaces, which were occasionally used; we also had a couple of paraffin heaters. The main cooker, in the kitchen, like the fridge, ran off Calor gas, so their cylinders, and spares, were very much a feature of our lives.

Despite the four doors, the living room did provide adequate space for us all. The dining-table stood against the wall beside the door to the stairs, and was moved out for meals; otherwise, Rhoderick and I had the window-seats, my grandmother an armchair beside the stove, and there was a sort of short, folding sofa against the other wall, with a couple of 'floating' chairs in the middle of the room. The two dogs tended to occupy the floor in front of the Nurex, and the cat, or cats, had we brought them with us, perched on any willing lap. In the evening, my father might be making up casts at the table, my mother and grandmother reading or discussing what we would be doing the next day and the requirements for food, Rhoderick and I playing or reading, hoping not to be sent soon to bed, while the comfortably-hissing Tilley shed its soft light over us all.

The cottage, which is still there, lies across the narrow, inhabited part of the glen floor. Beyond the all-purpose shed, a short stretch of drystone-dyke led to the burn, here a series of long peaty pools with short rapids. Its gentle murmuring (except at times of spate) was the constant background to our lives. It flowed down the middle of the glen, and the ground on the other side was comparatively rough and boggy, occupied by a multitude of small birches and willows. Beside and below the cottage, taller alders gave deep shade to the dark water, where small trout jumped in the evening. Our side of the glen was the inhabited and cultivated part, and the cottage itself formed part of the boundary between its two sections: the Front and Back Park. The word park was, and still is, used in the Highlands and Islands to denote any enclosed and serviceable ground, where animals might be pastured and crops grown.

The Front Park was the lower and boggier; our track ran through it, past the combined barn and byre, up to the new Shepherd's House beside the winding, single-track road. The drier part was good green grass, where you could still see the long ridges which are misleadingly known as 'lazy-beds', old cultivation strips, with their pattern of ditches. Below our track, it was generally wetter, a mass of tall rushes; but up by the byre, close to the manure heap, was an elder bush, with a single, graceful, small willow between us and it. The Front Park was delineated by some fencing, which ran along the foot of the steep glen side, dense with hazel and birch bushes, low enough in places for us to watch the occasional car making the steep ascent out of the glen, heading towards Kylesku.

Where that road ran in the other direction, after the Shepherd's House and neatly-arched bridge over a pool of the burn, it crossed the very low ground on a somewhat elevated causeway before reaching higher flattish land which we soon began to refer to as 'The Point'. The causeway described a wide loop around an area of salt flats, which we boys adopted very rapidly as one of our playgrounds. The broad burn ran down one side of the rather blue-green flats, but an equally wide, much shallower and slower-moving backwater, almost a creek, looped back towards the road, before narrowing in the sticky, squidgy, short-grassed turf of the flats which were heavily criss-crossed by thin ditches and cracks. One of our great pastimes here was to search for the small creatures which occupied the channels and gravelly pools. If you walked across the brackish creek, tiny speckled flatfish broke cover and scooted ahead, leaving a short muddy wake. They were very hard to catch with our shrimping nets; the three-spine sticklebacks, neat, silvery, swimming in shoals, were certainly much easier. There were often elvers, perhaps three inches long and steel-grey. Fast and wriggling madly, they weren't easy to catch either. I also recall tiny prawn-like creatures, perhaps an inch long, almost entirely transparent; and miniature shrimps which often swam on their sides, sometimes clutching a baby underneath. These all inhabited the brackish water of the flats – unless we transferred them for a while to the pale blue baby's bath which we had long outgrown but had brought with us. This would be positioned at the back of the cottage, but we were always worried that one of the dogs might absent-mindedly drink from it, or that one of the sinister herons from the sea-loch would notice it when flying over the cottage and decide to investigate.

Our other activity down on the flats involved the sailing of model boats. My brother normally had a little yacht, I remember he had a rather basic blue one with a metal keel and one that was larger, much fancier, with a pale hull and simulated wooden deck. I favoured motor boats – of the elementary, clockwork variety – and had a beautifully-modelled motor torpedo boat. I was very sad when its engine ceased to work, and it was replaced by a very much more ordinary cabin cruiser. We could sail these in the creek, but occasionally would borrow a small spade, and widen or deepen a few of the narrow channels through the flats, damming them in places to form new 'navigable' stretches.

The instinct to play with water, or in water, and particularly to build dams seems an inevitable part of boyhood, and we had noticed that across the road, up by the Shepherd's House, there was a very small burn – probably just a ditch, but rather more attractive than that suggests. Inevitably we dammed it, with stones and turf, probably with the assistance of the two boys, Alan and Angus, from that house. On one occasion, they approached us looking rather mysterious, saying we should

5

have a look at our little dam and see what we had trapped; it now contained a somewhat irritated little brown trout, the size we always called 'tiddlers', which another, older boy, Murdo, from the nearest township of Nedd, had caught while fishing the Bridge Pool. Instead of throwing it back in the main burn, he had transferred it to our tiny pool, for which it was really far too large. I cannot believe that it survived very long.

At some stage, we ventured across the main burn, and found an attractive little tributary which descended through a minia-ture gorge, with a large rock in the middle dividing the flow. This, like most of the glen down here, was in dense woodland, mostly birch, where there was an amazingly luxuriant growth of ferns and moss. With gathered stones, and much of the moss, we here constructed our most romantic-looking dam to date, trying to make it look as natural as possible. In later life, I rather ruefully discovered that some of what we blithely considered to be 'merely moss' and had uprooted to make the dam, was actually quite a special rarity, called Wilson's Filmy Fern. Here we were just across the main burn from the cottage, but could hardly even see the white of its thick walls, so dense were the low-growing trees; it was another world, a place of our own.

As I have mentioned, the area of ground behind the cottage was called the Back Park. Along its length, on one side it was simply bounded by the main burn, which was fairly broad, and in places ran quite deep. From the gate by the other gable of the cottage, a substantial and well-built drystone dyke ascended the side of the glen, below the climbing road, before eventually curving down again to the waterside just below the First Falls. It enclosed a substantial area, much of which was hazel woodland, with open stretches of good meadow-grass, and a little bracken around the edges. But its most important feature, really, was the stretch of flat, dry, sweet turf which stretched behind the cottage. That first summer, it was grazed by the large black cow called Daisy, which belonged to Dannie McCrimmon, the shepherd, and Colleen his wife, who was the teacher in the local Drumbeg School. Dannie I remember as tall, long-striding, soft-voiced; Colleen was slim, and as my mother remarked one morning could run like a deer. She had seen this when Dannie had set off for the hill, forgetting his piece, and Colleen had grabbed his bag and sprinted after him.

I was already keen on photography, and in that very first day or two, I took, on my Brownie 127 camera, a snapshot which I still possess, of Daisy grazing peacefully behind the cottage; the unblemished expanse of the lovely meadow is quite clear. But Daisy had some bad habits, including that of chasing small boys, whom she disliked, and very early on, Dannie arrived one morning with posts and wire, to give us an enclosed area safe from her depredations. This we very much appreciated and was typical of the kindness we invariably received from the inhabitants of the house up by the road, on whom we depended in many little ways – there were only the two houses in the glen in those days. An area of hard standing, unfenced, gave us room to park whatever cars we had at the front of the cottage, where we might sometimes have tea if we were around at that time of a fine day; a short stretch of grass led down to one of the burn's deeper pools, and the big alders which lined its banks.

This little area, the cottage within the relatively open spaces of the Front and Back Parks, with the salt-marsh beyond, lay within the long, narrow, wooded confines of the lower stretches of the glen, which in fact swept on towards the open sea of Eddrachillis Bay, enclosing the narrow waters of Loch Nedd itself within dense woodland. All this, and much more, was part of our New World.

# 2

# Walks from Our Door

During the summer, Daisy was not always in the Back Park, and it became the location for our basic, minimal, daily walk for the dogs. Often they did much better but, if the plans for the day were not particularly dog-friendly, we took them for a circuit behind the cottage. At this time, and indeed for many of the Glenleraig years, we had two dogs – a black Labrador called Tigger, and my grandmother's Skye terrier, Struie. Tigger was a very beautiful dog, quite big for a Labrador nowadays, but without the heavy, square build that larger Labs now often have. He had the wonderful Labrador temperament but was also very intelligent (perhaps less common now!), and we felt that he might have collie somewhere in his ancestry, as he had a line of white on his chest. Struie was of a breed that was rare even then – much rarer now – and which my grandmother and her father had kept when living at their family farm of Auchindoune, near Cawdor. The Skyes you see nowadays tend to be hugely hairy, which Struie was not, but he certainly shared their very distinctive shape: not in fact a small dog, quite strongly built, but with short legs. His temperament was not quite as good as Tigger's, but he was very little trouble when out on a good walk.

Within the confines of the Back Park the dogs could generally run free, but we tended to call them back to heel at times, partly just to remind them that they were actually quite well-trained, but also in case a sheep might have managed to get into the Park and was concealed by the bracken or thick hazels. The habit sheep have of starting off in a panic could tempt even the best-behaved dogs to follow, and being in this area of sheep-farms and crofts, we were determined that the dogs would be instantly obedient – for their own sakes. We all knew very well that shepherds had, and exercised, the right to shoot dogs they saw chasing sheep, and we were anxious that we would never have cause to worry, making sure that Dannie saw how obedient ours were.

The first part of that standard walk was along the meadow section of the Back Park to a small rise, where a low but abrupt cliff rose above the amber waters of the long, tranquil Holly Pool of the burn. The holly which gave the pool its name grew at the foot of the leaning cliff; the narrow grass bank below also had some slender, inclined birches and a rowan, draped with honeysuckle. After this, the way descended again to where a wooden footbridge crossed the burn. Our regular route continued close to the burn, through hazels and alders; here the dark water was broken, in small rapids, with lots of stones and boulders, while ahead we could hear the roar of the First Falls, sometimes even see a curtain of spray if there had been heavy rain the night before. But we could not continue along this bank, as the high dyke came down the hill here and ended abruptly on a rock above the rushing water. At this point, we made quite a steep little climb before starting to loop back towards the cottage. Here we were quite close to the dyke; above it ran the road, and in those days traffic was rare enough (and my interest in cars already beginning) for us to take note of the vehicles that did pass by. We were particularly critical of any caravans; down by the flats there was a sign indicating the gradient of the hill ahead, and with climbs of 1 in 5 and 1 in 4, as well as significant hairpin bends (the worst of which was not yet even tarred), the single-track road was denoted as being 'unsuitable for caravans'. When some did attempt it the result was often disastrous, with frequent burnt-out clutches. The inability of some of the drivers to reverse was then, as now, a constant source of complaint, but with good reason: if the road were blocked, as sometimes it was, the necessary detour could involve an extra hour's driving or more.

Near the highest point of the enclosing dyke was a wide gate and, close by, a small stone pen against the main wall. From here the way began to descend, almost in steps, until we stood on a level just above the back of the cottage. On its very edge, standing sentinel, was our own guardian rowan, but before we reached it, there was a visual treat to enjoy. When, after a few years, the estate gave up running the sheep-farm, and Daisy departed in the wake of the McCrimmons, the grazing pattern changed – there were no more cows for some years, while sheep continued to occupy the Parks only at specific periods. By the time we would arrive for the summer, they had been out on the open hill for some months and the growth of the meadows, within the Back Park especially, was astonishing. Once again, my camera came out and, once again, I still have the pictures.

By this time, I had a more sophisticated camera, given to me by my much-loved godfather, and I enjoyed playing with the focus when I was moved to take photographs of the little alp above the cottage. The first was simply of the distant view over the Shepherd's House towards Loch Nedd, while in the second I brought the foreground into close focus, leaving the distance hazy. What I was anxious to capture was the richness of the hay-meadow flowers in front of me. I had started off very young with an interest in garden flowers, having my own little garden at home in Fife from at least five years old; this interest had widened rapidly to include wildflowers, as we all, especially my father who was a very keen botanist, enjoyed their delicate beauty.

The pictures are old, but the density of the flowers is very noticeable. Most of the flowers are quite common, but here they are in profusion; there are yellow hawkweeds, the delicate (despite its name) umbel of pignut and white ox-eye daisies at the highest level, with a remarkable amount of red clover at the lower, along with buttercups. There were also white clover and yellow rattle here, and drifts of various eyebrights at the lowest. Scattered about, there was also knapweed, and the steep slope below this level grew bell-heather, the lovely slender St John's wort and lady's bedstraw. I remember that, whenever the sun was shining, we would hear grasshoppers on this slope. In front of the cottage, in the damper areas among the rushes, there were orchids, both the crimson spikes of the northern marsh, and the pinker of the heath-spotted and, in a ditch beyond, there was the luxuriant, almost tropical, yellow mimulus or monkey-flower, with occasional patches of the deliciously-scented meadowsweet. The banks of the burn had the same hawkweeds and daisies, with the addition of great tangles of purple-blue vetch. It was all truly lovely, and on a fine day buzzed with bumblebees while butterflies danced over the magic carpet of flowers.

Some decades later I was giving a talk to the very active Assynt Field Club (a body which had appeared while I was living away from the parish), and I included these pictures, contrasting them with what these little alps had now become. As I shifted the slides from past to present, the audience actually gasped, it was so hard to believe it was the same location; only the buildings in the photographs made that clear. All the wildflowers had completely disappeared. In their place, at precisely the same time of year, was a dense growth of bracken, reaching to my head height – and I am precisely six feet tall. I could not walk through it; you would have needed a machete to forge a path where once I was used to strolling downhill. The area was only 'enlivened' by the tangle of some brambles. After spending a while looking carefully around, it had become obvious to me that the whole lower part of the glen was now lacking many of the flowers we had known. The monkey flower in the ditches in front of the cottage had gone too, and the splendidly ebullient vetch on the banks of the burn was equally nowhere to be seen. The Assynt landscape may look stark, unyielding, unchanging, but there is always change, sometimes subtle, sometimes not, even here . . .

There was another regular walk which could start within the Back Park, leaving it via the top gate, or we would take the almost-track which ran along the outside of the Park dyke up to a bend on the road above us. From here, there was a defined track which zigzagged its way up the hill face, which was partly grass and heather, with some encroaching bracken beginning to obscure the drystone ruins of several houses, barns and byres. It was evident that there had been quite a significant township up here. The slope eventually ran into a boggy level, but the path, which had been well made, was dry for the most part, although there were a few places – probably where culverts had collapsed – where we had to negotiate some much wetter stretches. On our left as we walked over we could clearly see the old banks where peat had been cut until quite recently; we had been told that the folk of the nearby township of Nedd had the right to cut peats from around here, but it was only the banks which were much more convenient for the road which were now used.

We walked this way often, but one day in particular sticks in my mind – or, more likely, a series of days. Within a few years of starting to holiday in Glenleraig, we had acquired a very characterful Siamese cat, and, as an experiment, brought him with us one summer. Kandi sometimes behaved more like a dog than a cat, and loved coming for walks with us, but he found it hard to keep up with Tigger and Struie, both of whom had a remarkable turn of speed. I can see him running along, complaining loudly that the dogs were going too fast, while making it quite clear that he disapproved totally of the damper patches along the way. Kandi hated getting his feet wet, and would shake each individual damp paw at intervals, quite clearly swearing as he did so.

So the Nobles merrily proceeded along the path towards an attractive small loch, which was on one bank overhung with delicate birches. As ever, we made an effort to learn the local place names, and this small loch was called Loch Torr an Lochain; we knew well what all the elements in that name meant, and were amused to find that one of the small, craggy hills above it was named Torr an Lochain. I always wondered whether this apparent circularity was simply a bit of local

Gaelic humour, blithely fed to an uncomprehending, monoglot cartographer, and have since found other similar instances.

The path eventually steepened, winding its way up a slope past a small waterfall, onto a higher, wet level, where it simply seemed to disappear into the peat. This was often the point at which we turned for home; it provided good views over the open, island-dotted bay of Eddrachillis and the pale northern hills of the Reay Forest. The track had presumably originally continued towards the next deep inlet of the sea at Ardvar, where one isolated white lodge could be easily seen from the road, but not so easily approached. There was a footpath which led there from the road; the only alternative was to take a boat, and the boat that was used for this purpose was sometimes seen at the very head of our own Loch Nedd. It was a launch called *White Heather*, and it sat on a trolley which ran on rails set in concrete on the shore. We often walked past it when giving the dogs a road-walk, partly to remind them that they were trained to walk to heel on the lead, and partly to wear down their claws a bit.

That walk always started with a halt on the bridge over the burn to look down into the pool. We learnt to do this quite soon, as there might often be a small shoal of sea trout that had swum up that far on a high tide but were held in the pool if the burn was running low. At the head of the pool there was a shallow, diagonal rapid which crossed from bank to bank, and the fish needed a reasonable flow of water to get over this obstacle. Dannie told us that there was often a run of salmon in the autumn – he himself had caught a nine-pound grilse in the Holly Pool, with a hayfork – and at high tides the seals would come up as far as the bridge in pursuit of the run of fish.

This walk continued along the causeway over the flats to the slight rise we called The Point; it was grassy with some small birch and willows and was at times used by campers. The elevated ground tailed away towards the shore of the sea-loch, and the shingle beach there, close to where *White Heather* sat on her trolley, always fascinated us. When the tide was rising, from between the shingle stones in several places there would rise a fountain of bubbles, rather like a spring but composed simply of trapped air. Across the narrow head of the loch, the long hillside, swathed in trees, rose steeply; the line of rocks at its rough foot was light grey-to-white, above a line of black, itself above a line of seaweed of a vivid ochre colour. It seemed there were always herons along that shore, and as we approached, they lifted into the air on their long wings, with that sudden harsh cry.

Immediately after *White Heather*, or simply the rails and trolley if someone was in residence at Ardvar, the road did a steep rise to a sharp little blind summit, immediately descending almost to the water. This little hill we named 'Boat Brae', because at its foot a large wooden boat – a lifeboat, we understood, from a small puffer which had sunk in the loch – was stranded on the gravelly shore. From here the narrow road rose again, with an almost vertical rock and hanging wood above it, and the wooded loch shore below. There was a small building close to the road shortly after this; it was always called the 'Wool Shed', as the wool from the Nedd and Ardvar sheep used to be stored there until the puffer which had served this remote coast had come to collect it. From here the road continued to rise until it reached a small level, with a cattle grid, which signalled the beginning of the crofts of the township of Nedd, where we would often turn back in order to avoid any close encounter with the local collies.

# 3

# Boating and the Sea

Glenleraig was very much our holiday-home. We lived for most of the year in Cupar, a small, quiet, market town in agricultural Fife, where our architecturally elaborate – if not downright pretentious – but attractive Regency villa sat between two roads out of town, guarded from view by high stone walls. Here our family doctor was one Doctor Stevenson (generally known as 'Stevie' to us; occasionally, I suspect, even to his face). Stevie was keen on sailing, and my father sometimes crewed for him, until one cold day in April their dinghy capsized in a squall from the hills around Loch Earn. It so happened both that they were leading the race at the time, and that virtually everyone else had capsized, too. Help was eventually forthcoming, but it reached my father and Dr Stevenson last, as they clung to the upturned hull in the freezing waters. While my father watched the doctor turning blue, he realised that any first-aid techniques he had ever learnt were irrelevant to their current situation, and that trying to keep the good doctor talking was about as much as he could hope for.

They both survived the ordeal and, the next summer, Stevie and family came north to Assynt, to Achmelvich sands, where they camped, and Stevie and his boys sailed on the turquoise sea. One day we went down to see them, and both my parents ventured out with him – separately, as I remember, because the dinghy was not that large. I photographed my mother, looking very sporting in bright yellow oilskin shorts, top and life-jacket, before she set out on the water.

Our own boating from Glenleraig had a less than auspicious

start. A friend of my father had presented us with what was definitely a very homemade, small rowing dinghy, with a flat bottom and rather garish paint scheme. It was really intended for Rhoderick and me, and we duly launched it in the burn pool beside the cottage. This was, however, rather small, and we moved up the hill to a roadside loch. We had christened our strange craft the '*Boojum*', and the *Boojum*, with us in it, duly sailed off among the waterlilies. It rapidly transpired that the flat bottom of the dinghy was not very well attached to the sides, and we began, quite rapidly, to sink. We were not yet in deep water, and no harm was actually done, but the *Boojum*'s short career with us was certainly ended; my father began to think about a proper boat.

The result of this cogitation and much research duly appeared the next year; it was a fourteen-foot, graceful, fibreglass dinghy of a particularly attractive pale blue, which we promptly christened *Periwinkle*. Lots of things duly appeared with her, of course, and the lean-to shed became satisfactorily full of boating bits and pieces, especially when she was not on the water. We had a Seagull outboard, and I can still hear the sound it made, which carried so well over the sheltered water of Loch Nedd. When not in use, the outboard sat up on a stand, accompanied by fuel tanks, oars, bottom boards, buoys, balers, rowlocks and ropes of most kinds and colours. Curleen, the thin, strong, orange twine, became a staple of life, not only used for nautical purposes but for tying up gaps in fences, strengthening collapsing clothes-lines and a myriad of other things.

*Periwinkle* had been towed north on her trolley, and could be launched from it, but the ease of launching or recovery was very dependent on the state of the tide and demanded quite a lot of physical strength. While my father, nearly six foot two and broad-shouldered, was a very strong man, and my mother in those days pretty strong for a woman, my brother and I were still young and flimsy in build, and couldn't help much where sheer physical effort was needed. My father therefore decided that *Periwinkle* should normally be moored, but in a location where she could be brought into shore on the rope, rather than needing yet another dinghy to reach her. After consultation with the crofters in Nedd, whom we were beginning to know, a location was found which fitted the bill. It was, however, not quite perfect; true, the water where the mooring was placed was satisfactorily well-sheltered and deep, and the many birch trees leaning over the water served excellently for tying ropes. The problem was the nature of the shore at that point. It was a splendidly smooth, steeply-sloping mass of rock, the lower half densely cloaked in the slipperiest of seaweed. With the aid of the various ropes, it was perfectly feasible to clamber up or down, holding buckets or whatever, but a degree of agility was definitely needed and, just occasionally, the ascent or descent did not go according to plan. I remember best an occasion some years on, when a dear young girl-cousin was staying with us. She had a superb sense of fun, and was a great favourite with everyone; one of her engaging habits was to dissolve into such torrents of giggles that she could only slide down the nearest wall and collapse on the floor. On one occasion it was her turn to climb up the slippery rock; halfway up her feet went from under her, and it was only her hold on the rope that saved her from sliding down into Loch Nedd. At this point, she got the giggles and could move no more, so my father, for some strange reason clutching a bucket at the time, went to her aid. Although he put his arms round her (so that he was now clutching her, the rope and the bucket) she could still not move, and her wild giggles infected him until he too could not move for giggling. I was on the shore and could only watch this performance, being quite determined not to go to their assistance and be similarly affected.

Loch Nedd is narrow, and very well-sheltered in this area of prevailing westerlies, being only open to the north. Its waters are rather secretive and dark, as its steep sides are mostly very wooded, indeed overhung by trees. It is effectively in two parts, divided by a projecting headland: the outer and the inner, where *Periwinkle* was moored. There was also one small rocky island, with a few neighbouring rocks, the wreck to which I have already referred, and there were then only three other boats: the *Red Earl*, which boasted an actual cabin and belonged to regular holidaymakers from northern England, *White Heather* (already mentioned), and *Catriona*, which was owned by one Frank Ross, who at that time lived in Edinburgh, I think, but came from Nedd. A few other boats began to appear very soon after we arrived, and we all found the quiet waters a delightful place in which to potter about. As we grew and became stronger, my mother, Rhoderick and I might sometimes just row quietly around, looking out for the porpoises which sometimes approached us very closely, their little fins rotating as if set on a wheel, their dark eyes watching us. There was often a seal or two hauled out on the little island, and nearly always the herons lined up along the shore.

At very low tide, the look of the loch changed enormously, and it could clearly be seen that our burn had, over thousands of years no doubt, carried down a great quantity of material, a mixture of organic matter, peat and gravel, which extended over a large part of the inmost loch. Here we went looking at times for shellfish – not that my parents were ever that brave in eating this food for free – and found great quantities of opened, empty oyster shells. My father did love oysters, and that inspired him once to undertake a thorough search of this intertidal zone, which produced yet more empty shells and only one, probably still living, oyster. The shell was so large, encrusted and dark, that its inhabitant remained unmolested. We were later told that many bays like Loch Nedd, especially neighbouring Ardvar, and others all around the coast had been well-known for their oyster-beds, which had at some date succumbed to a fatal disease.

At this time, I was working my way through the family copy of Gavin Maxwell's *Ring of Bright Water* and was fascinated to discover that he too had found old oyster-beds at Camusfearna, but none living, despite constant searching. He did say that perhaps this actually was just as well, for if a bed of living oysters were to have been found, it might rapidly have succumbed to his gluttony. (Many years later, when I was living in Sleat of Skye, much closer to Camusfearna, I did discover my own wonderful shellfish bank, with healthy living razor clams, scallops and oysters; it was only revealed at exceptional tides, which provided the necessary limitation on my own exploitation – but they did taste remarkably good!).

Outer Loch Nedd was guarded by one rather sinister rock, but beyond that was the expanse of Eddrachillis, well-provided with jagged headlands, rocky islets and several more major rocks. My father of course acquired the relevant chart, which he enjoyed studying on the dining-room table in the soft light of the Tilley, but he wisely decided to enlist some local help and advice before we ventured out across this much more open water. We had by then got to know Colleen MacCrimmon's father, whom we always knew as 'old Angus Munro'; he was a short, square man who must have been very strong in his youth. His face, with its thin, high-bridged Highland nose and luxuriant moustache, reminded me of a picture of Thomas Hardy in old age (we had been studying some of his poems at school). Old Angus knew the local waters well, and he guided us on our first venture out from Loch Nedd, which was to the exquisite double beach on Oldany Island, which then became a favourite destination for us all. From that day on, explorations in *Periwinkle* were one of the happiest features of our holidays.

After a year or two, my mother's elderly aunt made us a present at Christmas of three lobster-pots, which in time came north on the roof of the car – probably, by that time, a big old Humber, which we all adored. We checked with the local crab-and-lobster fishermen that the presence of three creels would be acceptable to them, and having duly got the nod that it was fine, we set about getting organised. We knew roughly where to place them, mostly in the outer loch, close to rocks (which put something of a premium on the calmer days), preferably on a patch of sand, but close to weed; to see this we again needed the better weather. A bait barrel was acquired, but for a while we were unsure what we would use for the bait itself. My father's loch-fishing soon provided the answer; he loved walking the complex Assynt hinterland, carrying his rod and fishing in all the trout lochs he encountered during these long days. Many of the lochs were somewhat under-fished, and therefore full of tiddlers. He decided that it would be both beneficial to the size of the future catch, and answer the question of the supply of bait, if he brought home each day's tiddler catch, to be salted in the bait barrel. Thus equipped, and with a serviceable boat-hook for catching the line of floating corks which indicated where the creels were, we began to try to catch lobsters.

In the end, we did, from time to time, bring up a pot with a lobster in it, but the big edible crabs were far more common – and very tasty. They could be quite large, at least the size across the shell of the span of a big man's hand, and if there were several within the pot, it could be rather heavy to haul up from the sea floor. On one occasion there were no fewer than thirteen in the pot, and it took my father all his very significant strength to bring the crowded creel to the surface and get it over the side into the boat. Then there was the very real problem of removing the crabs; they looked sinister and menacing, and had impressive armoured claws waving towards the questing, unprotected, human hand. My father afterwards claimed that it was the bravest moment of his life (and he had been on active service in the Navy during the war) when he started to try to extract these crabs, and I photographed him doing it. At times the pot would contain other, less useful catches; quite often a spider crab and sometimes a dogfish, shaped like the small shark it is, with a spotted skin that was as rough as sandpaper.

We tried to do the pots every day or two, so it was quite often a job to be done early in the morning, although the state of the tide could complicate matters. We had, very soon, realised that they should not be done on Sunday. The surrounding community was, in those days, firmly Sabbatarian in its views, and we tried hard not to upset local feelings by doing anything too conspicu-ous on the Sabbath. Initially, my father was occasionally tempted to try his luck, and one Sunday crept out of the back of the cottage, in order to go to fish a small, largely invisible loch in the hills. He returned in an hour or two, so wet that we thought he must have fallen in. This, it transpired, was not the case; he had walked up to the loch through the concealing wood, and, once on the bank, had put up his rod and started casting. Whereupon, according to him, a small, dense cloud had appeared out of a blazing blue sky and moved across it, until directly above him. It had then rained, briskly and efficiently, on the loch and him, before disappearing. He had not taken any waterproofs, was duly soaked, gave up and returned to the cottage, where we were lazily basking in glorious sunshine. We looked at him in disbelief: he shrugged his soaking shoulders, assured us it was entirely true, and that he would never again fish on a Sunday. 'The Lord has spoken,' he said, and that was that.

We fished, too, from *Periwinkle*, either at the mouth of the loch where there might be mackerel in shoals, or, further out, around the small, rocky Meall Islands in Eddrachillis where we might catch cuddies (coalfish), or the big golden lythe (pollack). Once or twice we landed one of the oddest fish I have ever seen, a gurnard, with its armoured and spiny head and bulging eyes. We decided not to tackle these strange creatures and returned them to the sea; I seem to recall that one squeaked as it was being cautiously handled. Codling were more common, and highly valued. The dashing and colourful mackerel were always eaten fresh on the day of catching, or if small, salted for bait, while my mother made the other species into a totally delicious, creamy fish pie. I can still see it arriving on the table; under the pastry, the fish was coloured yellow by the turmeric she used to add extra flavour. An Abu smoker had been added to our capabilities, and smoked trout was duly put on the regular menu, in addition to the fresh or the sweet-pickled version. We did not live off the land, but did garner quite a lot of our food from the lochs and the sea. We had great fun catching it (quite often getting some exercise in the process), and the meals were very tasty and nourishing; it was like someone's definition of an idyll.

# 4

# Out with Dannie

Dannie the shepherd was very much responsible for getting us involved with some of the activities which went on in the surrounding wonderful landscape. I had begun to explore it a bit myself, just setting off for an hour or two on my own. Given the nature of the area, I think my parents were amazingly calm and sensible about that; I was never warned not to drown in the burn or a loch, not to fall over a cliff or into a bog, and there were plenty of such hazards around. Nor was I ever told not to get lost; they knew I could easily find the burn or the road and would follow either home. On one occasion Dannie took the four of us, me and Rhoderick, Alan and Angus, with him when he was out on the hill. We set off up the road, the beginning of many a good walk, and where it levelled out, we branched off, so that we were walking just above the long woodland in its deep glen, vaguely parallel with the burn, and heading for the ranked cliffs of Quinag. We stopped, I remember, when we were overlooking the first of the two beautiful lochs, through which our burn flowed on its way from the mighty cliffs to the sea. I recall saying that I had been there, pointing to the shore of the first loch, to which Dannie replied, 'My, you're hardy', a compliment I hugged to myself for the rest of the day and much longer.

Perhaps because I was older, and my legs were longer than the others', he took me alone with him one day when he was going out looking for foxes – or at least, their dens. I was aware that this was also a compliment but was somewhat unsure as to exactly what was going to happen during the day, mainly because of the gun he carried, of which I was very wary. Dannie also took his brindled Cairn terrier, Duich, a dog I liked very much, which in some way reassured me. We went to a neighbouring narrow glen, the one which led down to Ardvar, and walked for a while in its wooded depths, until we came to a rockfall area under a low cliff, a feature which is very much part of the Assynt landscape. Here in all the tumbled boulders Dannie thought there might be a den; we listened at various holes and definitely heard squeaking from one. Dannie decided not to put Duich down into the hole, probably, I think, because he had decided against shooting any fox-cubs the Cairn might bring out, or a bolting vixen, in front of me, and we walked back to the road. I did hear, some while later, that he had gone back subsequently, and it transpired that it was not fox cubs which we had heard but young badgers; these were the first badgers anyone had heard of in Assynt.

Another time, he took the four of us up to where he cut peat for the fire and their own equivalent of the Nurex stove. The peats were now dry and it was time to stack them; he showed us how to do it, and while he and his boys started on one stack, Rhoderick and I were entrusted with another. Both of us were good with our hands, neat and precise in how we did things, and when he came over to see our stable, tidy, growing edifice, he was full of praise; when we got back to their house, later that afternoon, we sat in the kitchen while Dannie wrote for each of us a certificate saying that we were good peat-stackers, and signed it. These were later framed, and I still have them, although they are by now badly faded and difficult to read.

In those days, Assynt was very much sheep country, populated by a mix of Blackfaces and Cheviots; Nedd was a crofting community with sheep, and Ardvar was an estate-owned and run sheep farm, with Dannie as shepherd. In terms of sheer acreage, Ardvar was a large sheep-run, and while Dannie was the sole full-time shepherd, he could call on men from Nedd, and even Drumbeg, to assist with major events in the shepherding calendar; during the summer when we were at Glenleraig, these were generally the dipping and clipping. Both the dipping and clipping were preceded by the gathering, rounding up all the sheep on the very complex terrain of Ardvar, and requiring many men and attendant boys like us, and several dogs, some barking madly, so it was a great day out for us. I described in my book *North and West* (Scottish Cultural Press, 2003) a clipping which took place in front of Ardvar Lodge, when several folk, male and female, from the nearby townships, participated. By taking part in such important communal activities, especially as we grew and became physically more useful, Rhoderick and I became known to many folk around who we might well not otherwise have become acquainted with.

Dannie was very kind to us, and as we became more used to walking the hill with him, he decided that we needed a proper shepherd's crook, and he made us each one, with a hazel shaft and the curved handle of sheep's horn. To form the shape he wanted, and to enable him to carve a small thistle at the very end, he warmed the horn above the Tilley lamp, and said it was that which gave the lovely golden glow in the handle. I was very proud of my stick, which lasted for decades of long walks, and I remember, shortly after I was given it, resting on it while standing on the bridge close to Dannie's house, at the start of a day's gathering. As I waited, one of the crofters from Nedd, Johnnie Kerr, came over the causeway above the flats, long-strided, with his crook and his dog reflected in the waters of a high tide, gilded by the morning light, a picture I have never forgotten.

Sometimes, clippings and other events were held elsewhere on Ardvar. Across the loch from the Lodge, at the foot of the part-wooded hill and far below the modern road, was a very substantial sheep-fank, with quite a large, general gathering area and a complex pattern of compartments opening off a central run, each equipped with a gate which could be swung across in order to divert selected sheep into that particular compartment. It was very well built, the walls quite broad, so that we could walk along them, and fairly high; they were topped with heathery turf. This was backed by a substantial building, with one door, and a fireplace in one gable. Much of the walls was of hard sandstone, not the complex rock from immediately around, and it made for quite an impressive location. Down on the shore, you could see an area of flattish stones that lay prone on the damp heather, and marked, we were told, the extent of a small graveyard from the time when a complete community had lived around the loch. Out in the water, especially clear at high tide, there was a small, circular islet, crowned by the tumbled walls of a round Iron-Age fort. The map marked it as a broch, the locals referred to it as a 'dunain', and I remember it was the crofter Johnnie Kerr who told me that 'dunain' meant a 'Pictish fort'. My slightly sceptical consulting of a Gaelic dictionary ultimately proved that he was wrong (in that there is no reference to the Picts in the name), which rather disappointed me.

The big wool bags were hung from the rafters of the imposing shed, and the fleeces, once tidied and rolled, were packed into them by being trodden down. After a few hours spent rolling fleeces, our hands were softened by the lanolin in the wool, but I imagine that we must have smelt rather of sheep! Keeping our clothes clean during a summer of such activities must have been quite a problem, but at least for sheets and towels there existed the Lairg Laundry (at a considerable distance, about fifty miles we always used to say), and the parcels of laundry could be conveyed there on the Mails. As to cleaning us, the Nurex did a splendid job in heating the water which came from a small burn on the hill; if there had been lots of rain, and the water was peaty, the bathwater could be so dark that it was hard to imagine that immersion in it would actually clean you. Meanwhile, outside, our burn, swollen to the size of a small river and now the colour of whisky, roared past the gable of the cottage.

As I have said, it was our participation in these communal activities which helped us get to know many of the people who lived around us. Quite early on, Rhoderick and I started a ritual, which took place as soon as possible after we had arrived at Glenleraig for the holidays. Often it was the very next day that we set out on our walkabout, to let everyone know we were there. Although in the first few years I think we must have taken the easiest route up to Nedd, by road, after a while we went through the woods and over the open hill. This was because our first port of call was hardly actually in Nedd, but up the narrow road from the main cluster of houses, then up a small glen, close to the township fank, which was picturesquely placed beneath a dramatic rock. In order to get there, we had first of all to cross our burn; we could always have gone via our track to the road and used the bridge there, but just below our cottage there was an island and we usually crossed there. The stream on our side of the island was fairly shallow and would not go over the top of the gumboots we nearly always wore (calling them 'wellies' came much later!), and we would then wend our way through the small trees on the little island to the narrowest point of the other channel, which, in theory at least, we could jump. We generally managed this; we had no wish to fall in, as this narrower flow was correspondingly deeper and faster, so we took the jump seriously, with as much of a run-up as there was room for on the confined island, and with something of a lurch of the heart as we took off. Having made it safely across, we worked our way through the swampy scrub till we reached the glen-side and the small tributary where we made the moss dams. This little burn we followed up through the wood until we reached the higher, more open ground, where we slowly clambered uphill, through boggy flat spaces and over heathery knolls, until at last the gradient eased off, and we could see the green tract of ground which began just around the walls of the Nedd fank and extended down as far as the shore. We duly crossed the next, wide bog to this, and wandered downhill to the first white house, set below the narrow road.

This belonged to a lovely old couple, Johnnie Kerr and his rosy-cheeked, always black-skirted wife, Hughac (plus dogs), who made us welcome in their gentle voices. Eventually we would leave and stroll down the little road, the hill above it hanging with birch and hazel as we descended towards the main group of houses. We passed a ruin on the right, then the road described a curve about another one which was being restored by a family of loyal holidaymakers like ourselves, before we joined the through-road.

Close to the junction, there sat above the road, and surrounded by a lovingly-tended garden, the house of the 'Miss Stuarts' as we always called them. (I realise of course that it should be the 'Misses Stuart', but it is far too late to change the habit now.) They were Hughac's sisters, and Peggy, the more talkative of the two, must have been very beautiful in her youth; she had spent much of her life as a nurse-companion in Nice, and spoke fluent French. Sometimes we would actually visit them, or perhaps only chat for a while outside if Peggy was in the garden.

Then it was time to cross the road to a somewhat larger house which sat in a corner of its own green park, and was owned by Colleen's parents, old Angus and Dollie Munro, who always entertained us, and asked how everyone in the family was. While Angus' voice was quiet and slow, Dollie's was much quicker, almost shrill; she darted around like a bird and was as kind as he was. The final visit was again across the road to a substantial house which stood impressively above the road, and belonged to the Stewart family. Old Mrs Stewart, Agnes, tiny but quick-witted and determined, was Angus Munro's sister, and she lived there with her daughter Katie-Anne, and son Kenny who was the local electrician and had a shop in Lochinver (which meant that we virtually never saw him at the house).

I do not think that at this age Rhoderick and I ever gave any thought to the nature, or the ages, of the households we visited; these were the folk around us, and that was enough – they populated our world. Most of the older generation would then have been in their seventies, so around my grandmother's age, and, like her, their lives would have been seriously disrupted by the Great War. There were enough names on the War

Memorial in Lochinver to show the toll on the townships of the parish; as evidence of this, there was one widow in Nedd with children around my parents' age, and two old women who had never married. Three old couples there were childless; in later years we saw middle-aged folk marry, too old to have children, but glad of the companionship – perhaps this was true of the people in Nedd, too. In some ways, therefore, it was the epitome of the declining Highland township, but its inhabitants had their own, ever-welcoming dignity – if they had troubles, they bore them quietly.

Within four years of our arrival in the glen, the Assynt Estate had decided to rent out the Ardvar sheep farm. The incoming tenant wished to employ a different shepherd, and so Dannie, Colleen, their boys Angus and Alan, plus dogs, left the Shepherd's House. With them went 'Daisy the coo', the source at least occasionally of our milk. From then on we got our milk from the Stewarts or, at least, from Katie-Anne's coos, and collecting it, often on foot or sometimes by car if we were passing, became as much a part of our regular routine as doing the lobster pots.

So Rhoderick and I made our ritual visits to three or four houses, and at each we were offered and duly consumed tea – often diluted with Carnation Milk, rather than fresh, to the extent that it gradually became one of the most evocative tastes of our youthful holidays. Probably there would be some cakes, and certainly the homemade scones which everyone locally called pancakes, and we 'drop-scones'. The names did not matter – they were delicious, especially when freshly made. Our mother used to make them for us sometimes, too; on one occasion I ate twenty-six, to Rhoderick's puny eighteen. In my defence, I should perhaps add that hers were much smaller than the shop-bought ones you may have seen. We were indeed quite full as we half-jogged down the road to the head of Loch Nedd and our cosy glen, and full of delight; our world knew that we were back for the summer, and a vision of golden days stretched ahead.

Again, early on, my parents had wonderfully decided that Glenleraig was the perfect place to bring up boys, and that we would spend virtually all our long summer holidays there. My father would be up for his three weeks (eventually four) and some weekends; when he had to go away, either my mother or grandmother might go south to look after him, but in time he worked out how he could 'cope' in their absence; he merely ensured that all his friends knew that he was on his own at home, and the invitations flooded in. The most he ever learned to cook for himself, at times of dire need, was scrambled eggs.

# 5

# Into the Trees

I had no idea in those days that the walk gently uphill past the location of our filmy-fern dam, would, in later years, become really significant, and that I would take a number of people this way, in order to look carefully at the surrounding trees which in my youth I rather took for granted. Even in my early adult life, Glenleraig was never far from my thoughts, and I had begun to think about, then to study closely, the nature of those encircling woods. Eventually, having made the acquaintance of many like-minded enthusiasts, I slowly acquired some sort of reputation as an 'expert' on far-northern woods, and found myself, on occasion, leading groups around them.

We would climb the fence, go into the birches, crossing and then following the little burn which Rhoderick and I had had such fun damming. It is an easy walk uphill, and in spring, with willow warblers singing from every bush, and the vivid energy of redpolls overhead, it is a lovely one. There may be a few primroses still in bloom, and, mercifully, the bracken is only just beginning to arch up from the short grass. With few leaves on the trees and bushes, it is the best time of the year to see the nature of the ground itself, and very soon you may see the 'ghost' of cultivation ridges ahead; in the past, crops were grown here. Some of it was presumably fenced, and you will spy the hint of a dyke along the burnside. Growing out of it is a complex tree, which on close inspection turns out to be a low-pollarded alder, closely integrated with a hazel – perhaps their stems were used for the fencing?

Our way continues to gain height slowly among widely-spaced birches, with the odd hazel and rowan, rather unremarkable woodland. Once rather higher than the little burn, we can see very clearly a significantly taller birch pollard, cut to regrow above the possibility of grazing by the stock which would have frequented these woods in the past. Sadly, a few years ago, one of its branches broke off in a gale, which has rather spoiled its look, but the basic shape remains, and a few other similarly-sized trees also show signs of management. Just a bit uphill, over to our right, is a most remarkable tree; short, thick, massive, but horizontal. This is, strangely enough, a hazel.

The normal form of growth of a hazel is what I call the 'basket of sticks', a whole collection of pretty thin stems (like those Dannie had used for our crooks) with, perhaps, a few thicker ones somewhere in the middle. The individual stems are often so thin that you can close your fingers and thumb around them, and there will be many such. This particular hazel, however, has one single stem which is so thick that one cannot reach one's arms around it; it is wonderfully covered, like most of its neighbours, in moss, a comfortable place to sit. It seems very secure – or did, the last time I was there; I used it as a seat and ate my lunch sandwiches in the soft sunshine! Obviously, it was once upright, and pollarded; you can see where it was cut and the new growth came. It is a very strange tree.

We continue up by the wee burn, into what might be called a sylvan dell in England, enclosed by a wall, out of which more old trees grow. Then into an open space, damp underfoot and only moderately heathery, looking north with a lovely view to the mouth of Loch Nedd. This space was devoid of even seedling birches when I first found it as a boy, and when I last went there it was still bare, despite the presence of many birches along its edges. Other heathery places were showing a good growth of regeneration, and it may simply be that this area is just that little bit too wet for the birch to colonise it. We walk a little way down this clearing, then head again into the woods on our right, making a sharp little descent (sometimes very damp and skiddy!), into a grove of hazels. These are nearly all strange; thick-stemmed, again with an obvious point of cutting. Such trees, like the one first encountered on this walk, seem rather unstable, and one has completely blown out of the ground, something which would be most unusual for an ordinary hazel. The root plate of this one is now vertical but the tree is certainly alive, shooting in new directions, proof that enough of the roots have remained viable. I am always amazed by the sheer tenacity of our native trees, even this far north, where the winter winds can be ferocious.

And, importantly, there is continuing evidence that these trees were harvested until quite recently; a cushion of moss perfectly preserves a saw-cut face, where a branch was once removed. I have wondered, did Dannie come up here one day to get just the right stem of hazel for a new stick?

Not far away in this up-and-down hillside wood, on a boss of rock, there stands possibly the finest widest-spreading downy birch I have ever seen. And I have constantly pondered: its top has the typical shape of a pollard – surely this is far too high to have been reached? (Probably . . . but then I have since seen remarkably high pollarded trees in France.) Then again, perhaps it just broke in the wind, and regrew in the perfect shape.

Once below it, you find yourself in another grove, another group of the extraordinary hazels; all thick-stemmed, all with an obvious point of cutting, all with comparatively spindly regrowth above that point. These are single-stemmed pollarded hazels, and there are enough of them, in Assynt and in that important 'ashwood' at Rassal by Kishorn, to make it clear that they are an important feature of our ancient, pre-Clearance woodlands. There is another group close to Drumbeg. Their location, close to long-established crofting townships, with individual trees still preserving clearly the marks of quite recent saw cuts, makes it evident that to maintain, as some do, that their strange shape is simply the product of heavy grazing, is far from convincing. These trees were used by crofters, as you would expect.

All these veteran trees are effectively hidden by regeneration of birch, rowan and willow around the old woods, and even although the mosses, lichens and liverworts within them were surveyed many years ago, no-one really seems to have looked at the trees; often these woods were simply dismissed as 'birch scrub'. In all these woods, the trees and even the rocks are covered with an extraordinary profusion of low growth (including the filmy-fern), a luxuriant vegetation which has provided the 'excuse' for describing these places as the 'Celtic Rain Forest', a term, like the 'Highland Tiger' for the wildcat, which no Celt or Highlander has ever used. I much prefer 'Atlantic Oakwood' which may sound less evocative but is simple and accurately descriptive.

It is a real shame that early, ecologically-minded visitors, mostly from England and used to the magnificent, wide-spreading oaks of the south, when first entering the Highlands dismissed much of this precious woodland as 'scrub', and devoted their attention to the areas of old Scots pine, which became the focus of much attention as surviving patches of what was called the 'Caledonian Pine Forest'. It is this which has come to represent the presumed natural vegetation of much of the Highlands, while the oak woods have only begun fairly recently to be recognised for what they are. It is a fact that many tiny remnants, in the least likely of places (or sometimes the most obvious, such as the fringes of the popular seaside village of Ullapool), are scattered over the area and are still without recognition or, most crucially, protection from grazing which would give them the chance to regenerate.

There are none now, but there were some sheep in these extensive woods when Rhoderick and I were exploring them. On one occasion which I recall, we did the walk in reverse, down this little valley rather than up. We had been fishing for much of the day with our father. Mum had given us a lift up to Johnnie and Hughac Kerr's, at the top of Nedd, and after a gentle chat with them both, we walked up past the fank to the bealach and down the long slope to the first beautiful loch. This is simply 'Loch a' Bhraighe', the 'Loch of the Brae', as I was pleased to be able to inform my father and brother; languages were beginning to interest me, and I was irritated to discover that my great-grandfather had been a native Gaelic speaker, but had not thought it worthwhile to pass on the language to his daughters; my grandmother could easily have taught me.

This day we had the use of the boat which belonged to the Drumbeg Hotel, well-known in those days for its extensive fishing. The boat was quite old, wooden, clinker-built, but looked very sturdy; it needed some bailing before we settled ourselves in it, one boy in the bow, charged with looking out for rocks, one in the stern, and, not surprisingly, my father at the oars. This loch has a couple of islets, a few small rocks, and attractive bays; it is one of three, closely linked, which almost encircle one of Assynt's characteristic little rocky eminences; around the sheets of water are more of the same, higher and barer.

We certainly had a lovely time, and caught a few fish, but in a way, for me, the highlight of the day was the journey home. It had been agreed that we should walk back to the cottage, and my father was certainly thinking of taking the little side-road down to Nedd, and then the familiar way down to the head of the loch. I, however, had other ideas, and to my surprise, I got his agreement that we could take the shorter, more direct route through the woods. He had no idea where we should head, and was, I think, surprised at the confidence with which I took the lead down through the trees. I already had what my family used to call a 'bump of locality', a good sense of direction, and was undeniably pleased to lead us to a slight eminence just above the tidal flats and the road. There was the cottage, and soon the trout we had caught would make a delicious supper.

# 6

# Fishing the Burn

It was the next family in the Shepherd's House who really spurred on my interest in fishing the burn, and thereby exploring further the core of the glen. It is true that I had made one or two fishing trips with my father even before we arrived in Glenleraig, but the catching of fish did not assume much importance till later. It had, however, become our constant habit, whenever up by the road, or walking along it, to look over the bridge into the pool. It was always a thrill to see a small shoal of sea trout, perhaps a maximum of a dozen or fifteen, holding position across the gentle current of the shaded water, but it only slowly occurred to me that I might one day try to catch one.

The next family to be installed in the roadside house were the MacLeods, Jockan and his wife Johan, who was normally called Joey. He was thin, hard-working and lively, always smiling and laughing, while Joey was quieter, perhaps a deeper thinker. We very rapidly became the best of friends with them; they were always welcoming and kind, and possessed of the wickedest sense of humour, being somewhat inclined to practical jokes. All but the youngest of their four children, red-headed to one degree or other, were pretty well grown-up and away, although they visited at regular intervals, so it was their youngest daughter Violet whom we got to know best. She was four years older than me, a great tease, and rapidly becoming extremely attractive, with hair of a deep red and a beautiful complexion. She was also very keen on fishing, and soon we were great rivals in seeing who could get a sea trout out of the burn.

To give it the name by which it then appeared on the one-inch Ordnance Survey map, the Amhainn Gleann Leireag was of a middling size, somewhere really between a burn and a small river, with some attractive falls and dark pools. For much of its lower course, it ran through the deep woodland which surrounded us, and these pools tended to be much overhung by birch, rowan and alder. To add to the difficulties, one or two of the most attractive sections were effectively blocked by fallen trees, so any attempt at conventional fly-fishing was ruled out. The way to catch the fish was to use a worm, and I was given a short fibreglass rod specifically intended for fishing the burn. With this, a small landing-net, hooks and nylon and lead weights, clad generally in waterproofs and gumboots, I was equipped to catch fish – in theory at least. The crucial bait, the worms, were found by digging in the damp ground immediately around the manure heap beside the byre. (Rather to my surprise, looking back over so many years, I seemed perfectly able to cope with the business of impaling the live worm on the hook, a task I doubt I would like now.) Much of this fishing I recall doing in the rain; the point being that the rain would bring the river up in spate, providing enough depth of water to let the waiting sea trout up from the Bridge Pool, and help them through various shallow rapids. But all this water meant that the current at the favoured locations, the base of the various falls, was fast, and the lead weights were needed to get the worm down below the surface.

So there I would be, perched sometimes rather precariously above the fast-flowing stream, dampened either by the spray or the rain, trying to chuck the weighted, wormed hook across the pool, in order to reel it in across the flow, waiting tensely (I can feel it now), for the tug which meant that a fish was investigating and might take. At some point, you had to decide whether to strike, to lift the tip of the rod abruptly, hoping properly to hook the fish; all too often, of course, you did it too soon, and the line went slack. If you did hook the fish, it would often dive down towards the base of the pool, where no doubt all sorts of sharp boulders and stranded branches lay invisible in the black water, the line would snag on one of these obstacles, and you would lose the fish. If, however, you eventually exhausted it (a small sea trout of about a pound in weight would put up a fierce fight), you had the awkward task, often enough, of trying to get yourself close enough to net it, without yourself falling into the fast-flowing burn. (As I write this, more than fifty years later, I can hear the constant roar of the falls and the rain dripping from my black sou'wester on to my waterproof jacket.) If the rain ever stopped on such days, it might often mean the end of the evening's fishing as the midges would come out in their millions, until my hands were black with them, and I had to give up the struggle.

As will be gathered, fishing the burn on these days was very much for the enthusiast; even just walking upriver was something of a problem, as there were many low trees and lots of hazel bushes, and you had to make your way under their sodden canopies, trying to avoid catching the rod and line on a branch, or receiving a face-full of water as you walked into yet more soaking leaves. Part of the way lay over an area of old cultivation ridges (the so-called 'lazybeds' of the Highlands and Islands); between each was a wet, peaty ditch, which often needed jumping, while the actual ridges were densely overgrown with hazel, lurking amongst which was the occasional spiky wild rose and a few blackthorn, which were even more hazardous. If, despite all these obstacles, I succeeded in catching one or more of the beautiful sea trout, my sense of achievement was immense; I photographed the catch, my mother would cook it, fresh from the burn, for my supper, served with hot salad cream and, of course, I had run to tell Violet of my success. (I am fairly sure that she caught more than I did, which only spurred me on to greater effort!) The taste of those fish, caught after such struggles, was absolutely sublime; I was in seventh heaven.

The peaty waters contained other fish; once, much to all our surprise, my mother caught a flounder up at the First Falls. It was on the drier days, when I had little expectation of sea trout, that I would search for the other tasty inhabitants of the burn. These were the brown trout, golden to dark-brown in colour (instead of the silver of the sea trout), with handsome red spots, but in the waters of the burn they tended to an average weight of about half a pound. Fishing for these on a dry day, perhaps with a reasonable breeze to keep the midges away, was extremely pleasant; it also required some skill. With the water being lower, and the pools running more slowly and far more transparent, you had to approach the bank with real caution, as the fish were quite wary, and might be alarmed by a heavy footfall, or the casting of a shadow over the water.

I enjoyed fishing the comparatively long Holly Pool this way, crouching low on the far bank, or, further up, below the Third Falls, a pool to which I had given the name of the 'Dark Green Pool'; it was backed by a low cliff, itself overhung by trees which cast a green shade, and was virtually never touched by sunlight. Below this, the burn widened and shallowed before dividing and enclosing a narrow island. Here, too, a tributary joined, issuing from a deep little gorge that descended the glen side; this whole corner was picturesque with slender young birches, their black-and-white stems as bright as the foaming falls. I did occasionally fish such rapids; there was a longer one under the alders downstream from the Holly Pool, and standing at its head I would gently let line out, sending the worm down the burn, then very slowly winding it back in, bringing it up against the current. This virtually always caught something, frequently the tiddlers which I might perhaps keep for bait for the lobster-pots, but also quite often, and much more difficult to deal with, an eel. These averaged at least a foot long, would always have swallowed the worm and hook completely, wriggled wildly and with significant strength, were slimy and slippery, and, as I discovered during one exhausting and exasperating session, almost impossible to kill with the standard quick blow to the back of the head, which we used to despatch the trout. In the end I gave up, and if I ever hooked another eel,

I simply cut the nylon, and let the creature go; it did not seem an ideal solution, but it was the only feasible one.

Walking quite a distance upstream, you emerged eventually from most of the woodland, into a broader, more open area, where there were gentle rapids, and lots of stones and small boulders scattered across the wider water. While the woodland birds mostly tended to elude me, there was often one here that I managed to see properly and identify; it was a dipper, even at times a pair of dippers, often only revealed by the bobbing white patch of the breast, as the rest of the body was as dark as the stones on which they perched. Just above this area, the burn had quite a different character, slow, dark and mysterious as it meandered around a level marsh below a wooded crag. On this, for some years, herons nested; I still recall the fright I got the first time I discovered them there. I was walking warily beside the oily water, careful not to fall on the very tussocky bog, when something, enormous and black against the sun, launched itself from the projecting rock with a loud, harsh cry.

I did know what it must be, not in fact a pterodactyl, but a heron, as we were accustomed to its slow, heavy flapping and occasional cry as it made its way over the cottage, up from the shore of Loch Nedd to its chosen nesting site; but I still think I was lucky not to fall into one of those deep pools in the immediate fright. My father once brought a rope and a brick up with him on an afternoon walk and tried to estimate the depth of the deep pots through which the burn flowed up here. His best guess was about twenty-four feet.

There was nearly always a pair of buzzards planing over the cottage; their mewing was almost as much a part of the daily soundtrack as the noise of the outboard engine, or the murmur of the burn as it passed the cottage. Once at least, however, it was not a buzzard; I remember we were all still in bed one morning, when my mother called to us to get outside quickly, as there was a golden eagle above the cottage. So, dressed as we were in our pyjamas, the whole Noble family lined up outside the front door, binoculars in hand. We had a magnificent view of the great bird; and our neighbours probably had their existing views of our eccentricity more than confirmed!

Further up, above the slow, deep meanders, was another typical Highland-burn section, with rapids, small falls and some pools; you could follow this up to the first of the lochs. At one place, there was a low fall, with, immediately below and beside it, a small, dark, backwater, where the foam from the fall described its slow circle, moving, counter-intuitively, apparently upstream, against the direction of the main current. I was across the burn at this point, but reckoned that I could drop a worm right in the middle of this gentle circle; it seemed likely that a trout would lie precisely there. That is exactly what I did, and found my objective first time; the worm was taken immediately, totally to my surprise, and when striking I completely overdid it, and the poor trout, extremely well-hooked, flew over my head to land some yards behind me in the thin heather. It weighed almost exactly half a pound and I had it, as usual, fresh for my supper that night.

With my father regularly fishing so many of the lochs, and my own, lesser efforts, my mother was faced with how to deal with all the trout of edible size we caught. We quite often would have them fresh for supper that same night, but, as I have mentioned, the smoker more than came into its own when we had a glut, and smoked trout was a much-appreciated delicacy. My mother also found a recipe for a sweet pickle for trout, and that was also very popular.

Just occasionally we had an equal glut of a rather superior kind. This was not a generous harvest from the pots of lobsters (though of those we caught a few, at intervals, enough to give us all the occasional luxurious meal or starter), but of salmon. My grandmother had long been separated from her second husband, with whom she had had really very little in common. But they had never divorced, and maintained a somewhat stately, but courteous distance, meeting up from time to time, without any real appearance of constraint. He was an expert of world repute on the salmon, as well as a very skilled fisherman, and his salmon-fishing provided an annual occasion for such a meeting. He never retired properly, continuing to work as a most respected consultant between spells of fishing, and one of his favoured locations was Loch Stack on the extensive Westminster Estates. He would stay at the Garbet Hotel, Kinlochbervie, and thither we would be invited, perhaps for lunch on a Sunday, or for dinner. The latter was quite a serious jaunt, as we would head north to Kinlochbervie via the Kylesku Ferry (and, originally, the very slow road beyond that), but the ferry would have tied up for the night before we could possibly get back there; this necessitated a return journey of at least a hundred miles home via Lairg, virtually on the east coast of the big county of Sutherland. Sometimes we might head up for the afternoon, waiting for Grandpa to come off the loch at the end of the day's fishing. The sight of the boat approaching across the dark water of the wide loch, backed by the desperate, angled screes of Arkle, remains with me, and with it, the sense of excitement: what had he caught? Often, the answer was several salmon, and on a number of occasions, we were given some to take home with us.

Such a bounty of salmon, when we only had a small, gas-powered fridge and no deep-freeze, could be difficult to cope with. We would give a few away to friends, but we would still have plenty for ourselves, and could be tempted to experiment with them. My father was half-Danish, and his Scandinavian memories included gravadlax. We looked up recipes, managed to obtain quantities of dill (from goodness knows where in those long-ago days), duly stuffed the chosen raw fish with the herb, wrapped it in tinfoil, and buried it for some days in the ground behind the cottage. The result, when exhumed and tasted, was universally declared to be absolutely disgusting; I suspect the cat got the rest of it.

Nowadays, of course, the idea of having either a 'glut' or a 'bounty' of salmon is extraordinary; the Atlantic salmon has seen such a decline in numbers as to make 'catch-and-release' the order of the day on many rivers. And the sea trout which

I used to catch in the burn have pretty well disappeared; there may well be fewer brown trout, too. One cause has clearly been the emergence of salmon farms, which may be seen in many of the sea-lochs up and down the West Coast and in the Islands. The feeding of countless salmon in the cages led to a high concentration of the parasitic sea-lice which adversely affected local populations, that we know; but we are also now all too well aware of the slow, insidious effect of acid precipitation during the centuries since the Industrial Revolution began. It is very probable that this will have altered the chemistry of the rain- and river-water over the years, leading to fundamental changes in these systems.

One of the visits by my grandfather to the Garbet Hotel, quite early on, gave us proof of the extraordinary nature of the local grapevine. One day, we were out around Nedd, when we met Johnnie Kerr. He told us that there had been a serious fire the night before, up at Kinlochbervie, and the Garbet had burnt down. All the guests had got out of the building safely; 'Don't worry,' he said, 'Mr Menzies got out unharmed.' This was in fact quite extraordinary. Kinlochbervie was some distance away, on a slow road, and we knew that Johnnie had no car, nor a phone in his house. It was true that he might have seen flames of the fire at night from the rising road that led to his home, and made inquiries the next morning, but we had never mentioned the fact that my grandmother had a husband living, and no-one had any particular reason, as far as we knew, to believe that the Jock Menzies who had escaped the burning hotel, along with several other people, had any connection with us. But Johnnie knew that he did.

# 7

# The Great Outdoors

A new phase in our regular activities began when my father acquired another, smaller fibreglass dinghy for loch-fishing. It was christened '*Troutbridge*', after the much-abused ship in the radio comedy programme called 'The Navy Lark' which we all loved (partly, I suppose, because both my parents came from naval families). He got permission to put it on a large and beautiful loch in the Assynt hinterland, Loch Poll, which was not visible from the road, but only a shortish walk from it. We managed to park the car in a passing place, carefully ensuring that we did not deny its use to any traffic, and would walk across a flat, boggy area to small rocky hills from which we descended a long slope to the loch-side and our waiting craft. The loch was extensive, with some nice wooded shores, gentle birches leaning out over the peaty water, and a group of attractive islands roughly halfway towards its distant head, where a fine, short waterfall indicated the burn which flowed through the long chain of lochs, so characteristic of this part of the Assynt landscape. We once landed there towards the end of a long summer holiday and saw that a number of fish were jumping the falls. It was quite an easy matter to catch a few in a landing-net, and we were slightly surprised to discover that they were brown trout migrating through the system to spawn upstream; I had not, until then, realised that they too were migratory, like the eels, sea trout and salmon, but within the more limited confines of the fresh water.

The fishing on Loch Poll was quite varied, because of its attractive topography, and it became another popular day out for all of us, save my grandmother, who did not feel equal to the climb back up to the road. I was interested in the burn which flowed from the north end of the loch (close to where we kept the boat), the short distance to the sea at Oldany; it was of a similar size to our own one, but its lower pools ran through much more open ground, far less encumbered by overhanging trees, which meant that it should be feasible to fish with a fly rather than the worm. We passed this section every time we fished Loch Poll, as well as on every trip to Lochinver for supplies, or on our regular jaunts to one of the fine beaches which are such a delightful feature of the coast. I must have talked constantly about my desire to fish the Oldany burn, until my mother suggested that perhaps I should write to the people who had the fishing of it; we did at least know their name, and that they lived in the nearby lodge high above the road. Eventually I did, actually writing after the holidays from my boarding-school; the idea gave me something concrete, connected to Assynt, to look forward to, and helped me, briefly, to forget how little I enjoyed the school. I received a courteous reply from a Brigadier Mandleberg, inviting me to visit him and his wife when we were next in Assynt. This was duly done, and the meeting ushered in a real friendship with the splendid old couple, widened significantly our acquaintance in the area, and gave us access to yet more fishing.

I often think of those wonderful old people when passing Oldany; the house they lived in, and the nearby farmhouse, stand above the road and are easily seen. Nowadays both are holiday-homes and often empty. In our day they were full-time homes; there are several other examples.

My parents were very hospitable, and frequently invited cousins of our age to stay; girls slept in the little boxroom downstairs, and boys up in the spacious loft with us. Later on, as my father's business activities widened (he made Haig's whisky in vast quantities, eventually becoming the Production Director), he travelled all over Europe, meeting the distributors in various countries. In those days, when giving of gifts by business contacts like cases of champagne at Christmas, or doing some other kind of favour was regarded as quite normal, some of them would ask if they could send over a son (it never seemed to be a daughter) to get some experience at my father's works, and improve their English at the same time. My parents would often invite such boys to join us on holiday for a week or so, and I eventually made a couple of good friends at the dreaded school, and felt secure enough in our holiday fastness to invite them similarly. In addition, some relations or good friends would come up to Assynt for their own holidays and, staying locally in the Drumbeg Hotel or a B&B, would join in with some of our activities, like the routine lobster-pots, or a day fishing on Loch Poll. One of the things I remember most from such days is the noise of the water slapping gently against the side of the boat, as we fished down a promising shore in the perfect breeze. One cousin, who came a few times with his brother, both being mad on fishing, gained everlasting fame as he was on his way over the bog before the descent to the boat; not looking where he was going, he fell spectacularly into a dark, wet, peaty pool, which became 'Paul's Hole' forevermore.

As far as I was concerned, one of the few good things about my boarding-school was its location on the very edge of the Highlands, and the fact that on Saturday afternoons in the Summer Term, we were allowed to escape into the local hills. I had been given a dreadful old bicycle (one pedal kept on coming off, however tightly I tried to put it back on), and on this contraption I braved the summer traffic, heading for an empty glen between rounded hills. Here at least I could wander at will, often on my own, but at other times with the two boys from my House – Angus and Niall – with whom I shared a love of open spaces. After a while, I did realise that the very individual mountains of Assynt were in every way superior to these rather lumpy summits, and I resolved that the next summer holiday would see me venturing higher than before.

From then on, climbing these wonderful peaks became a regular part of the summer programme; fortunately my father was (almost) equally keen, as I dragged him each summer up the great hills. We started each season with Quinag. It was our tradition to do this from sea-level, from the cottage, walking out of the door and up the brae to the road which we followed for a while. The main ascent up to the first peak was really steep, and a significant effort, but the route thereafter ran along a beautiful ridge, linking separate peaks and providing incomparable views. It was equally traditional to descend from the very highest point to the flat sandstone pavement which terminated abruptly in the vertiginous cliffs of the Barrel Buttress of Sail Garbh. Here we always stopped, put down our rucksacks, sat down close to the edge, and looked gingerly down the precipitous drop.

Returning to the Centre Peak, we had one of the finest views of the day, that of our final two, very shapely summits, rising ahead of us across the deep bealach. We would pause before descending to its floor, at a spring that issued from high on the ridge. By now we would be quite tired, hot and thirsty, and its ice-cold water was bracing and refreshing. On these hills of Torridonian sandstone, the tiny streams that flow from such springs are crystal-clear, pink with eroded sand, bordered by tiny cushions of the darkest moss, made enchanting by the delicate flowers of starry saxifrage, one of my father's favourites. While up here, we were listening, too, for the extraordinary calls of the ptarmigan, watching for the occasional mountain hare, searching the skies for eagles.

It was always a wonderful day – and a long one too, by the time we had climbed the last two peaks, and then retraced our steps to the same bealach, before descending the rough, steep slopes to the head of our own glen, and the long walk home. At this stage, after some four thousand feet of ascent and ultimately fourteen miles, we were definitely hot and weary, and my father would muse aloud on the long, refreshing gin-and-tonic he intended to drink as soon as we were back at the cottage, exhausted and sweaty but exultant.

Through the ensuing years we climbed all the prominent sandstone hills in Assynt and the neighbouring similar parish of

Coigach. On one occasion, in my father's absence, when we had our cousins Paul and his brother James staying, I think my mother must have felt the strain of coping with all this young teenage energy, and so decided to take us all up the long, rough slope of Canisp, a single conical peak visible from many directions, giving the most splendid views over its spectacular neighbour, Suilven. Suilven, too, was climbed, by me, Dad, and, as I remember, my school friend Niall. On that occasion I decided that the scrambling involved in tackling its subsidiary summit, which is ringed with crags, was more than I really enjoyed – going up was fine, but descending, with at one stage, a good view of an attractive loch between my feet but hundreds of feet below, was not!

Our longer boat trips in *Periwinkle* were also very special. We were fortunate in our location in Loch Nedd, which is part of the large and attractive Eddrachillis Bay, and sheltered from prevailing westerlies by the high Point of Stoer. It has a very varied shoreline, and contains a number of groups of rocky islands, including Oldany with its beautiful double beach, a real favourite of ours; usually we had it to ourselves, and a picnic lunch on the short sweet turf by the old salmon-fishers' bothy, looking down the sand to the clear enamel of the water, across a rocky headland to the high peaks and domes of Quinag, was a time of extraordinary beauty and peace.

To the north, and nearly always visible, was Handa Island. To visit it was a significantly longer voyage, which we undertook at least once. It was on a day of warmth and flat calm, with the occasional bank of fog that enabled my father to show off his navigational skills, as all the familiar seamarks, like the Meall Islands around which we often fished, disappeared from view. We had visited Handa from Tarbet on the nearby coast on a number of occasions, but circling the sandstone island, looking up at its crowded and noisy cliffs, with puffins, guillemots, razorbills, kittiwakes, shags and, still almost rare in those days, fulmars, all flying overhead, was unforgettable. This was Nature, in all its exuberance and at its apparently most chaotic, in a magnificent setting – and not that far from home.

From the innermost part of the wide bay of Eddrachillis, there reaches inland a system of sea-lochs which, certainly in their furthest reaches, deserve to be called fjords. We made, too, a number of sorties in this direction, frequently with Rhoderick, me and Dad (and probably some visiting friend or relation). We would take the boat round the rocky coast, past the narrow inlet into Ardvar and the lonely house of Kerrachar, along the wide channel of Loch a' Chairn Bhain to the islands and the narrows which in those days were crossed by the Kylesku ferry. Here we would halt, go into the slip and pick up the remainder of the party, certainly my mother and grandmother (with the dogs and the all-important picnic) and generally one or two others.

Somewhat low in the water thereafter, we headed out into the wider expanse by Unapool, after which the two real fjords reach inland between high hills. These, Lochs Glencoul and Glendhu, reached only by boat or on foot, are quiet and impressive, each with a lone house and outbuildings near its head, into which rivers flow. A great sheet of rock looms over the head of Glendhu, while off the steep side of Glencoul there leaps the long fall of Eas a' Chuil Aluinn, the highest waterfall in Britain and, in those days, very little known. It is fed by a rather small burn and needs to be viewed after some days of heavy rain, when its near 600-foot drop is magnificent. This is splendid, wild territory, the hills looming and precipitous, and as it was part of the Westminster Estate's deer forests, we would see stags and hinds, in those long-ago days a real novelty.

As a young boy, I was a romantic and emotional soul, and something in me responded to the very special atmosphere of these far-inland seas. I had already, around the age of nine, written my own bird book, and now I began to try my hand at romantic historical fiction, embellished with my own drawings (as the bird book had been). In it, I tried to recreate the life, in some unspecified but thrilling past century, of a small commu-nity living here around the seaweed-girt shores, to the endless soundtrack of the long waterfall. The hero, a boy of my age, and almost my name, attired in his kilt, was forever standing by the shore, looking at the setting sun across the loch, and musing on the joy of the morrow. His home was an unlikely, but wonderful, combination of substantial black-house and broch. Occasionally, our own cottage and glen provided that sort of romantic attraction, particularly when Jockan from the Shepherd's House played his pipes on the bridge, in the golden glow of a fine evening. I was hooked – and forever, as it turned out.

# 8

# Past and Present

My grandmother was an interesting, if occasionally difficult, woman. Her life, like that of so many, had been totally disrupted by the First World War, which left her a young widow of only a few months, and also destroyed any chance she might have had of intellectual employment. I am not sure that she actually ever aspired to that, but she was both musical and artistic, with a whole range of interests which she pursued with energy. She read widely, had a considerable knowledge of Scottish history, and easily infected me with her new enthusiasms. Assynt gave her one, which was geology. This whole West Coast zone, from Durness in the north, to Sleat of Skye in the south, is an area of remarkably complex geology, known all over the world. Within that zone, Assynt is particularly famous. My grandmother was more interested than I in the appearance and textures of these different rocks, many of which she later polished and set in silver jewellery which she made, while I began to think more about how their varied nature led to the complex formations in the landscape which we were increasingly exploring.

Assynt gave her considerable scope for another of her long-established interests, which was archaeology, and she was instrumental in taking us to several sites, two of which inspired me to develop my own, lifelong interest in the past. These were very different, located in contrasting places, and completely captured my imagination. They were the Clachtoll Broch (which at the time we tended to call Stoer Broch, being ignorant of the precise boundaries of the neighbouring crofting townships) and, inland, the Bone Caves near Inchnadamph.

Eastern Assynt is quite unlike the coastal landscape, consisting mainly of long limestone corridors between high, grey, quartzite mountains. In the hinterland of Inchnadamph, two beautiful glens, of very different character, take you into the very special limestone landscape, characterised by such features as dry riverbeds, springs and caves. The turf, well-drained, is sweet and green, the rocks white, and the burns, where they run on the surface, are a clear amber, rather than the dark peat-colour of the Leraig. These places harbour very special flowers, our favourite of which was the gorgeous, daisy-like mountain avens. My father was a very keen botanist, and in later years, he and my mother used to come up to the cottage for a week in mid-June to explore the wildflowers at their early best. Now as I write, decades later, those same flowers are in bloom above the road along the Loch Assynt shore, sometimes in the first week of May; clear proof of climate change.

A little to the south of Inchnadamph, where the long line of cliffs peters out, a narrow, high-sided glen leads one of these burns down from the higher hills. The burn itself, though substantial, does not last long, as, after a short distance, it flows out of the hillside from an unobtrusive spring which is just beside the path. There is something rather odd about standing in the middle of the path there, and having a significant amount of water quietly welling up just below you. From there on up, the way continues beside a dry, stony stream bed, and all the time, ahead of you, there looms a superb, complex crag of limestone. Below the great lump of rock itself, steep grassy slopes lead down to the floor of the glen, and it was up these inclines that we used to labour in order to explore the three or four Bone Caves. They are quite impressive, extending some distance back into the hill, and tall enough for you to stand up straight in places. The view out across the glen is fine, and it was quite easy to start to try to think yourself back in time. What we did know about the caves was that they had been excavated many years ago, that the excavation reports had never been fully published, and some crucial finds had been lost, but their importance, despite these rather negative aspects, was clear. There had been discovered, in the cave system, the bones of several animals which belonged to a post-glacial fauna: arctic fox, lemming, reindeer and bear. There was no doubting the human use of the caves, but some question as to when exactly, and how, they were occupied. There were said to have been traces of hearths, and here my romantic inclinations tended to override any lack of precision in the archaeological record: there must have been cave-dwellers in this remarkable location, following the animals that retreated northwards along with the ice, perhaps after the final fling of the last Ice Age.

Clachtoll Broch was very different, but equally imposing. We would park on the flat Stoer Green, walk down to the sand beach (which occasionally disappeared in winter storms) and head for the prominent monument to the south. On the way, we had to negotiate a high beach of tossed red boulders, where I was always worried that my grandmother would fall heavily on the stones.

The Broch tower, of Iron-Age date, rises on its rocky eminence, still impressive despite a great tumble of stones which must have fallen from its upper walls. Its courtyard was then full of more debris, but within the thick double walls you could trace an internal gallery. The most significant feature remains the single entrance, with its great triangular lintel over the beginning of the passage through to the courtyard. Here, too, are visible passages off on either side. The way up to the entrance seems to have led between subsidiary structures, all contained with a massive outer rampart. Despite the enormous jumble of sandstone boulders, the site gives an impression of great strength, and again gave my romantic nature a great deal of scope for weaving knowledge with heroic fantasy. Rhoderick and I would crawl into the side passages, braving spiders' webs and the dark, conscious of the size of the lintels above us, and the length of time they had remained in place.

Decades later, I began to revisit this fine site on a regular basis; it was partly that its location was in complete contrast to the wooded fastness of my glen, but also because brochs had always fascinated me, and this one raised several questions in my mind. Its characteristics became very clear to me through these repeated visits; the first and most important was that it is, by any standards, a major site: there is a fine, double-walled, circular tower, obviously well-preserved despite the collapse of its upper reaches (which had pretty well filled in its courtyard), the clear remains of at least two enfolding ramparts, enclosing also perhaps two house structures, and some kind of forework at the broch entrance. Secondly, it is a crazy site: probably even when it was built, too close to the sea which has destroyed part of the circuit of the walls, but it is also far from level, necessitating some really awkward construction work. And, finally, I began to see that the imposing tower was in danger of collapse; it had obviously suffered from structural problems in the past (but it took John Barber of AOC Archaeology group to point out to us that the splendid triangular lintel had been reset at some stage, the wrong way up); and it had several stress cracks in the individual boulders of which it was built. Increasingly, too, it was obvious that people were casually digging into the structure.

All this suggested that a major effort was needed to secure its future, and it is very pleasing now to be able to write that after an immense amount of hard work over many years, the project is almost finished, and we have a much better appreciation of what is a magnificent, and stabilised, Iron Age monument. It is a great tribute to Historic Assynt, one of the energetic community bodies which exists in this remote parish with its small and ageing population, that this could be achieved, in partnership with many organisations and agencies.

The Assynt coast has a number of monuments from this period, most of them with obvious defensive features, some on really restricted and awkward sites. The dun on the tidal islet in Loch Ardvar I have already mentioned. Another fascinating site is on the big headland of the Point of Stoer, which is composed of the same sandstone as the high mountains, and has its own fine cliffs. Here, beyond the township of Culkein Stoer, an easy walk leads to a natural arch. This connects a low, but cliff-girt stack to the rest of the promontory; both sections have traces of old stone walls. Those on the stack are obviously coursed and carefully placed, and always looked more recent to me than the wall of massive boulders which cuts off the neck of the headland. That resembles the outer rampart of Clachtoll Broch, and it is more than probable that it derives from the same period. Apart from its undoubted archaeological interest, this is a wonderful viewpoint, looking over the wide expanse of Eddrachillis Bay north to Handa, backed by the pale hills of the Reay Forest. Once or twice I was brave enough to crawl across the narrow neck above the arch and look around the restricted area of the top of the stack; it does not extend far beyond the small, neat structure which stood there.

South of Lochinver, the coast road continues in Assynt as far as Inverkirkaig with its ephemeral sand beach and lovely dark river. Here it ventures south into the neighbouring Parish of Coigach, and this further section was known to us as the 'Lost Road of Ross-shire'. We always assumed that it was not visible on the road maps of the County Council, as for long enough virtually none of it was tarred. Eventually it was rediscovered, and slowly the tarmac extended its length, but it remains to this day very narrow and quite a challenge to drive. On one occasion my grandmother drove Rhoderick and me down it to Inverpolly, in order to locate and explore another promontory fort of probable Iron Age. The walk there was quite steep, and eventually my grandmother decided to wait behind while we ventured further. This monument was quite complex in plan, with some sort of circular 'citadel' from which further walls extended. These were only a few feet in height, but completely fascinating, as they were what is called 'vitrified'. This implied that the original dry-stone walls had been subject to great heat. Individual stones had fused, presenting a 'cemented' appearance, but the apparent cement was black and granular – the little, pink-flowering English stonecrop which grew on it had really dark leaves. Whether this heating process had been undertaken deliberately, in order to present a wall-face which could not be quarried, or was the result of some disastrous, accidental fire, was for us quite a subject for debate as we drove home along the intricate Assynt coast. Around this time, I started taking photographs of the archaeological sites we visited, and making notes in a school jotter, especially purchased for the purpose; my organised interest in, and enthusiasm for, archaeology was born.

The Point of Stoer is a smoother, more flowing landscape than the rugged, complex hinterland of Assynt, and it extends far out into the Minch, the channel between the northern mainland of Scotland and the Outer Hebrides, for which we always looked on the often grey horizon. It had, therefore, a more oceanic feel than the rest of the parish, felt indeed almost like an island, and gave wonderful walking above the high red cliffs. Unlike Handa, it had no vast seabird city, but was, around this time, increasingly home to a number of fulmars, and they, calm and confident masters of the air, would often come quite close to us. One day, I sat for a good while on a prominent little eminence which gave a wonderful view of the slender, top-heavy stack, the Old Man of Stoer, and waited. Sure enough, a fulmar appeared, gliding on those long, narrow wings, and started up a routine fly-past, getting closer and closer to me each time it passed. I sat patiently, photographing it each time it came close, and was very pleased with the results – which, of course, in those days of film, I only saw several weeks later. In the black-and-white photos, the bird's watchful, considering, large dark eye is quite clear; a bird of distinct character.

We were all very interested in birds, and there was certainly a considerable variety to be seen around us, from the lordly golden eagle to the many woodland birds which swarmed around the cottage. Close to the road, in every direction, in those days we would see wheatears, smart with their white-and-black rears, on rocks or clumps of heather. Small bushes would often hold the dapper stonechats, while the shores of Loch Nedd had the statuesque herons, with a few noisy oyster-catchers and the more musical curlews. The loch obviously provided plenty of food, and a number of birds flew over the cottage while on their way to their breeding-grounds from the sea. Among these, the divers, red- and black-throated, really symbolised the north for us. While the smaller red-throat would breed on very small bodies of water, it could often be seen on the larger lochs, perhaps feeding or 'just visiting' – frequently they could be watched for ages as they slept on the water – where the larger, more dramatically-patterned black-throats nested. Their ululating call, and the complex caterwauling of their smaller relative, was emotionally important to us, part of the soundtrack to our precious holidays, just like the mewing of the buzzard as it quartered the hillside above us almost every day.

Of mammals, we saw very much less. As my brother and I explored the wooded glen, we frequently had the briefest of glimpses of the wary red and roe deer, which rarely ventured into the open ground. Once as I walked with one of the shep-herds gathering sheep above the wooded peninsula between Lochs Nedd and Ardvar, the dogs flushed several roe deer; their circular white rumps bounced away from us as they headed for deeper cover. At the other extreme, we heard several shrews squeak among the rushes at the front of the cottage. And that, in those days, was about it, which nowadays sounds rather strange. It must be remembered that many of the shepherds then effectively worked as part-time gamekeepers, and foxes, in particular, were relentlessly pursued; we knew that there were some about, but I do not recall that we ever saw one. Almost every house, too, had its dogs, ours included, so most animals would keep well away. On one occasion, Kandi, who had been out in the dusk, came bolting back to the cottage, every hair standing on end, ears flat, glinting blue eyes narrowed and evil, making the most appalling noise which can best be described as a high-pitched growling. He clearly had an awful fright; we conjectured that he might have met a wildcat and kept him in during the following evenings.

It will be clear that these years began my lifelong interest in the natural world. When I returned to Assynt in 1995, after some fifteen years living elsewhere, the ecological diversity of the parish was much more celebrated than it had been in my childhood. The Assynt Countryside Ranger Service was in place, and extremely effective. There was a flourishing Field Club, which of course I joined, with many areas of interest, and several enthusiasts with their own expertise. In this context, while it is somewhat invidious to single out just two names, I must do so. Pat and Ian Evans of Nedd devoted many years, great energy and wide-ranging knowledge to their studies of Assynt, which resulted, among so much, in the splendid *Flora of Assynt*, a book which is authoritative, comprehensive and simply beautiful. It is well-illustrated and well-written, the product of years of passion. It cannot really be summarised, and is one of the great works of the parish. When my father, then elderly and living in retirement, got his copy, he found it deeply satisfying. He had always loved wildflowers, and the beautiful pictures of the landscape and its varied flora reminded him of the years when he had wandered free over our glorious hinterland.

I cannot resist noting that I had the great pleasure of adding one flowering plant to the authoritative list compiled by Ian and Pat. It is probably the smallest of all, or very nearly, and certainly inconspicuous; it is called moschatel, *Adoxa moschatellina*, and has an attractive, minute flower, greeny-yellow, which has given it its name of 'clock tower'. I was walking one fine day in the hinterland of Inchnadamph, and just happened to see a limestone crag, with a touch of green at its base. I thought to myself: 'A botanist would go and look there,' and I did; there was the moschatel, one of my all-time favourite flowers.

# 9

# People and Places Around

In 1966, Jockan's employer gave up the tenancy of Ardvar, and the Macleod family left the Shepherd's House up by the road. We were very sorry to see them go, but they did not go far – simply to Clashnessie where they had come from originally. Here they had a substantial house and lovely croft, and we were frequent visitors. Rhoderick and I were growing, and we could be more use now with crofting tasks. In fact, as 'the Noble boys' we were beginning to achieve our own separate identity, and established new links between the family and the communities around us. One of the tasks which helped us achieve this was the haymaking at Bordans, Jockan and Joey's croft above the burn in Clashnessie, which had the most beautiful hay-meadow. Here we worked on a lovely day, turning the sweet cut grass with long wooden rakes, looking across to the other white houses of the township, or down across the pale pink sands and shallow, enamelled sea to the cliffs of Handa on the far horizon.

Any day spent working at Clashnessie was wonderful, enlivened by constant joking and laughter; the villagers, most of whom turned out to help in these crucial tasks, seemed all to be possessed by a lively sense of humour and of the ridiculous. Friendly teasing was constant, and we revelled in it. I remember one day at Bordans in particular; it was hot, and Joey brought out a great tray of iced lemonade which we drank while sitting on the short grass below the house. Another day also sticks in my mind, when we went to gather in the oats growing on a croft on the other side of the bay. This belonged to a wonderful old brother and sister, and was harder work than the haymaking. Johnnie cut the oats with the tractor, and we had to gather them up and tie them into sheaves. Again, it was a hot day, but in contrast to the soft new-cut hay, the oats were prickly and irritating to the skin; we had to keep our shirts on to handle them, which made us even hotter. But the comments and jokes, with more than a few innuendoes which we were beginning to be old enough to understand, made the time fly past.

We had always enjoyed our contacts with the folk of the place; the community in Nedd I have already mentioned, but we were equally reliant on the people of the next township of Drumbeg. Here was the nearest Post Office, run by a woman who had the softest, loveliest voice I have ever known; I can still hear her calling out the names of the gathered locals as she sorted the mail. If we did not collect it the late afternoon it arrived, it was delivered the next day by the friendly, burly local postie, a really nice man from Kylesku. And Drumbeg had the village shop, well-stocked and welcoming. Kitty Ross, who ran it, rapidly became a great ally of ours. On one occasion, I gave Joey a lift up to the shop, where we found that Kitty was attending to two girls from a nearby lodge, who were talking, it seemed to me, rather unnecessarily loudly about Edmonton in Canada. Joey and I waited quietly at the other end of the shop, but I noticed the occasional, very quick, slightly ironic glance between my two friends, and when the clearly well-travelled girls left the store with their purchases, I said: 'Come on, you two, what was that all about?'. What the two girls could not know was that Joey and Kitty were closely related; her brother was married to Kitty's sister, and they lived in Canada, in Edmonton. Both Joey and Kitty had made several trips to see their siblings there and knew the city rather better than the girls who, we suspected, had been trying rather hard to impress the locals. (As it happened, Joey had another close relationship: her sister was married to Jockan's rather more precise brother Felix, and Felix ghillied for my grandfather on Loch Stack – it was a small world in some ways.) Drumbeg's other amenity was the fishing hotel; while my parents were not great pub-goers, the Drumbeg Hotel was cosy and friendly, and my father really enjoyed the company of the landlord, Andrew Mackay, who had been a Chief Petty Officer.

Further afield, there was another shop and Post Office in Stoer, and my brother and I were keen to stop there as often as possible. This was because Neil Angus who ran it kept different ice-creams from those we could get in Drumbeg, and one of these was my all-time favourite. I still recall exactly its various flavours, which seemed very exotic to me at the time.

Many of these folk were elderly, quiet and modest, but with depths and knowledge of which one might easily be ignorant. Brigadier Mandleberg had told us that during the winter he corresponded with Neil Angus – in ancient Greek. According to the Brigadier, a handsome and charming man, educated at Harrow, Neil Angus, lean and quiet and educated in Assynt, had by far the better grasp of the subject.

Perhaps about thirty-five or forty minutes away on the twisty, single-track road was Lochinver, the fishing village and main hub of Assynt, with a number of shops, the bank, the garage, a good chandlery and other amenities. A visit here was generally good fun, as we always bumped into someone we knew, perhaps lots of folk, and it could become quite a social event. Assynt at this time was mostly owned by the Vesteys, and the Estate Office was attached to the Factor's House, which had a splendid view out over the bay. We became friendly with successive Factors and Assistant Factors and their families, which increased the social nature of our trips to Lochinver through time. All were very good to us, and we had one or two memorable days through their kindness: on one occasion, we were given the landlord's section of the River Inver to fish; it is rather like a larger version of the Leraig, with rapids and falls and dark pools, except where a vast slow area with deep pools was created with dams and croys, which should provide splendid fishing on the right sort of day. We, sadly, did not have the right sort of day. It was warm and brilliantly sunny, and although the river was quite high after overnight rain, and there were certainly fish in it, they were completely uninterested in the various colourful flies with which we patiently tried to tempt them. I think my father connected briefly with one, but although the entire family, including my grandmother, tried constantly all day, we met with no success, which was very frustrating.

Another time, when my father was away, the rest of us were lent the Estate's attractive launch, the *Blue Star*, and her boatman, Kenny. Given free rein as to where we would go, we elected to cruise down through Enard Bay, round the low cliffs of Rhu Coigach, to the Summer Isles, where we landed on Tanera Mor, the largest of the group. At this time it was virtually uninhabited, and very quiet. *Blue Star* anchored out in the bay, Kenny rowed us to the shore, and we wandered around the ruins where Frank Fraser Darling and his wife had lived and created the farm which he wrote about in his book *Island Farm*. We all knew the book (and others by the same author) very well, and so were familiar with the fact that they had returned what was derelict land to cultivation, and tidied the nearby picturesque ruins, as well as undertaking the formidable task of restoring the handsome sandstone pier. It was quite a significant lesson in the temporary nature of man's involvement in any location on the West Coast. The pier and ruins were again deteriorating, while the former farmland, where drains were blocking, was reverting to rushes and the dark soil becoming waterlogged. Were Fraser Darling to have decided to return, he would pretty well have had to start again from scratch.

On the way back to Lochinver, we fished for mackerel, rocking gently on a calm sea, as we looked across to the craggy coastal islands, the view dominated by the improbable, vertical, western peak of Suilven which reared up from the rocky hinterland. We were quite late back to the cottage that night, and tired, but it had been a very special day – and the mackerel tasted fantastic!

Another, much larger and more famous ship caused some excitement and amusement in later years, when neighbouring Ardvar had been bought by one Aubrey Buxton, about whom we knew rather little, except that he came from Norfolk – or at least somewhere very southern. We discovered that he was also a friend of the Royal Family when, one summer, we found the royal yacht *Britannia* anchored just along the coast from us. Ardvar by now had a Land Rover track, and we passed the Buxtons' vehicle one day when we were going up to Nedd to collect the milk from the Stewarts, as the Buxtons also usually did. Arriving at the house, we found Katie-Anne slightly puzzled, saying that they had just been visited by a girl who looked very like Princess Anne. We were able to assure her that it actually had been Princess Anne, which left her rather crest-fallen, as she was not sure whether she had 'behaved properly'. On this we could certainly reassure her; it was impossible to imagine Katie-Anne behaving improperly.

Another day around the same time, my mother was driving us eastwards; I no longer remember where we were going, but we were just leaving our glen, at a point on the hill where you can see oncoming vehicles for some distance. The Ardvar Land Rover came in sight, being driven rather fast as usual, and my mother said: 'There's that bloody boy again, I am not going to be terrorised by him.' Buxton had been employing a lad to do various jobs about the place, and he, 'that bloody boy' had been in the habit of driving the Land Rover too fast and almost pushing people in ordinary cars off the road – everyone was fed up with it. So my mother, a determined woman, put her foot down, the prow of the Humber rose and we swept imperiously up the hill. The driver of the Land Rover failed to brake when he should have and passed the nearest passing place by a few yards. My mother stopped, and pointed, firmly: 'Back!' she said, 'Back!' There was a grunt of gears, and the Land Rover duly retreated to where it should have stopped. On reaching it, my mother halted again and wound down her window to address a few pithy words to the 'bloody boy'. When the Land

Rover window was also wound down, she found, not the boy, but Prince Philip, looking rather startled. My mother did, as she later said, the only thing that seemed possible; she smiled charmingly, said 'Thank you so much!' and accelerated away. Reliving it in gales of laughter later that same evening, she remarked: 'Bang goes my invitation to Buck House.' (There she was wrong, but that is quite another story.)

By this time, there were new folk in the house by the road; an ex-RAF family had taken on the farm, and it was no longer only a sheep-run, but a mixed agricultural enterprise, with several cattle, geese and hens, and later, a single horse. While it was undeniably true that the greater scale of this farming activity did rather impinge on us in the cottage, and in particular, on our access (as our track went through what could be described as the very heart of the farm), we found the new family to be very friendly, and our little glen, with its two houses, was as happy a place as before. We were in and out of the house by the road as much as we ever had been.

Quite soon, that same road was where I learned to drive; I had actually had lessons in Fife, but failed my test when I tried it there. I then spent the next summer driving on our narrow, twisty road which gave me plenty of practice with all sorts of manoeuvres, especially that of reversing, which was a crucial skill. First of all, I drove the small Triumph estate which we had acquired; that was easy enough, but the big, broad Humber was more of a problem. It had an imposing bonnet which seemed as wide as the road itself, and, when going uphill as on the abrupt little 'Boat Brae' near the cottage, provided some paralysing seconds when all the driver could actually see was the bonnet and sky. Eventually all the practice paid off, and at the next attempt at the test I passed.

Once I had done so, and having two friends from school with the same interest in climbing, the three of us decided to travel north by car one winter and spend a few days in the cottage, with a view to making some winter ascents of my beloved hills. Niall, who, like me, now had his licence, borrowed his mother's

Cortina, and came north from Cheshire to pick up Angus and me. From Fife, we travelled up an increasingly wintry A9, eventually, after quite a long and eventful day, arriving at a rather cold cottage. We managed to get all relevant systems working, and the place became very cosy, an isolated pocket of warmth and golden light in a deep, dark, cold glen. The weather was not very helpful during our short days there. On the first, we set off to climb Quinag, and had managed to scale the first summit when the cloud very firmly came down, and we could only see a few feet ahead. Fortunately, I knew the mountain very well by this time, and led; when we reached a point where the ridge narrowed abruptly and changed direction, I called a halt. From here on, the ridge was bounded by huge cliffs and buttresses on the 'homeward' side, and we would be committed, effectively, to a major expedition in thick mist. This seemed dangerous, and we retreated.

The next day, too, the cloud was firmly down, and all the big hills totally obscured. We went for a walk over the Point of Stoer, and when we were at the highest point, they obligingly cleared and we could at least see our objectives. We had a superb tea, courtesy of the MacLeods at Clashnessie, and as we returned home, the evening sky was a glacial duck-egg blue, and the temperature tumbling. We were in for a heavy frost, and, with luck, the next day would be clear and cold.

So it was. We were up early, to find there had been a fall of new snow during the night, which had stayed powdery in the deep cold. The Cortina was terribly light in the tail end, and we slithered our way along on the coast road, not daring to risk the steep hills between the cottage and Kylesku, nor the high pass over to Inchnadamph, which was our goal. We got there, and spent a magnificent winter day, clambering through deep and endless drifts of the finest powdery snow; these persisted until we were over three thousand feet, and we could at last walk more briskly. The short winter daylight was already failing when we reached the summit of Conival, one of the two Munros here. We had hoped also for the other, Ben More Assynt, but there clearly was no possibility of this, and we had to make do with a glorious view of its long, rocky, snow-covered ridge, before turning back the long way we had come. It was almost as arduous going down the steep back of Conival, and we were tired when we regained the car, before setting off on the skiddy homeward drive. As we eventually reached and passed the farmhouse, a window opened, a voice yelled to us to stop, and dear Nina handed out to us a hot, new-made shepherd's pie. That, most gratefully received, was duly consumed, followed by a probably illicit amount of whisky, and three exhausted, happy teenagers slept extremely well that night – another very special evening spent in the glen.

# 10

# Time Passes

As the years passed, and we grew older, rather inevitably some of the oldest inhabitants of the glen began to grow frail or die. Assynt was still a very traditional place in those days, and funerals were held in the home of the person who had died. As they were generally attended by almost everyone from the neighbourhood, that meant, of course, that a large number of those attending actually stood outside, and might hear nothing other than the, to us, strange and mournful traditional psalm-singing. When the service in the house was over, the coffin was carried off the croft ground which had been the home of the departed, and, in the case of the small, neighbouring township of Nedd, straight up the steep hill road to the high graveyard. The female relatives in those days never followed the coffin up the hill; the whole interment was left to the men. My father, I think, found attending some of these funerals quite hard, and, partly because he did not know the community as I did, enlisted my company at such events, once I was in my late teens. I, too, being at that age both emotional and impressionable, found them quite hard going, and well recall being somewhat aghast when, up in the small and obviously rather crowded Nedd graveyard, the earth which was being shovelled over the newly interred coffin visibly contained a couple of skulls and odd bones. I think my father allowed me the traditional small dram once we were back at the cottage on that occasion.

Other than these inevitable departures, nothing much really seemed to change in Assynt while we were there. The few shops remained the same, and the narrow road with passing places which connected us all together remained unchanged (as indeed it does to this day, apart from the addition of many more passing places and much more traffic). The outside world was, however, soon to be given the opportunity to impinge much more on all our lives.

The 1960s may have been remarkable elsewhere for other things, but for us in the Highlands it was the beginning of the great era of new roadbuilding. This carried on over many years and, looking back, it all seemed rather haphazard, the result, I fancy, of difficulties experienced by the road authorities in agreeing new routes and compensation with the relevant land-owners along the way. At a practical level, to us as we ventured north each successive year, it seemed that the routine was to remove the surface from the old road, then, and only then, to begin the slow process of building a new one – in lengths of a number of miles. This impression may be unjust, I admit, but one aspect I do well remember. The Highlands may often be famous for wet summers, but during those years, the rain seemed torrential, and what was left of the old roads was constantly awash so that the extremely deep potholes in what remained of their original surface were invisible, and we wallowed in and out of them, or, sometimes, crashed into their unguessed depths. On one occasion, the well-laden Humber fell victim to such a deep hole and broke a spring – although we were able to continue to the cottage. The friendly men in the small garage in Lochinver had it all repaired in record time; there was a lot to be said for the mechanical simplicity of cars in those days. They only seemed to have one pit, and some simple bits and pieces of tools and parts, but Andrew and Norman put a new engine into my grandmother's old Austin, when she had continued to drive it, despite having gone off the narrow road and putting a hole in the sump.

Out of all the mess and travail, there ultimately emerged smooth new sections of highway, and there was no doubt that communication with the outside world was generally easier and faster – provided you went by Ullapool. Further south, the A9 remained much the same, with some small improvements, but there was beginning to be talk of providing a completely new, fast road out of the Highlands. Life was beginning to change all over the North, and this certainly had its useful moments, such as during the holiday when my brother was rushed to hospital in Inverness with viral meningitis.

The improving access encouraged us to use the cottage more frequently. We had never (sensibly, I think) contemplated a Christmas or New Year there, mainly because of the lack of electricity, but we did make visits at other times of the year. I rather grumbled, I know, when my parents took to having a week there on their own, around the middle of June. This was in term time, so there was no way that either my brother or I could have come with them, but it often gave them the best weather of the year, and I longed to be there too. The main reason for choosing that particular time of year was my father's interest in botany. There were some special flowers to look for at that season; perhaps the loveliest of these was what we nearly always referred to as *Dryas octopetala*, better known perhaps as mountain avens.

We certainly made the journey north for a few Easters. I remember one when high pressure must have positioned itself over Assynt for the entire week we were there. It was calm, mildly frosty in the mornings, and even the high hills only had thin tracings of snow. The lower ground was, in the brilliant light, sharply delineated, but only in different shades of ochre to brown; there was only a hint of green in the cropped grass around the cottage. While out walking, I took quite a few land-scape photos and once back (reluctantly, of course) at school, I found myself showing a selection of the slides to my tutorial group. I recall being somewhat taken aback when some of the boys, used to more southern landscapes, commented on the harshness of the country which I so loved.

School life was, of course, punctuated at regular intervals by the horror of exams, and my A-Level year eventually arrived.

I spent the Lent term, the one which begins with the New Year, on an exchange at a school in France, which I very much enjoyed. (This turned out to be the beginning of very much another story in my life.) But I had to leave the great expanses of the Normandy plain just as spring was beginning to steal on the scene, and return to Scotland, first to Fife where my mother took me to see a small cottage on to which an enormous oak had fallen in a great winter storm. Then I headed further north, but from my boarding school, and in the company of a couple of masters and some other boys. My school had an institution, the Cadet Corps, which I thoroughly disliked. In theory it was voluntary, but I never heard of any boy being able to wriggle out of it, and each boy was supposed to spend one week during his period at the school at a summer cadet camp, which would have eaten into my precious holidays in Glenleraig. There was, however, one way out. It was labelled, ominously, 'Arduous Training', a week spent during the Easter break, hill-walking, somewhere in the Highlands. This particular year, it was in Torridon, based in the primitive Altroy Bothy near Kinlochewe, and the weather chose to be particularly grim. I do recall that one day we were simply reduced to walking along the road, and even then could hardly see where we were going in the whirling snow. We did have one decent, actually rather wonderful day, to which I referred in an earlier book of mine, *Castles in the Mist*. On this occasion we participated in an annual deer count, and Niall and I walked with a keeper deep into the big hills of this magnificent landscape, where many years later I was to have some glorious days.

After this one good day, the weather was slightly better than it had been before, and when at the end of the week the rest of the school party headed south, I stayed there and got a lift to Poolewe on the nearby coast, where cousins lived at the famous Inverewe Gardens. That evening, my mother arrived in the Humber with my brother, and the next day we headed round the coast to Ullapool, and north to the cottage, where we would stay for another week. The roads were by this time clear, but there was plenty of snow lying, and the countryside looked magnificent. The dreaded spectre of school receded rapidly; we were back where we belonged.

I had a particular task to perform that Easter, one of the few things connected with my school that I did not mind carrying out. Of school subjects, I had always enjoyed Geography, inevitably perhaps the Physical Geography with its glacial, riverine and coastal features, and as part of my A-Levels had to produce a geography project, which of course I decided had to feature aspects of Assynt. And so we spent a few days driving around, with me hopping out of the car at regular intervals to take the photographs which were to provide much of the content of the project. The snow had further retreated, leaving just enough to emphasise particular landforms, and the traces of old land usage, like the lazy-beds, field walls and clearance-cairns. In time (this being an age of film) I was to see that the photographs had come out very well, and writing the project, featuring these pictures of the much-loved landscape, became simply a pleasure rather than a chore. I am unable to resist passing on the information that I got an A grade in the Geography A-Level, and the project was highly commended; shows what real interest in a subject can achieve!

But we had another job to do that Easter; our cottage had once been Snowcemed, and was, in theory, white. That was rather a long time ago and, as the photographs I took of it in the snow when we arrived show all too clearly, the Snowcem had largely worn away, and the cottage walls were, simply, dirty. We were well aware of that, and our other task was to restore it to a pristine, shining white. So, one fine day towards the end of the week, we laboured outside, mixing the powder with water in various buckets, and applying it to the walls with assorted brushes. The old walls were rough, and the labourers got splashed as they worked; Rhoderick ended up in an old pinny and a black sou'wester. When you included the shed, there was quite a length of wall to repaint, but by the end of the day we had done it, except on the one gable where we had not been able to reach to the roofline. At the back, the corrugated-iron extension was already beautifully painted in grey, which spared us quite a lot of effort. All the next summer, every time we looked at our spotless abode, we remembered that tiring but happy day when we had transformed its appearance. That night, in the soft light of the Tilley, warmed by the stove, the three of us were sleepy, content that the job was done, but also aware that we were shortly to return south.

We never really liked the return to what was, I suppose, 'normal life'. In fact, I remember one day when Rhoderick burst into tears at bedtime in the house in Fife, after the day's journey down. My mother came and sat on his bed, and sang him to sleep, I still remember the song. And there was one treat on that way down the long road south. Sometimes, in fact, there were two: if it was hot, we would stop for Capaldi's Ice Creams, I think it was in Kingussie. But we always stopped in Dunkeld for chips, partly as it would be too late for supper when we eventually reached our destination, and partly because we all adored the chips this particular place produced. I can see myself standing there with my father, against the counter, smelling that wonderful (and for us, pretty rare – they were a special treat) smell, hearing my father ask for 'double vinegar for everyone'. No-one ever complained that the car smelt of chips for a few days afterwards . . .

A few days after that, I would be packing again, gloomily getting ready for school. That year, the particular and inevitable gloom was delayed for another two weeks, as my mother suddenly produced scarlet fever, and I was in quarantine – the school did not want me back. When that extra relief came to an end, as it was bound to do, I packed, as ever, the precious photographs of my parents, my grandmother, the dogs and cat, and, almost above all, the cottage and Quinag, my lifeline to better times.

# 11

# The End of the Idyll

There were other intimations of change, too. The farm by this time had become very busy, and as the only way to the cottage lay through its heart, life could at times become fraught. There were far more creatures around us; where occasionally Daisy or some sheep had grazed, sometimes now more than thirty cattle would be impounded. We knew that at times we were in the way of the farming, while equally, at times, the farming was in our way, but we never fell out with the family in the farmhouse, who were very friendly – although, equally, it would be idle to deny that the occasional neighbourly dram or two definitely helped to keep the peace!

But there was a more fundamental problem: the new landlord, Mr Buxton, did not wish to renew our lease when it expired, the date of which was now on the horizon. On his part, this was fairly understandable, as the 'estate', as it was now beginning to be called, possessed, when he purchased it, only its remote lodge, the farmhouse, and our cottage, apart from a few sheds. Should he wish, as he did, to employ anyone to live and work on the estate, the quickest way of finding a home for the said employee would be to resume possession of our cottage. So, in the last year or two of our tenancy, we began to look around for alternatives; that we wanted to stay in the area was undoubted, but, twelve years or so on, there were far fewer possibilities for this than we had been offered all those years ago.

I was not very happy about the situation, but pushed the thought of our eventual departure from the glen out of my mind. I had, in any case, other thoughts to push away, to try to forget. With the first of the wonderful long summer vacations from university came the inevitable realisation that they too, would come to an end, and then I would have to face – what I did rather realise deserved capital letters – Real Life, and I was in no rush to get there.

I did, therefore, face my long vacations in the most positive of moods, determined to do as much as possible within the allotted time. My father was by now making valiant efforts to interest me in some sort of career, although in those days his idea of a 'proper job' was rather limited, and I spent a few weeks one summer working in a Land Agent's office in Elgin. This I quite enjoyed; I stayed with a friendly and lively family, I was allowed occasionally to drive the senior partner's rather fast car, and I got to know Moray quite well. Historically it was an important province of Scotland, with an interesting history and some important ancient buildings, which I loved. Its countryside, in those days, did not do so much for me, as fertile landscapes held little attraction; but there was, importantly, another local interest, as Violet's beautiful elder sister lived nearby, and I visited her several times.

My summer vacations were so long that I could fit in a spell elsewhere, in this manner, without reducing my time in Assynt. Another year, I took myself off, in my little car, to Orkney, a group of islands which fascinated me, and with which my mother and her family had important connections. (This I have written about in my book *Sagas of Salt and Stone*, published by Saraband.)

Eventually, I reached my last such vacation, and with it two other approaching milestones, about which I was more than equivocal: I was to attain my twenty-first birthday (Real Life, here I come!), and it would be our last summer in the cottage in Glenleraig. This all appeared momentous, in every sense a new epoch, and I resolved to write a little journal to record how it progressed; it was as well I did, as it turned out a much more complex summer than any of us had anticipated. I have the little brick-red notebook beside me now.

I was by then very determinedly following up some of my many interests, and once back in Fife I took myself on a jaunt, by train, to Glasgow, simply in order to visit Glasgow Cathedral, a superb building which is still far less well known than it deserves. Glasgow itself, at this stage, was far from its best, and I was not impressed by it, but the Cathedral I adored – and still do.

In complete contrast, my next trip in my little car, a Morris Minor convertible, was for ten days mostly spent in Harris and Lewis, reaching there via Skye. It was frequently rather wet, and I seem to have lived off fish and chips. There were, inevitably, a few damp, cold and slightly lonely moments, but there were high spots too, like Dun Carloway and the amazing Callanish Stones. I also encountered for the first time the full glory of the flower-carpeted machair, although, as I drove north to Ness one fine day with the roof down, it brought on an amazing attack of hay fever, and I sneezed all the way up the road. The best campsite was north of Stornoway, at Garry Beach, where one early morning the sun awoke me, and I went skinny-dipping in the cold Minch. I lay on the sands; the sun was rising in a grey-pink sky, the calm sea was grey-yellow, and the warming beach was again grey-pink, shot with silver. Across the Minch rose the familiar hills of Assynt; prominent among them was the astounding sharp profile of Suilven.

I was in Fife for less than two weeks before we all travelled north again, back to those very hills. Because the A9 was by now so congested, we had got into the habit of leaving Cupar early, and managed on this occasion to depart soon after 5 in the morning, reaching Glenleraig by 2.30 p.m., having avoided any traffic jams – definitely a record. The first week back was mostly spent in preparing for the celebrations of my twenty-first. People began to arrive: Angus, my friend from school, my adored godmother, and a young master from the same school, with his wife and three small boys, who had also become firm family friends. Angus stayed, as before, in the long loft of the cottage with us boys, while the others were 'parked' close by, my godmother having B&B in the friendly farmhouse.

My birthday was celebrated in two parts; separate 'bashes', I suppose one might say. The first was comparatively stately, frankly for the local posh folk, with cousins coming down from their own holidays at Oldshoremore. It was held in my parent's bedroom, with the bed removed for the occasion, which actually was very enjoyable. We knew everyone very well, and I took custody of an unexpected number of presents.

The second part could best, I think, be described as a riot. There was, early on, a moment of anxiety, when Kenny Stewart from Nedd arrived well in advance of the specified time, when several of us were half-dressed at best, only to announce that he had a terrible cold and would not be coming. When the others did arrive, it was chaotic, and absolutely wonderful – also quite noisy! In the confines of the cottage (we used pretty well all the rooms for this occasion) we had two pipers playing, although, mercifully, not at the same time. The MacLeods were there in force (apart from Joey who was babysitting). Jockan was one of the pipers, and their son Alastair played the accordion superbly. Nina from the farmhouse played her auto-harp, and a group of Norwegian girls they had staying sang in beautiful harmony. Hughie from Drumbeg, who had a good voice, sang a lovely local Gaelic song, Airigh Culchinn, and I contributed a few others. In the somewhat confined space, lit by the soft light of the oil-lamps, we danced: an eightsome, a foursome, schottische, Gay Gordons and others. The whisky flowed and there were gales of laughter. For me, as the centre of attention (including being 'bumped' on the floor twenty-one times!), it was all quite emotional. My dear godmother, who loved a good party, had a wonderful time and made many friends; she was also observant and remarked on my attraction to the 'pretty girls'. Violet and her sister Anne were both there, and looked completely stunning; I was deeply fond of them both. In fact, everyone who mattered to me at that stage in my life was there.

When our life did return to the holiday normal, it was still quite busy, as people came and went. Danish cousins visited and some of us took *Periwinkle* around Oldany Island, to meet the others on the gorgeous Clashnessie sands, where a few of us swam, and we had a splendid picnic. Characteristically, my parents had offered hospitality to the son of one of my father's French distributors, and Ben became part of our lives for a few weeks. One brilliant, hot day, Angus and Ben and I climbed the fine southern peaks of Quinag, returning to the car by the dark corrie loch. Here, inevitably, I went skinny-dipping and Ben swam in his smart blue pants, while Angus bathed his feet. On another occasion, Ben, Dad, Rhoderick and I took the boat to the Oldany beach, where again I ended up in the water. It was a glorious day, and the view of Quinag from the beach, across the shallow, sandy bay, was sublime. For a while we shared the shore with another party, but once they left, I succumbed to the childish joy of constructing the most elaborate sandcastle on an outcrop of rock, complete with a death-defying single-track road to it; I was doing quite well in keeping the spectre of 'Real Life' at bay.

There were very different occasions, too: family and clan events. My grandmother had been born a Munro, and, amongst many achievements, her very energetic father had founded the Clan Munro Association. We all dutifully attended a clan gathering at the beautiful Foulis Castle, near Evanton, to celebrate the twenty-first birthday of Hector, the son of the Chief; and my grandmother, looking splendid, made a speech and presented him with the gifts from the clan.

Back on our own West Coast, we went north one day to Kinlochbervie, visiting the ebullient cousins who were holiday-ing there, and having lunch with my grandfather, who had, as every year, been fishing Loch Stack, and had done rather well. He seemed pretty fit for one of his age, despite serious arthritis. The summer season was progressing well, and we had some glorious days.

I spent quite a lot of time walking on my own, sometimes

just up the glen, enjoying the colours of the birches, the pale ochre of the many mosses, the subtly different greens of the grasses, ferns and bracken, the splash and sparkle of the peaty burn. On hot days, I stripped to run over the soft woodland floor, then cooled off in the dark pools, watching the sunbeams playing through the overhanging leaves. Further up the burn, I swam in the beautiful big loch at its head, watching the great mountain sailing like a ship over the open moors, backed by fluffy white clouds on a deep blue sky.

And it was a few days later that my mother saw a golden eagle from her bedroom window, and we all charged out in our pyjamas to watch it soaring majestically in the early morning sun.

Then we had a few rather more complicated weeks. These included a quick trip south for Rhoderick and me, going to a ball in Stirling Castle, organised by Angus, whose father had been a soldier. We had to collect our dance partners en route, and, after the ball was over, return them both to different locations; the weather helped by providing torrential rain almost throughout, and I had a nasty allergy fit. The ball was predictably stately, but enjoyable.

Shortly after, my parents had a quick jaunt to Germany, work-related, yet apparently very pleasant; but again, it was not the simplest thing to begin the journey from Assynt. And, in between times, my grandfather died unexpectedly, followed by two more elderly members of our extended family. There were, therefore, a number of departures, hospitals to visit, funerals to attend, and one or two arrivals, planned some time before all this began. Somehow, in all this confusion, the last days of the family holiday went by, and I was left there on my own.

Despite the fact that I had wanted this, and had planned it, initially I did feel very lonely; but a wonderful day walking around the head of the glen under Quinag, and yet more swimming, rapidly restored my spirits. Then I went, as I had very occasionally before, up to the wonderful Drumbeg pub, where I made a new friend and, inevitably, drank rather too much. There were no parental eyes to watch as I returned to the cottage and strolled around the Back Park in the moonlight . . .

A few other similar days followed, out on the hill or crossing to the just about tidal Oldany Island during the day, walking, running and swimming, followed by a visit to the pub in the evening, or to friends for supper. I was very much enjoying establishing my own identity in this land, and among the community which I had known for so long; I was no longer just one of 'the Noble boys', I was myself, Robin (however strange an entity that really was, even I did not know!).

One day, I drove to Inverness to pick up Simon, a friend from my Cambridge college who belonged to St Andrews, only some nine miles from Cupar. We were to spend the next week mostly in the hills, and the weather did more than just cooperate; it was glorious. We climbed Quinag, Suilven, Ben More Coigach and Stac Pollaidh. At the end of each one but the last, being hot and relaxed, I had my swim and walked around in the sun to dry off. Simon stayed on land but seemed to cope happily with my regular fits of nakedness.

We also had some wonderful social occasions, hosted by very good friends: a rather alcoholic lunch, an evening in Clashnessie with the MacLeods, and a great ceilidh in Drumbeg. It was, for me at least, the perfect boys' week in the cottage.

At its end, we had to get up early so that I could drive Simon to Lairg to catch the train. We saw a male hen harrier very close to the road, near Ledmore Junction; they were often spotted there in those days. On my return, the exhaust fell off the car and I had to go via Lochinver in order to get it re-attached. And on the way home from there, a hen belonging to the Stoer Free Church minister (of whom I was rather scared) ran under my wheels and died. Fortunately, the minister was not at home, and his wife was very nice about it.

Then, suddenly, that was it; time was up. I spent two quick days, packing and saying goodbyes. I took a final walk up the glen, and the next day I shut the door of the cottage and drove south.

During that busy summer, the Assynt Estate, from whom we had leased the Glenleraig cottage, offered my parents the tenancy of another one they owned. It was actually further south, on the way to Ullapool, over the border from Sutherland into Wester Ross, and in the parish – just about – of Coigach. It had been a shepherd's cottage, but the estate had decided to take the sheep off the hills of the Drumrunie Forest and move the shepherd and his family elsewhere.

At first sight, it was not particularly inviting. Although the views to the southwest, of the peaks of Ben More Coigach, were splendid from the distance, its own position, where the long dip-slope of Cul Beag disappeared into a large area of bog, was bleak. It did, however, improve on closer acquaintance. It sat quite snug below the road, and the ground in front of it ran down to a rushing burn, significantly smaller than the Leraig, but pretty. It got quite a lot of sun, and there was fishing nearby, in a few small lochs, and one much larger one, Loch Lurgain, which ran westwards between the lovely peaks of the Coigach hills. To the west was Coigach proper, and Achiltibuie with the Summer Isles; Ullapool was an easy drive to the south on one of the good new roads. Access from Cupar would be much easier than to Glenleraig, and this may have been the deciding factor; my parents took on the lease.

I had by now been in the habit of venturing north (always by train) for New Year, which I spent, with the greatest enjoyment, in Clashnessie. A year or so after that last summer in the glen, while up there in midwinter, I asked Jockan if he could give me a lift along the coast to Glenleraig so that I could go for a short walk, perhaps just around the Back Park. He did exactly that, and left me for a while. I walked past the farmhouse (there was no-one there at that particular moment), past the byre and barn, and along to the empty, silent cottage. I went down to the burn, dark and running high, and around to the back, to the small patch of ground which Dannie had fenced for us so many years before.

I knew well, by then, that I was an emotional youth, but I was surprised to find myself leaning against the short length of dyke, with tears running down my face. Jockan had referred to it as my old home; he was quite right, but it had been, in effect, so much more than that, and it seemed that I would never get back. Eden had been found . . . and then left behind.

# 12

# Back to the Land

Within three years, I was back living full-time in Assynt. By then, a lot had changed. I was married, and we had a very young child. We had been living and working in Inverness, and had enjoyed getting to know the Capital of the Highlands from the perhaps more real perspective of the resident worker, as opposed to that of the visitor. It is a lovely city, in part at least, and in a beautiful setting, and we had made some good friends. But the work in the Highlands and Islands Development Board had its very real frustrations for me, and I had realised that an office job, despite the security that it offered, also guaranteed something which I still find difficult – being confined indoors in spells of good weather. Not being entirely sure what we really wanted to do, we then decided to go where we actually wanted to be and find some way to do that. And there was no doubt: we wanted to live in Assynt.

We ended up somewhere very different from the coastal area I knew so well from my youth. This was partly because we got the chance of a small croft: Jockan had some relations who had lived in the inland community of Elphin, where they still had a croft and a somewhat derelict little house, which had been their old family home. They had no wish simply to sell the place to the highest bidder but were looking for people who would try to make something of actually living there; and, fortunately, they decided that they liked us. The process of acquiring a croft can be somewhat cumbersome, but eventually it was completed, and we could take stock of what was to be our home for the next several years.

In some ways, it was not all that enticing. The little house had been built close to the old single-track road and had rather suffered when that had been significantly widened and made much faster. It did look east but was rather squashed into a high bank at the back, to the west and to the north; this did at least provide quite a lot of shelter from the prevailing winds. There was some space by the southern gable, and the remains of a garden; sadly any view on this side was blocked by the local telephone exchange. The house and garden were at the very corner of the small, three-acre croft, which lifted gently from the road and levelled out before shading into what seemed like an endless expanse of bog.

The really good news was that the land itself, of the croft and also the garden, was very good; Elphin is on limestone, and therefore unlike much of the rest of Assynt, being an island of real green grass and white rock. The view from our rather small windows, over the road, was of a row of good fields rising into a fine hill with pale crags; where our croft became bog marked the very end of the porous limestone and of the fertile ground.

The surrounding landscape, best seen from the higher hill, is magnificent. To the west, so often seen against the setting sun, we could see the fine peaks of Cul Beag, Cul Mor, Suilven (which looks amazing from any direction) and the long slope of Canisp. Elphin and its neighbouring township of Knockan lie to the south of the parish of Assynt, close to its boundary with the parish of Coigach, which is geologically fairly similar, and endowed with the same type of fine scenery, although its big hills cluster rather closer together. To the south, a highish pass, steep on its northern side, took the new main road quite quickly to the junction at Drumrunie. Perhaps a mile along the road to Achiltibuie was my parents' new cottage, which they had set about enlarging so that they could take advantage of the easier access, using it more often than they had Glenleraig.

Being higher in elevation, and in the open, less-populated country of the interior, meant that Elphin had a slightly isolated feel, but at the same time it was also quite convenient for travel in all directions: westward to Achiltibuie as described, to the east from Ledmore Junction and down the Oykell, south to Ullapool and beyond (including Inverness, where we all went when the list of things-we-need-to-get reached a certain length), and north to Lochinver, or over Skiag to Kylesku and, ultimately, Kinlochbervie, Durness and the north coast. So, as a location in which to live, it was in fact significantly more practical and accessible than the remote peninsula or island of which we might have been dreaming.

We had some ideas about how, eventually, to earn a living, but having a small financial cushion from the advantageous sale of our cottage in Glen Urquhart, our main concern was to restore the little Elphin house, and to work the long-neglected garden and three-and-a-bit-acre croft. We were both fully signed-up members of the contemporary back-to-the-land, practical self-sufficiency, do-it-yourself and grow-it-yourself movement. I suspect we were regarded as hippies by some of those around us, but we fairly rapidly met others in Assynt with the same motivation, and hugely enjoyed the freedom to get on with the various jobs involved. We had one firm rule, to which we stuck as closely as possible; if the weather was good, we worked outside, and if it was not, we worked inside. And, importantly, we did take afternoons, or days, off, whether it was to enjoy the countryside around, or to go and see friends or relations – my parents, brother and grandmother especially, if they were at Drumrunie. I always felt that a sensible work/life balance was crucial in the long term, and have stuck to the principle, sometimes in the face of a degree of criticism from others, ever since.

Before moving in, we had stayed a few days at Drumrunie with friends, who very kindly helped with the initial decoration and organisation which would make most of the little house habitable. We therefore began our spell of residence in the house with a tidy, if tiny, little bedroom for Mairi, our almost-toddler, a decent bedroom for us, a bathroom which had only needed repainting, a sitting-room and a kitchen/dining-room. This last was fine apart from the damp gable, which we had had reharled on the outside, while we stripped it on the inside, scraped away much of the damp mortar, and left the stonework to dry out. The damp had badly affected the landing and the bedroom above the kitchen; as weather permitted, I worked my way along the landing and into the rather grim bedroom which had not been habitable for years, possibly decades.

I had very little knowledge of, or aptitude for, carpentry, and was somewhat averse to precise measurement – on the rather sensible grounds that to try to fit square cupboards precisely into a space defined by wonky walls, floor and roof, was only going to lead to the necessity of filling in the result- ing inevitable gaps. I soon discovered why the floors were wonky; stripping away the worm-eaten pitch-pine lining and floorboards revealed that damp had seriously affected the floor- joists where they ran into the wall. The roof had been renewed at some stage, so they were now dry, but clearly rotten. I was, I decided, not capable of carrying out any of the conventional and rather major work to solve the problem and was wonder- ing what to do when I discovered that, unlike the floor-joists, the roof-timbers were not simply sound, but as hard as rock. I therefore devised the neat expedient of hanging the beams in the floor from those in the roof, and hiding the result behind some rather informal cupboards, retaining, sensibly I thought, a hatch, through which I could inspect the success, or other- wise, of my carpentry. Others might criticise the look of the cupboards, and no doubt did; I was more concerned to ensure that the floor never gave way – and it did not!

Soon after moving in, during the early winter, we were invited to the Primary School party; we knew that this would be hugely enjoyed by our very sociable toddler, Mairi, that we would probably enjoy it, and that it would provide a very useful introduction to the community around. It worked out very well; we had a good time and made the acquaintance of a number of folk who were to become real friends. Among them were Bill and Ingrid Ritchie, with their sons, the quicksilver, blonde Colin and the quieter, dark Paul. Although it was mainly a party for the kids, a certain amount of whisky seemed to be circulating quietly and it became a good west coast ceilidh; we were glad that we could easily walk home.

This party was actually held in the Old Elphin School, a solid stone building of the type which may be seen throughout the Highlands, the gabled schoolhouse attached to the big schoolroom, which always had high windows so that the pupils within should not be distracted by the sight of the enticing world outside. This school had in fact been closed, and children from Knockan and Elphin were taken by car to Inchnadamph. In those days, there were similar primaries in the parish at Unapool, Drumbeg where Colleen McCrimmon had taught, Stoer and Lochinver. Now, roughly fifty years later, only the one in Lochinver remains. The others closed as the number of school-age children slowly declined, which shows very clearly that while the actual number of people in Assynt may not have changed very much over the decades, the nature and age of the population have done so very definitely.

Outside our little house by the road, the tasks were many, and it was hard to know where to start. The walls and roof of the house needed painting, old flowerbeds against the walls which were holding damp soil had to be removed, space had to be dug to enable us to park the car tidily, and the area in front of the house, adjoining the road, had to be fenced, gated and generally made safe for our about-to-be toddler, and various pets. Fish lorries thundering past made the house shake, so the protection needed to be real.

The sloping, roughly rectangular vegetable garden had to be dug and laid out in beds and paths. Its soil was dense and black and proved to be very fertile; we planted pretty well as we dug, and strawberry bed, raspberry cage, blackcurrant bushes, lines of vegetables and herbs began to grow as the new gravel path made its way from the gate to the house up to the gate to the croft. That year we had a wonderful February, soft, dry and warm, and the rather longer days helped us make great progress. By the time the Easter snows came I had sown peas, and they were sprouting green; I protected the new shoots under the snow in inverted jam-jars, and as soon as the warmth came again, they were released. We were soon shelling fresh garden peas in the open air, and revelling in our own produce.

The lovely green ground of our croft was only fenced on two of the four sides, and I started slowly, bit by bit, to enclose part of it, and subdivide that so that we had, in effect, two fields. A little gate gave access to the damp heather of the Common Grazing, in which we had a share. In most of the other crofters' minds, that share was for sheep, but we had other ideas and, as soon as was practical, we acquired two lovely white goats, christened Alpha and Beta after one of our dearest friends and her sister (we knew they were the sort of people who would appreciate the compliment, which was meant sincerely). They were enchanting animals – friendly, clean, and very easy to handle – and provided genuinely lovely milk, from which my wife also made various cheeses and yoghurt. We could rotate their grazing in the two fields, and release them, particularly in the winter, onto the Common Grazing where they relished the heather. The dream was becoming reality, and the brown hens added a touch both homely and practical, with the added bonus of delicious eggs.

An incredibly friendly and helpful man, the lovely John Venters, who lived with his family in Elphin, came and cut the unfenced meadow for us, and we had perfect drying weather for the hay, which was to be an important part of the winter food for the goats. In the warm breeze, the flower-and-herb-rich grass dried rapidly, and we were soon taking it into the stone barn-and-byre which stood roughly in the middle of the croft. Haymaking in such conditions was a most enjoyable task and rendered all the happier by the flaxen-haired Mairi, now very much running about, delighting in the company of the dog and the goats, and even in that of the hens.

We had been shown the peat-banks that went with our croft, and in dry April weather I had cut a good store of peat for the winter. Peat-cutting is not as romantic an occupation as some may think, being fairly back-breaking, and in addition, I had to carry each bag of dry peat to the road. But slowly, peat accumulated in the barn and on the outside stack, while I gathered wood from various sources at intervals. We had installed a solid-fuel cooker in the kitchen, and a little wood-burner in the sitting-room, so plenty of fuel was required.

We worked hard that long summer, and good weather extended right to the middle of November, by which time I had virtually finished the long task of repainting the corrugated iron of the roof; we had no wish for our roof to be one of the many of rusted iron which characterised Elphin in those years, picturesque though they might look. The vegetables in the long-uncultivated ground of the garden had grown spectacularly, and we had to fold the outer leaves of some of the cabbages to get them through the front door; we did think of emulating the Findhorn Community, which rather fascinated us, and forming a cult based on the magical properties of our ground, but never quite got around to it . . .

When winter did arrive, we were actually ready for it, and settled back into the routine work of improving the interior of the house. There were two or three spells of heavy snow, and at times we were cut off, at least from the world to the south, as the northern aspect of the hill we all simply called 'Knockan' could hold a lot of snow. This did not matter much to us, most of the time. We were, typically, making our own bread, drinking our own milk, eating our own eggs, vegetables and cheese . . . and were very content.

I kept a very sporadic diary that first year or two, and during one cold spell that winter, made a few notes. One day, I climbed up Cnoc Breac, the prominent limestone hill which was high above us. At first, I got good views of our much-improved little house with its garden and partly-fenced croft, but then it began to snow heavily. Soon it was a virtual white-out, of the densest, softest snow I had ever known. There was no wind, not even a breeze, and the heavy flakes fell thickly, straight to the white ground. It was magical, and I was elated; I stripped and ran around in the ice-feathers of the falling snow, rolled over and over in the deep drifts, until my skin glowed with life. Eventually I dressed and returned to the warm and cosy little oasis which was our home. This was indeed the Good Life.

# 13

# The People of the Place

The process of getting to know the Assynt community all the year round, as opposed to being simply a summer visitor (albeit one who had happily taken to spending New Year in Clashnessie) was fascinating and got off to a quick start when John Venters called around one afternoon. He was going that evening to a meeting of the Assynt Crofters' Union, and did I want to come? It seemed, rather vaguely, to be quite a good thing, and so, later that day, off we went. I was quite at ease during the evening's proceedings, as I knew the Chairman and some members of the Committee fairly well. Towards the end of the meeting, I was rather taken aback when I was put forward for the vacant position of Secretary – proposed by dear John himself! Once again it seemed, rather vaguely, to be quite a good thing to do, and so I returned home that night clutching some old files, and with some official standing in the community, however small.

As it happened, the Crofters' Union was quite a lively organisation, and soon had an important role to play in publicising the effects of changes to the legislation which governed the complexities of crofting tenure. These were far-reaching and controversial, with a number of folk forecasting that, however desirable they might be in some ways, giving to crofters the automatic right to purchase their house-and-garden ground (with the eventual possibility of unrestricted selling-on) would be the ultimate death-knell of crofting as it was then known.

As, decades later, I travel the coast road through the familiar townships, past all the new houses, most of which are not occupied all year, it is hard not to agree with that view; but then again, some families have survived economically just because they could sell a house, or a site, to someone with money from elsewhere. And it is crucial to remember that individual crofts were never intended to be viable economic units (our own was just a little over three acres in extent); they were always the basis for part-time activity.

The Union duly held a number of meetings in scattered village halls, which I attended, often with the role of introducing our local Crofting Commissioner (who, of course, everyone knew!), sometimes having to run the meeting and explain the changes myself. These were interesting and friendly occasions and, as a result, I soon knew the principal elements of the legislation by heart. This should have been very helpful much later when it came to me, as a crofter, making some changes to the status of a small part of my tiny croft, but as the then landlord of Elphin and Inchnadamph (not at that time part of the Assynt Estate) had no such knowledge, she objected to my perfectly legal intention, and we were close to arguing the case in a session of the Land Court before she withdrew her entirely illegitimate objections. The whole process, for me, was not much more than a moral victory; it had cost me time and money and should never have happened. Up until then, I had rather taken for granted the way our Highland countryside was owned and controlled, but from then on, I began to be significantly more aware, and questioning.

A couple of years earlier my father had had some difficulty in finalising the tenancy of the cottage at Drumrunie. As the Assynt Estate would never, in those days, sell any property, and my parents were sure that they wanted to use the place for many years to come, they asked for, and were rapidly granted, a long lease. The problem, when it arrived, was the wording of the lease, which required my parents to return all buildings, at the close of the tenancy, to the condition in which they had been found at the beginning. As my father briskly pointed out, this was ridiculous; one of the ground floor rooms was damp, which they proposed to remedy – was the damp to be restored at the close of the tenancy? And there was a disused barn and byre which they intended to turn into extra accommodation (the basic cottage was indeed significantly smaller than Glenleraig) – was this to be demolished when the lease came to an end?

The initial answer, illogical though it seemed to us, was yes. Of course, my father objected to that, and letters flew back and forth until at last sense was seen and intelligent phrasing replaced the original provisions. Now, my father was not only quite obstinate, he was also well-educated and articulate, and it had taken him a considerable effort to get a reasonable result; he remarked to me that you could see why many people might just give up in the face of such a nonsensical provision. In fact, we discovered from friends in a few townships that exactly this had been happening on a number of occasions, and young folk, who had wished to stay in the parish, had eventually given up and moved away from Assynt which, sadly, now had a fairly elderly and dwindling population.

As I got to know that population better, I became amazed at the number of lively community bodies there were, and at the busy social scene outwith the summer season – splendid dinner-dances in Drumbeg and Lochinver, for instance – and the extraordinary generosity of the community in supporting numerous good causes. Some of this could be anticipated; I joined the Cancer Relief committee, and we put a lot of effort into fundraising. Even then, most of us knew someone with cancer and there was, for all of us, an undeniable feeling of self-interest as we helped with yet another bring-and-buy sale. But that factor could not account for the astonishing sum of money which Assynt raised for the Queen's Silver Jubilee; I remember working out that if the British population had raised the same amount per head as the small and not exactly prosperous parish of Assynt had done, the total would have been around three times what was actually achieved.

Looking back at that time, and that community, I am struck by the fact that although so many of the people we knew would qualify, by any standard, as hard up, they were always hospitable, and very generous with their time towards any casual visitor. I think we virtually never telephoned in advance to say that we were thinking of coming over, let us say, that Sunday afternoon. If they were in, and we turned up, we were always welcome, although there were some amusing moments. We went often to Clashnessie, as Violet, living at the time with her parents, now had two small, engaging, red-haired kids, and on one occasion we headed, as ever, for the back door – which was the one used by friends; only strangers would go around to the less accessible front door. As usual, we went straight in, just calling out as we shepherded our two youngsters through the door. There was nobody in the back kitchen, just an ironing board, and a pile of ironing. Joey had fled at the sound of the door and did not return to view until she was sure who was coming in; this was a time when the Sabbath was still a day when even such basic tasks as washing and ironing could not be countenanced by some of the more devout. Fortunately Joey's washing line was invisible to all, hidden in a sort of little courtyard, surrounded by sheds.

We had friends in pretty well every direction: northwards to Unapool (near Kylesku), along the coast via Drumbeg and Clashnessie to Achmelvich (where we enjoyed some wonderful musical evenings), or southwards to Ullapool where relations of old Brigadier Mandleberg lived; they, too, with their young children, became close friends and introduced us to others. And when I started to work at the Highland Stoneware Pottery in Lochinver, with its team of artists and craftsfolk, that extended our social circle still further. We were all pretty adept at carting our children around in the evening, and putting them to bed in strange houses (although ours seemed the most reluctant of all actually to go to sleep – Mairi, in particular, loved a good party from a very early age!). Drinking and driving was still commonplace, so I look back on that free-and-easy era with very mixed feelings; the sad truth is that there were some fatal accidents which hit our small communities hard.

With the animals, the croft and vegetable garden, the house and, soon, two young children, my work in the pottery as well as my own work as an artist painting local landscapes, these were busy and happy years. Each was punctuated by the regular visits of my family to nearby Drumrunie, and activities which became almost ritual: Sunday lunch with all the family (my mother was a superb cook); summer trips out in one of my father's small boats, one on a little loch with a sandy beach near the house, the other moored at Old Dornie from where we could cruise through the islands; and a regular, end-of-autumn visit which included a magnificent dinner at the famed Summer Isles Hotel in Achiltibuie. We knew the owner, Robert Irvine, quite well – he had bought some of my pictures for the hotel – and my father really enjoyed teasing his daughter, Lucy, when she was doing a spell as a waitress there. By this time of the year, the landscape was at its most spectacular; there is not much heather, and in the late autumn the vegetation of grasses and sedges turns a remarkable tawny-red, sometimes highlighted by the late flame colours of rowan berries and the last leaves – irresistible to any artist.

After some years, I inherited some money from an elderly relation, and we decided to build a little house up on the croft and away from the road. This seemed a reasonable enough idea, but I soon discovered that our landlord, apparently, had other ideas. I was informed that there was an estate objection to the project; a letter had been sent, stating that our little house right beside the busy road was 'adequate', which rather riled me, and so I went to see the landlord's representative who lived at the time in Inchnadamph Lodge. There, in a drawing room which was rather larger, it seemed to me, than the ground floor of my cottage, I was told that I could not, on any account, have access to the owner of the estate, which did little to improve my mood.

Eventually, despite this unpromising start, we got our way, and in record time a little timber-framed kit house was built near the western boundary of the croft, with all the amazing views we had for so long enjoyed, but only when we were out and about. Winter sunsets, when the great hills were covered in snow, were absolutely stunning, although the fierce gales which were common were experienced in all their fury in a way we had hitherto avoided. There were times when I watched the two picture windows, which looked to Cul Mor and Suilven, flexing in the storms, and did wonder . . . but they never actually broke.

The ground floor of the old house we turned into a little craft shop and art gallery; the latter was full of my own pictures, and in the first year of it being open we did rather well. I soon discovered that there was an unexpected problem in the popularity of some views. I had painted the snowy peaks of the mountains against the spectacular sunset colours, and the pictures sold as I was placing them on the gallery wall; other folk who were in the room at the time immediately asked if I would paint others of the same scene. I did so, to begin with, but decided, reluctantly, that I would not do so again – the second version was never as good as the first.

I quite enjoyed being in the shop, as I could work in the nearby garden if there were no potential customers around. And I also got to know some of the customers quite well; it was surprising to realise exactly how many foreign visitors to Assynt there actually were, even then, and my ability with languages stood me in good stead. It may have encouraged folk to make a return visit to the shop and gallery within just a couple of days; certainly a number did so, and even sent me postcards when they returned to France or Holland or Sweden – some remained in touch for several years.

One real benefit of moving from our bedrooms down by the road was that we found ourselves further from the corncrakes. There were a few inhabiting the underused fields across the road, and they made a remarkable racket through the summer evenings and nights. For a small, almost invisible, skulking brown bird, they made their presence felt in no uncertain terms, and often kept us awake for hours, especially when they had newly returned to us from Africa, and were just 'tuning-up'. I had spent some time in the fields out of curiosity, keen to see the creature which could make such a din, but never had more than the briefest glimpse.

In June and July, of course, the nights were very short, and we did have lovely spells of weather. I found it almost impossible to go to bed on these wonderful light evenings, and would leave the croft, cross the road and walk up the fields to the limestone crags, from which I could look down on our garden and fields, backed by the amazing hills. If I went, as I often did, much further east across the elevated limestone ground, I might stay out until it was genuinely twilight, and the white rocks glowed. There were masses of flowers in bloom, mostly the lovely, daisy-like *Dryas*, and they too gave back the fading light like tiny moons. Looking west, the last light touched the long, almost canal-like length of Loch Veyatie, and the ancient hills grew blue-black as the sun briefly set. It was pure heaven.

# 14

# Life Moves On

Being part of a small community, as I knew from Glenleraig days, meant that we felt the deaths of old friends very strongly, and early on during our time in Elphin, dear Hughac from Nedd and the wonderful old Brigadier Mandleberg from Oldany had died. That same year, Jockan had a bad heart attack, and was very ill for some anxious months, but he made a remarkable recovery, and carried on much as before for some more years, before falling ill again. This time he did not survive, and we joined with his grieving family in the croft where he had, over so many years, made us wonderfully welcome. At most funerals in Assynt, it was then, as it often still is, the custom to sing the Twenty-Third Psalm 'The Lord's my Shepherd' to the local tune which most people know from 'Amazing Grace'. I had, and still have, a strong voice, and had always sung, so, without in any way wishing to, I began to find myself leading the otherwise unaccompanied singing at such house funerals. It was extremely hard to do so on this occasion; Jockan had been the most wonderful man, gentle and kind, but with a wicked sense of humour, and I had known him so well for many years. Not surprisingly, this was another occasion when I found myself at the back of an old house, leaning over a dyke, crying my eyes out.

Another very sad occasion was tragic in a way that Jockan's death, although he was no great age, was not. We had good friends at Achmelvich, Ian and Penny, whom I had known since we were in Glenleraig, and as they had young children, and were very musical and hospitable, we had become very close to them. Penny became ill, and the problem turned out to be a brain tumour; she survived one operation, and we visited her in Edinburgh while she was recovering and staying with her parents. The problem sadly recurred; she had another operation but was never the same person and died fairly soon after. I vividly remember her funeral at the new graveyard on Stoer Green by the sea; her siblings linked hands and looked up at the sky as she was laid to rest, tragically young, leaving Ian with two small children.

In face of such tragedies, we did find comfort in those people around us, and also in the beautiful landscape we inhabited. After Penny's funeral, on the way home, we stopped the car at a small parking area by a little burn which, running beside the single-track road for a distance, suddenly dives into the narrowest and rockiest of side-glens, past the ruins of a little mill from the same period as the one in Glenleraig. I wrote that visit up later the same evening:

> We went down the narrow little glen, with its grey rocks, to the old mill of Altnabradhan. Its walls are of gneiss, the mill-lade is well-preserved, and there are red millstones of sandstone and green ones of serpentine. Further down the little twisting glen, we came to Port Altnabradhan, a narrow inlet between rocky points of grey gneiss. The sky was now the opalescent colour of late afternoon, and across the soft grey of the Minch, we could see Harris clearly, even the snow on Clisham. There were a few fishing boats far out, and birds closer to hand; only a slight swell at the mouth of the inlet. Close in, the water was a cold, clear green, and the sand under it could be seen to extend quite far out. At its head were little sand beaches between rough, grey-pink rocks, and a small area of cropped, machair-type grass above a shingle beach. On the edge of this machair someone has

had the happy thought to lay out, in stones on the grass, a celtic and an ordinary cross, which point westwards to the islands. The place has a magic which just cannot be described. We kept very quiet and watched the sea curling over the sand.

Another lovely day, we walked down from the road to the inlet of Ardvar, and across, the tide being low, to the tumbled stones of what we always called the 'broch' (although personally I would now call it an islet dun) and looked at the lovely old fank and cottage building where I had worked as a boy. It was now all abandoned, being some distance from the road, but still largely intact. In this sheltered place, the birches were just going green, and all the birds were singing; summer was on the way, and life was good.

Whenever I could take the time away from everything else, I did take to the hills; this was only two or three times a year, but they were always special. My wife and family were not very keen on me climbing on my own, and this had meant that my solo trips, although enjoyable, tended to be fairly short days on relatively easy hills like Creag Liath which rose behind the nearby cottage at Lyne. When, however, Chris, a music-teacher from Ullapool School, had come to live in Knockan, the township next to Elphin, I had the chance to do some longer days out with him, as he was as keen and fit as me.

We set off one glorious October day to climb Ben More Assynt, leaving the car at the ford in Glen Bain which runs into the limestone landscape behind the hamlet of Inchnadamph. This first part of the walk was extremely familiar to me; we had brought the young Mairi up here when she first began to walk, and she had run with delight over the short green turf which leads down to the disappearing river of this enchanted area. This time, however, we were keen to gain height, and so left the more familiar ground, heading upwards. We had started about ten in the morning, and it was bright and cold, with frost still crisp in the shadows. We made our way up the side of Beinn an Fhurain, and into the little corrie down which tumbles the burn that separates that hill from Conival, the first of the big peaks. Here we saw our first deer, although we had been hearing them roaring all the time. We crossed the col and went up the steep rocky slopes to the summit ridge; I well remembered labouring up here in heavy snow with my school friends Angus and Niall on that wonderful winter boyhood expedition. We emerged from the shade into the brilliant sun, and reached the summit of Conival about midday, pausing briefly to admire the distant, hazy views. The east was blanketed in fog, but our goal was clear, and we did not dawdle on the awkward, grating piles of quartzite which lead to the summit of Ben More, below which we lunched, sheltered from the cold east wind. We had a glorious view to the northwest, over the great arched buttresses of Na Tuadhan, to the fine ridges of Quinag . . . and I recall excellent venison-and-juniper-sauce sandwiches!

After lunch, we went down the lovely ridge towards the south – soft, green, mossy grass and little towers and crags of twisted grey rock; the quartzite ends at the main summit in a shattered, steep little cone. The ridge narrows and presents the sort of amusing little moments I like, nothing too nerve-racking, but I could see that Chris was getting less and less happy, and he did not want to tackle the little pinnacle that provides the only, and brief, moment when total concentration is needed. So he went back to descend to the loch below via the sheets of hanging scree, and I rushed happily along the rest of the ridge to Carn nan Conbhairean, enjoying all the little towers on the way, although some downward steps across a small natural bridge needed care.

Then down the steep grass from this last summit, where I had taken a good long look back to Ben More and Conival, one of the loveliest mountain views I know. I chose a line of descent close in under the steep slopes of the hill, going down to the loch while avoiding all the troublesome slow peat hags, which I had encountered the first time I had ever come that way. Chris was not yet in sight, so I dawdled around the loch and sat for a while on a large boulder on the shore. I was sheltered from the cool breeze, and the loch was perfectly still, reflecting the brilliant green- and white-scored slopes, the pure white of the quartzite summit, and scree gullies where some stags were roaring, and the azure sky. It was perfection; Olympus, the haunt of the gods, a fancy made slightly more feasible by the fact that I had once found my favourite flower, the Grass of Parnassus, in bloom on the very slopes I had just trodden. I knew the water would be too cold for swimming, which is what I wanted to do, but instead, I beguiled the hour by catching some trout in the burn, by the simple expedient of driving them ashore. I wanted to ascertain whether, in fact, they might be arctic char, which inhabit exactly such remote lochs, but these did not seem to be.

Chris rejoined me and we walked, deer on all sides, down the attractive narrow glen of the Traligill; that suffix '-gill' is in fact Norse, indicating a small ravine, so the Vikings had trodden that way long before us. We came round one corner to see a golden eagle floating gently along the steep cliffs of Conival. Further down, we saw it again with its mate, and watched them soaring for at least half an hour, before they landed on Conival's summit, perhaps two thousand feet above us. There they stood, in the ultimate picturesque pose, gilded further by the evening sun. A fitting end to a truly glorious day.

The weather, of course, did play a major part in regulating what we did, and how we felt. At one end of the spectrum, there was, of course, the fabled summer of 1976. By then, I was working in the pottery in Lochinver, and enjoying the summer 'commute' in the moderately early morning, and the wildlife which I might see on the scenic way to the pottery. In particular, I quite often had views of black grouse, themselves fabulous birds, close by the Little Assynt Field, which in those days was cultivated. On the way home, in the really hot weather of that summer, I had the roof of my little Morris Minor down and enjoyed the amazing views from the open car. Once back home, I simply stopped by our house, collected my wife and Mairi, and continued on down the road to Drumrunie, going just a little way past my parents' house. There we halted in a wide passing place, and walked down the hill, on long sloping slabs of purple Torridonian sandstone, to the shore of the larger of the group of small lochs, where my father had the fishing, such as it was, and the small boat *Troutbridge*, which had been on the remote Loch Poll. On the narrow, sandy beach we would laze, play with the ever-laughing Mairi, wander in and out of the shallow water, even venture far enough out to swim.

Such high-summer bathing became a habit, and we quite often would take friends there; on one memorable occasion, we were on the beach with two of my university friends who were now living in Skye, and their little baby. They were, in many ways, very like-minded, and as we lazed and ate our picnic, not one of us had a stitch on while we revelled in the wonderful sunshine. Suddenly, unannounced, over the bank came my parents. We all remained totally calm, they continued forwards as if this sort of thing happened every day, and Duncan picked up his tiny daughter to introduce her to my mother. It transpired that they had decided to take the boat out, so Duncan and I duly pulled it into the water and helped them in. Only as they rowed tranquilly across the shining water, did the sound of happy laughter echo below the ranked, hazy peaks of Ben More Coigach.

The summers of 1978 and '79 were very different. For weeks, if not months, the rain poured, and the wind howled. John Venters once again cut our field of hay for us, but the actual haymaking, the drying of it, was extremely hard work. We had found long wooden hay rakes of traditional style in the barn, and with them, and hayforks, we tended the hay at least twice a day, turning and lifting and shaking the sodden mass which in no way would ever resemble the quickly dried, beautiful blue, herb-rich hay of previous years. Quite soon, we resorted to the Norwegian practice of hanging the wet weight over our boundary fences, hoping the constant wind would at last dry it enough for us to get it into the safety of the barn.

After backbreaking days, we achieved it, and there would be enough to keep the goats over the winter.

By this time, life had moved on; Mairi had a younger, even paler-haired sister, called Sunni, and our small croft was now quite well populated: we still had the hens, and the two goats had become four. We had acquired, without really wanting to, a few tame lambs, and in 'high-security' fencing beside the byre gable, we had two pigs. Our small garden was, as ever, densely packed with vegetables and fruit, although the wetter weather was not good for the latter; and a small enclosure was growing various cabbages for our own consumption – and occasionally, for the goats; too much cabbage could taint the milk, which was, on their diet of good grass and heather, naturally sweet. From one perspective, all looked good.

But the weather had given us other problems. It was often so foul, with thick, low cloud, and columns of water sweeping across the drenched fields and flowing road through Elphin, that I doubt if anyone ever even noticed our shop and gallery. If they did, few stopped, and I could hardly blame them. The resulting reduction in trade had a nasty effect on our already low income, and when in 1979 the incoming government of Margaret Thatcher nearly doubled VAT and increased significantly the cost of fuel, the stream of cars heading into Assynt became a trickle. We could see that the writing was on the wall; we could not risk another bad year. We had been wondering for a while about living in Orkney, an archipelago which I knew and with which my family had many connections. When we saw an opportunity to make a living there, we decided, after a few visits, that we should take it, and duly set in motion the process of moving from Assynt. The 'Good Life' had indeed been good, but a new life beckoned.

# 15

# Home Thoughts from Overseas

Our new life in the islands was enjoyable, busy and fulfilling; we were running a former guesthouse which now was the home of the 'Orkney Field and Arts Centre'. I was, amongst other things, the teaching side of the Field Centre, and it launched me on a life of environmental education. The grey stone house was wonderfully situated on the wide Bay of Birsay, in the northwest corner of Mainland Orkney; it lies between the cliffs of Marwick Head and the tidal island of the Brough of Birsay. Despite all the attractions of our new and engaging life, we did not forget the county we had left, as on a very clear day we could see the north coast of Sutherland and its hills – especially Ben Hope and Ben Loyal, and the hills of Cape Wrath. At least once I was confident that I was looking at Foinaven, that great grey-white mountain of which we had such good views from above Glenleraig.

The sandstone landscape of Orkney is very different from that of Assynt: smooth, flowing, fertile, blessed in the summer with wonderful wildflowers and an enormous sky; I grew to love it, but it was in great contrast to where we had lived before. Once, maybe after a year or two in Orkney, we took a lovely family we had got to know to stay for a few nights in my parents' now somewhat enlarged cottage at Drumrunie. This was during the October school holidays, a time of year when Orkney is losing its vivid greens, and most of the leaves on its rather scarce trees have long gone. In contrast, the colours on the west coast were very strong, the magnificent hills a dark blue-grey above russet moors, the rowans aflame with crimson leaves and vivid berries. One fantastic day we all went for a walk up the valley of the River Kirkaig, which was running high after heavy rain the night before. We went beyond the roaring falls, where the lemon-yellow leaves of aspen were quivering, as far as the point where you get the wonderful views over the Fionn Loch, with Suilven rearing up in front of you, dramatic and fantastical. The clouds were scudding by, it was wild and magnificent, Assynt at its very best.

It was, somewhat paradoxically, during my happy years in Orkney that I began to develop a true passion for trees. There is no doubt that, despite all the other attractions of life in the enchanting archipelago, I did begin to miss trees as entities in the landscape. We were living on the very west coast of Mainland, which really is almost treeless; towards the more sheltered east there are plantations large and small, but in Birsay a willow that I had planted in the shelter of the large, rather rambling house, was soon the largest 'tree' in the village. I also began to have a recurring dream in which I, at last, was given the location of a secret wood which the Orcadians knew, but which did not appear on maps. (I can even describe now, all these years later, how you reached this area, and its geography!).

It was partly then, in this context, that I started one peaceful indoor winter day to sort out a box I had of prints of Quinag. I had always taken photographs, and Quinag appeared in many of them. A favourite view was at a point along the road towards Nedd, just where it left the causeway across the Flats and lifted slightly to the comparative height of the Point. It was a lovely picture, with the complex water and cropped turf of the salt-marsh in the foreground, and the long view of the high ridge of Quinag in the background. In the early photographs our cottage, white and neat, appears in the middle ground; it all makes a very attractive composition. Taking the photographs, it was nearly always my adored mountain that I concentrated on, and it was only when sorting out this box of prints, taken over more than two decades, that I fully took on board the fact that our cottage had disappeared from view by the time of the later pictures. Trees had grown up and hidden it; trees on the island and nearby banks.

This sent me to look at a very early photograph which I had taken on the Brownie 127, a view of the glen from higher ground, showing the setting of the two white houses. It also shows the burn running between them, and, although it is not very clear, it became obvious, when looked at very carefully, that there were at that time (almost certainly 1959 when we first arrived) lots of little bushes, infant birches, alders, rowans and willows. By 1980, these were at least fifteen feet in height, and growing quite close together, to the extent that the cottage had disappeared. I suddenly realised that this landscape I loved so much had been changing while I watched; that it was dynamic, evolving naturally. My interest in this place redoubled, and I resolved to study it in greater depth.

Accordingly, I renewed my intermittent researches, and it so happened that I was given, around this time, by Ian MacAulay of the farm in the glen, copies of the maps of the survey of Assynt done by John Home of Edinburgh for the Sutherland Estates; up till then I had simply used the rather less detailed map which had been drawn for the Spalding Club's volume which old Agnes Stewart in Nedd had insisted on giving me when she discovered how interested I was in the past of the parish. I found the 'new' maps fascinating; they were remarkably accurate, considering the complexity of the territory, and I could trace many of the places, the farms, the sheilings and the woods from memory – I knew it all so well from constant walking there. And then, logically enough, having grasped the dynamics of the landscape, I started to compare the areas of wood mapped in 1775 with those I had known as a child. This study I duly wrote up, circulated it to a few interested people, and in my search for knowledge, I began to correspond with one or two of them, and was, in due course, referred to others. I had chosen a good time; there were groups of people interested in the native woods of Scotland, and in time I was asked by a leading figure in this movement, Professor Chris Smout (among many other things, the Queen's Historiographer Royal in Scotland), to contribute a chapter to a volume on the history of our native woods, which he was editing at the time.

This volume, *Scottish Woodland History*, was eventually published by Scottish Cultural Press in 1997, and I found my contribution listed along with others written by luminaries in the field, such as Peter Quelch, David Breeze, Richard Tipping, Fiona Watson, Robin Callander and Tim Clifford, as well as Chris himself. Through the succeeding years I was privileged to work with these people to one extent or another, and to achieve some reputation in the field, but I also discovered eventually that some of what I had observed through the decades (and could prove with my photographs) was anathema to a class of 'eco-warrior' which was emerging around the same time. For some of them, all the woods of the Highlands must have been in decline since at least the Victorian period, and the fact that I had lived through a wave of regeneration in Assynt which began in the 1950s, when there were still plenty of sheep in exactly the same coastal area, was not what they wanted to hear. And my conclusion that neither the human population of the coast (well-populated in 1775 before the Clearances inland added to the numbers), nor those sheep of the 1950s, had done as much to limit the extent of the native woodlands as had the influence of climate in exposed areas (such as the Meallard headland between Lochs Nedd and Ardvar), may even now still be controversial in some quarters.

I still hold by those conclusions, and read, with some wry interest, what I wrote at the end of that chapter, under the heading of 'Implications'. 'If the above tentative conclusions are accepted, it could be suggested that in some instances, [climatic] conditions for the growth of healthy native woodlands on the West Coast are at present marginal. In the light of the predicted climatic deterioration which may follow global warming, for instance, it is now suggested that some time should be spent in assessing more precisely the climatic conditions pertaining at a number of woodland sites, ranging from healthy coastal sites to moribund and declining inland sites. Such information might allow new woodland and regeneration schemes to be located in those places where they would best be placed to survive future changes in climate.' (Not exactly spell-binding writing, but it seems like sense to me!)

As this interest developed, I made sure that at least once a year I made a quick visit to Assynt, partly, of course, to see important friends, but also to further my study of all aspects of its landscape. And, sometimes, inevitably, I would take a quick walk up the glen looking to see if there were any changes. Early on, the good level ground of the Back Park had been ploughed and sown with oats, which, of course, transformed its appearance; it was no longer (and presumably never would be again) the hay-meadow of our youth. Wondering whether I could return in the autumn to see the ripe crop, I remembered how, in years when the grass was short, my grandmother's Skye Terrier, Struie, would play football there with tremendous enthusiasm. He displayed remarkable agility when chasing the bright red ball, and on one occasion my grandfather, watching this performance, had wept with laughter, something we rarely saw as he could be somewhat forbidding.

And, later another year, when all the birches were golden and the bracken a rusty red, I was descending to the floor of the glen, a little further up it, when I saw from above a badger pottering along in the late sunshine. This was the first time I ever saw a badger in broad daylight, and his diurnal emergence was certainly not because he was short of food; he was ready for the winter, plump and happy. I supposed he must be descended from the cubs I had heard squeaking in the rockfall in Glen Ardvar, that time long ago with Dannie. I realised then that my connections with this glen were as deep as anyone's; I had no idea at that stage that they might become deeper still.

# 16

# Home Again

We had left Assynt for Orkney in 1980. I returned there fifteen years later, and in rather different circumstances, having reached something of a hiatus in my life. We had moved, with work and inclination, to Orkney, then to Strath Glass, then to Skye, but there were disappointments along the way; it culminated in my wife departing, taking the children with her. That left something of a mess to sort out, and decisions to take.

I knew what I wanted to do, which was to continue my environmental teaching all over the Highlands and Islands, but the main question to be addressed was where to base myself. After a year or so, I was sure that I wished to return to Assynt, to live again on that wonderful coastal strip which I had got to know as a child. There were many positive reasons for doing so; it was, for a start, as accessible as Skye (where I was at the time) or rather more so – everything in the Highlands really revolves around Inverness, and I would be closer to the Highland capital from anywhere on the Assynt coast than I was on the far Peninsula of Sleat. My parents were now retired, living full-time at nearby Drumrunie, and I still had a number of good friends in the area, with whom I had kept in touch. I knew that it was a remarkably beautiful and interesting area, and that I would find it endlessly fascinating.

I had, too, a real sense of unfinished business; I knew that I had to get to know Assynt again.

And so, at the beginning of September 1995, I found myself in Drumbeg, starting a new adventure. I had at that stage to rent accommodation, and in an area like this, it is often quite easy to get a winter let, but very hard not to be displaced in the summer to make way for the more lucrative summer visitors. At first I did find myself rather moving around, but after a while, to my great surprise and joy, the cottage in Glenleraig became available to rent, and I duly moved in. The day I finally did so was not one of unbridled joy, however; I went first to Dannie's funeral, and then stood by his graveside in the bitterly cold cemetery in Stoer, where so many of my old friends lie.

At first glance, perhaps, not much had changed in the glen; the burn still ran down the middle, the steep hillsides were still wooded, and the cottage stood there still, gable end to the peaty stream. But to my eyes, of course, virtually everything was changed, in particular the cottage itself. The clue to the changes was that another window had appeared in the frontage to the road, the view that everyone saw. It replaced what had been a rather damp cupboard in my grandmother's bedroom, and, in providing more light to that room, was decidedly welcome. The metamorphosis was, in fact, much more complete, the result of a complex process, the logic of which I did not entirely understand. The cottage had first of all been listed; in other words, placed on a list of protected buildings, intended to be preserved for their architectural character and interest. Subsequently, the cottage had been renovated, a process which totally transformed the interior. The corrugated iron and timber extension which had housed the bathroom and kitchen and gave us a back door, had been swept away, making the place significantly smaller, as those rooms had to be provided within the old stone structure, and depriving it of a door to the fenced area at the back, the notional garden, which was itself significantly larger than before, but otherwise quite wild and disorganised. Within, the entrance lobby, the living room and the loft were effectively the same, but much smarter, while the little old boxroom at the back had been enlarged, at the expense of what had been my parents' quite spacious bedroom, and had turned into a large new bathroom, entered from under the stairs. My grandmother's room, now pleasantly light, had become the new kitchen/dining room. This was my new space, and I settled my possessions into it very happily, and took up residence. At first I often slept upstairs in the summer, as, with the skylight open, I could hear the murmuring of the burn, just as in days of old. I was home; Quinag still presided over the wooded glen, and the burn still ran under the alders.

Another, more subtle aspect of change became clear to me after a while. It is almost hard to find the words; the very proportions of the place had changed, the feel of it was different. The difference was not due to that change in perspective we often get if we leave somewhere as a child and return much later in adulthood; I had been twenty-one when I spent the last summer in the glen, a six-foot adult. In fact, for a start, the area of trees close to the cottage had increased. In the Front Park, the hillside had first of all been cleared of its hazel bushes, then replanted with a mix of species, close together and never thinned, so they had become much taller than before, and some sycamores had been established along the old dyke, down to the gate into the Back Park. They had become quite large, spreading trees, and their top branches touched the cottage gable. The alders along the burnside had also grown considerably, and a number had appeared on the small island, growing to such a height that they hid the view of the road on its causeway where it crossed the flats, and you could not see the water covering that area even at the highest tide, although it could come up through the bridge, and flood part of the Front Park. The whole glen here felt more enclosed, more private, more my own world.

This was despite the other great change. Across the burn from the Back Park, where once there was an open, somewhat elevated flat area, there was now a salmon hatchery, part of a large fish-farm which was now based at Ardvar, itself now reached by a new road. This part of Assynt was the base for a new industry, one in which my own burn now played a significant part.

110

Quinag and Loch Nedd in early summer

The 'flats', saltmarsh in Glenleraig

Above the Second Falls on the burn

The cottage in winter 1968: definitely needing a clean-up!

The cottage in our childhood and adolescence, 1959–72

My father trying to extricate crabs from the pots

Ben leGrand and his lobsters

Jockan and Johan Macleod: the salt of the earth

Haymeadow flowers just above the cottage, 1965

The same view in 2000: impenetrable bracken

Elphin on its limestone 'island'

Life on the Elphin croft

My immediate surroundings in late winter

The cottage when it was my home, 1995–2010

An oak, coppiced and pollarded, near Culkein Drumbeg

A badger at the kitchen window

In the first few autumns and winters, I came to realise much more vividly than before how low-lying the cottage was. Much of the time, the waters of Loch Nedd seemed distant, but, as I have described, at the highest of tides they did approach the cottage. I decided that in such times, I was living at about two metres above the sea, at most. When there was a period of prolonged and heavy rain, or rapid melting of the snow high on the ridge of Quinag, the burn roared down the glen, burst its banks and spread over the flatter ground on either side. Where, just about by the cottage, it met the sea at the highest tides. The effect was to bring the foam-flecked, black waters to within a metre of the front door. I ended up getting sandbags, just in case, but never actually had to use them.

Yet another change became very obvious during my first autumn in residence, and every following autumn. When I was young, Ardvar had been a sheep farm, and the glen was an important part of that. In my later teenage years, the sheep farm had become a mixed farm, with many cattle in its heyday. Then, after the farm was given up and the 'estate' had been purchased by Buxton, it had been declared some sort of unofficial nature sanctuary. Now, by 1995, it was in effect a deer forest; there were red deer everywhere. In huge contrast to the days when we had had brief glimpses of a few, very shy red deer that came out into the Hanging Valley up the burn, at dusk, now I was actually having to shoo them away from the cottage and the car as I parked beside my own front door. If I wanted to grow anything in the garden I was trying to reclaim at the back, I had to protect it; as I could not bear the idea of erecting a deer fence between me and the gentle waters of the burn, I had, instead, to resort to the expedient of strange little protections for every bush or group of flowers that I planted.

It was during the autumn that the new inhabitants of the glen made their presence most felt. As many may know, during the rut – the mating season – red stags try to control, and mate with, as many hinds as possible, but they have, of course, many rivals. The general habit is for the stags to try to intimidate each other; the traditional way they do this is that the stags walk up and down an imaginary line, trying to look huge and impressive, and roaring with great power. This, for about three weeks, they did, having chosen not an imaginary line but my cottage as the theoretical frontier between them. And another would take up station just across the burn and roar away, presumably at both the contenders on our side. The ensuing noise was no doubt wonderfully primitive and evocative, but it was also a terrible racket and totally deprived me of sleep. More than once I leapt naked from my bed and ran out through the door, yelling and waving my arms; they dispersed, but not for long. It often seemed a real relief when winter came, and the stags became silent once more.

I quite quickly became established in my new life, set about being part of the community again, and explored anew the territory I had known as a child. As I did so, a feeling of contentment, literally a singing voice, re-established itself within me, and life in the cottage became all I wanted for now. Life, of course, still had its problems, but it was, once again, worth living. As a winter evening fell, I wrote these words:

> This evening, as ever, I shut the curtains as the light went; it was snowing outside, flurries of large flakes which drifted past the window. Through them, across the field, the massed birches glowed palely, reddish-purple, faint through the flying snow. Inside, the fire was going well, and its flickering warmth banished the cold outside.
>
> I live in a small cottage, deep in a wooded glen, in the far north-western Highlands. To some, my home must seem remote, but nobody's home can ever seem remote to them, and I only appreciate how it must seem to others when I drive the hundred miles south to Inverness, or look for it on a map of the British Isles.

It is my home indeed, perhaps the ultimate home of my heart, since first I walked in through its door, more than forty-five years ago. We did not own it then, and were not able to stay as long as we might have liked. The same is true now, as I do not own it, probably never will, and will not be permitted to live here forever. The irony is that no-one knows and loves this deep wooded glen or this cottage as much as I do; perhaps no-one ever will.

That I am here at all is due to a strange combination of what seems, at least, to be pure chance, the result of a pattern of people and places, a pattern, if you like, which has rooted me here in Assynt.

The contrast between such days of winter, and the summer, does seem very intense when you live outside as much as possible, as I always have. Later that year, I was again in reflective mood:

I should at this moment be feeling fit and active and on my way to the island fastnesses of Eigg and Rum. Lately, however, I have been somewhat mysteriously unwell, and as whatever is wrong has affected both my eyes and ears, producing sight and balance problems, it has seemed more than unwise to consider driving the two hundred miles to Mallaig, let alone taking charge of a group of folk that are keen to explore the islands.

I am, therefore, reluctantly taking it easy at home, sitting outside the cottage on the small patch of neatly-cut grass which leads down to the amber-coloured pool in the burn. Apart from that dark honeyed brown, and the flawless blue of the sky above me, everything else is now a midsummer green. The birches and multi-stemmed alders cast their deep shade over the murmuring waters, while, through the fence that borders my small patch of lawn, the damp meadow is full of rushes, dotted with the gold of buttercups and threaded with the delicate white of bedstraw. Along its edges, the white clover is dense and scented, and the red, large-blossomed and deep-coloured. Butterflies, mostly red admirals so far today, flit from it to the nettles at the back of the cottage, deliberately left for them. Lurking in the meadow grasses are the orchids, the deep crimson-to-purple of the northern marsh, and the vigorous, pinker strength of its hybrid with the heath-spotted.

There are birds all around, lost in the heavy foliage of the surrounding wood, calling continuously; chaffinch, willow warbler, tits, and, above all, the redpolls which chatter like clockwork toys as they ceaselessly loop from tree to tree. And, like glittering, miniature helicopters, the first of the summer dragonflies patrol the meadow-flowers in search of their prey.

I had the abundance and exuberance of nature all around me, and a whole world to explore; there was never enough time.

# 17

# The Natural World

As children, the spectacle of the Assynt wildlife had made a great impression on us; the regular soaring overhead of the local buzzards, the very rare and exciting appearance over our cottage of a golden eagle, the curious fulmars that came ever closer on the red cliffs of Stoer, these were the sightings that brightened our days. One splendid view I remember from my teens, fishing with my father on one of the innumerable lochs in the wonderful hinterland. We were fishing from the shore, sheltered by a low bank, when behind that bank we could hear a harsh cackling. Before we had time even to react to the noise (which we both recognised), two birds swept low overhead, still calling loudly, long necks outstretched, somehow almost reptilian in their complex and dramatic black and white. These were black-throated divers, and they were splendid, primitive, worthy denizens of their magnificent landscape.

I have always looked out for raptors, and still enjoyed the sight of the buzzards wheeling above the cottage as they climbed on the thermals. One day I was chopping wood when the noise of hoodie crows made me look up to see two of them audaciously mobbing a harassed immature eagle, which was heading up the glen as fast as he could. It was up there, towards the great sandstone cliffs of Quinag, that I sat one day on the damp ground, simply admiring the view across the two fine lochs, when I became aware of movement on the face of the isthmus between them. Through the binoculars I then watched, perhaps for the next half hour, a golden eagle, large and impressive, a female I think, walking around the rough bank and shore. Just occasionally, she flapped those great wings once or twice, to help her over some bushy heather, but most of the time she was actually walking, stiff-legged like an old man with bad knees. She spent a while poking her fine head, sun glinting on the gold, under the heather and a peaty bank. I could not imagine what she was doing, but a friend, wise in the ways of eagles and devoted to them, suggested she might be hunting for adders, which were certainly known in the glen – although I suppose she would not be averse to slow worms either. Once she went right down to the water's edge and dipped her beak in the loch. I presumed that this was simply drinking, but gather that such an action has very rarely been recorded.

There is no doubt that this was an unusual and privileged view of one of our greatest birds, but there is equally no doubt that it happened simply by chance, like most of my wonderful sightings at home. I was just there at the right time. This was equally true of some of the amazing views I had of mammals in these same years. Otters I saw at intervals, sometimes with even a year or so intervening, and in very different circumstances and locations. One leapt out of the seaweed-covered, ochre-yellow rocks as I rowed a dinghy silently in a tidal backwater, while the next I discovered quite far inland. I was walking in an area of rough heather ground on a hot day, and hauled myself up to a small summit in the chaos of gneiss hills, when I noticed something moving in a very narrow burn, almost a ditch but quite natural, a short and tiny watercourse that led from one wee lochan to another. There was something brown, speckled perhaps, splashing around, and I descended quietly to the burnside and walked slowly towards the commotion. At first I was thinking vaguely that it must be a female mallard, caught somehow, maybe in a snare, and making a real effort to escape. As I got closer, I realised that it was in fact an otter, or, at least, most of one, its head under the peaty bank much of the time as it energetically pursued – what? – a small fish perhaps, a vole, or even a frog. Eventually, inevitably, it looked up and at me; I was merely six feet away, perhaps within a critical distance as far as it was concerned. I remained immobile, trying not to breathe, and it looked at me in a very puzzled way, before moving slowly downstream. Three times it stopped, stood up and watched me, apparently still mystified as to what I might be, before returning to the safety of the dark waters of the nearby loch.

Much further inland, I saw another otter one cold winter day, and despite our closeness, I think it had no clue ever that I was there. I was engaged in the tricky task of crossing a much more substantial burn – almost a river, peaty waters swollen by recent snowfall – using some very slippery stepping-stones. Just as I stretched out my foot to the next, an otter swam fast down the river, head under, straight between my legs. I was very much surprised, and only my faithful old stick, providing extra and much-needed balance, prevented me from falling into the icy water.

Foxes I met rarely, always out on the open hill, but other species surrounded me in considerable numbers. I had actually, of course, been present when the first badger sett in the parish had been discovered, and in the intervening thirty or forty years, their numbers had considerably increased. They were now often seen in broad daylight, and again I delighted in trying to get close to them. While in the cottage one sunny day, I looked along the track towards the gate to the main road, only to see a pair of badgers approaching along it. They were obviously quite young, sleek and slim, and like puppies, jostled and shoved at each other until they dived off the track into the long meadow grass, where something seemed to occupy their attention. Determined to see what was going on, I went quietly outside and crept along the grass in the middle of the track until I was some six feet away, where I crouched and watched. The young animals, beautiful and clean in their black and white, were pulling at the flower heads of red clover which they ate with all the signs of real enjoyment. So fixed was their attention on this that I was eventually able to retreat towards the cottage without them seeing me.

I found it very interesting that within this period of, say, forty years maximum, and in the setting of the sparsely populated parish of Assynt, badgers had returned to a diurnal life, although I did still often see them in the car headlights at night, and some, sadly, were killed on the road. Another view of badgers close to was rather different. I was, again, outside, stacking wood, when I heard a truly horrible commotion somewhere behind the cottage, a noise between snarling and screaming. I went quietly through to the back field, where the steep hillside descends to the flat meadow, to see a pair of badgers ahead of me, rolling downhill, trying very hard to fix their powerful jaws around each other's necks. Again, they were so intent on this murderous task that they were quite unaware of me, and again I stopped when about six feet from them and watched. Quite soon, I could not stand the noise, so I said, quietly, 'Oh, do shut up, the pair of you,' or some such stupidity, at which they stopped instantly, took one look, and headed off fast in different directions, seemingly unharmed by their ferocious battle.

Many such sightings were of single or paired creatures, and, as I have indicated, they were often at really close quarters. Apart from providing me with an insight into aspects of their behaviour of which I had previously been unaware, they gave me a close view of their beauty, their strong sleek profiles (although badgers can look like plump little bears at times), their glossy pelts (or plumage), their fitness and alertness. But more than this aesthetic quality, there was almost always a feeling, on my side, that these were animals in their own landscape, competent and belonging in their own world in a way that we humans hardly ever do, a way that I craved, wanted so much for myself.

For me, as for many on the West Coast, it was the pine martens which gave most fun; they are exquisite little animals and can be readily persuaded to abandon the secretive habits that were forced on them during the years of persecution. I could tell that there were several of them around me, and a few judiciously dropped peanuts soon lured them into sight. It became quite common for me to look up from my desk to see a pine marten lolloping past the window, but one summer's activity often had me laughing out loud. That year, one mother who had taken to visiting had three young, two of which followed her closely and quickly, with hardly a squeak. The third, however, one of nature's fools, was always behind the others, late for everything. Just as the first group of three would be moving silently and sleekly under the car and around the corner of the cottage, he (I vaguely presumed such incompetence had to be male!) came round the corner by the old byre, maybe a hundred yards behind, yelling his head off, and so he continued right round the cottage gable till he caught up with the others where they scavenged below the bird table. This performance happened regularly that summer; they had moved on elsewhere when I returned from a holiday that autumn, and I often wondered whether he had ever learned to shut up.

It was the evening performance, however, that provided both the magic, and the interaction between species. I sat by my kitchen window many times that summer and watched, in the half light of the long evenings, the antics of the young martens. While mother was busily searching for the peanuts I had left scattered in the longer grass around the base of the bird table, the three youngsters took it in turns to rush up its supporting post, scoff some of the loose nuts on the flat top, and then jump off, legs spread like flying squirrels, landing in a supple heap before rushing to the post, jumping over mother, and repeating the whole process, over and over again. It appeared a hilarious game, and was certainly fun to watch, fun that did not entirely cease, to my surprise, when two badgers arrived and began their own search for nuts. Mother pine marten took one look at them, and leapt easily and scornfully on to the table-top where she continued to eat. The youngsters at first were cowed, but they watched the comparatively lumbering badgers carefully and resumed their game whenever they spied an opportunity. One actually did leap over a badger, and I saw the latter move as if to bite the flying marten which by then had reached complete safety. I was watching until darkness finally won, and even the striped heads of the badgers began to lose definition.

I had previously seen that the martens did accord the powerful badgers at least a modicum of respect; glancing out of the sitting room window one day, I saw a pine marten was moving rapidly along the track towards the cottage. Then, out of the other window, I saw that a badger was moving around the cottage from the back, presumably about to head in the opposing direction along the track. It did exactly that, and the marten, catching sight of this very obvious animal (it was, again, broad daylight) stopped, did a 'meerkat', in other words stood up on its hind legs, which they often do, and scuttled off the track to hide behind the luxuriant rhubarb which grew beside it. The badger apparently noticed nothing, presumably not even a scent, and passed by at a brisk trot, upon which the marten emerged, shook itself, and carried on its way unperturbed.

For many years, living in this quiet glen, I shared the world of these beautiful creatures.

# 18

# Exploring Home Territory

As soon as I was fairly well settled, I began a long programme of reacquainting myself with Assynt, a process which I hugely enjoyed. As I was working freelance much of the time, I managed to fit these exploratory trips in with the weather, which, my journals make clear, was exactly as unpredictable as you would expect of the far northwest Highlands of Scotland.

Assynt is a large, and largely empty, parish, and one road runs through it from Ullapool on Loch Broom to Kylesku on Loch a' Chairn Bhain, and northwards to Durness. This road enters Assynt at a high point under Knockan Crag, and from nearby Ledmore almost to Kylesku there extends to the east a long, rough, mountain ridge with white-grey high peaks almost hidden by their own foothills, and a few invisible, rather desolate glens. Perhaps the most unexpected aspect of this eastern part of Assynt are the occasional vivid green islands of limestone country, fertile and largely dry underfoot, with springs, sink holes, dry valleys, underground rivers and cave systems.

West of this single main road, a branch from which continues to Lochinver on the coast, is a chain of very individual mountains of Torridonian sandstone, best seen perhaps from that coast, from which they are often photographed. From places like Rubh' Stoer, the line-up is magnificent, extending from Ben More in Coigach to the south; in fact, only the last three in the great chain are in Assynt. The central of those peaks, Canisp, is a relatively gentle cone, an easy, if rough, walk, and a wonderful viewpoint for its spectacular neighbours, Suilven and Quinag. These are, without question, among the finest mountains in the land. Suilven is remarkably symmetrical, a narrow ridge with precipitous sides, a huge drum of a summit at the west, tapering to a vertiginous peak at the east. Quinag is on a grander scale, a range of peaks with long cliffs (from which my Glenleraig burn flows), bold buttresses and summits that are rounded, pyramidal, flat-topped like a castle tower, sharp like a tooth. Both these imposing mountains bestride their landscape, riding like huge ships a tempestuous sea of ancient Lewisian gneiss which extends to the intricate coastline itself. The gneiss forms a complex and intimate land, sometimes and very misleadingly called a plateau, of crag and rockfall, heather ridge and boggy flow, shining lochan and dark burn.

The narrow coastal road wriggles its way from inlet to inlet, over rocky height and through deep wooded glen; it is here that most people live. When I was young, they were still mostly crofters in an actively crofted land, but many things have changed since then, and in some of the townships many of the houses are unoccupied for more than half the year. Many new houses have been built too, but many of them, again, are simply holiday homes. Some of the sea-lochs are narrow and sheltered, others open and sandy, all bounded by the heaving complexities of the ancient rock, except for the big headland of Rubh' Stoer: here the sandstone reappears, and the bare peninsula is bounded by high cliffs.

The parish is, therefore, one of great scenic variety, and caters for many interests. My family were, passionately, country folk, and had wide interests. My Highland grandmother, who had long lived with us, was a keen birdwatcher and loved wild flowers; she was well informed about basic geology, archaeology and history, and had been a keen walker and fisher. My mother had inherited her love of birds and flowers, walking and fishing, while my father, who had read History at Cambridge, was a competent botanist in addition to all the above. He had been in the Navy during the war, and loved boats. As children, my brother Rhoderick and I were recipients, conscious and unconscious, of this huge resource of enthusiasm and know-ledge; we were extraordinarily lucky.

With this background of enthusiasm and happy memories, I set about relearning my landscape, from the coast to the high summits. Quinag, my local hill, I climbed at intervals from the cottage, as Dad and I had in my youth – a long but rewarding day. After a number of years, I made an important friendship, and together we climbed most of the popular hills, tending to avoid Suilven and the Munros, Ben More Assynt and Conival, which were by now much frequented, leading to a significant amount of erosion of their main paths – the fate of many Scottish hills. On my own, increasingly I headed for the less-visited ridges and peaks, where I could find perfect peace and solitude, wear exactly as much or as little as I wanted, and enjoy the less-disturbed wildlife.

I went, accordingly, one July day, up into the hills behind Inchnadamph, leaving the familiar limestone glen to ascend the steep face of Beinn an Fhurain, where I found cloudberry and dwarf cornel, plants which seemed to me to belong more to the eastern Highlands than the west. There were, of course, deer, but also good views of ring ouzels, the mountain black-birds, and two magnificent golden eagles. All through the day I tried to follow the easy leads of green turf, through the amaz-ing, daunting, scratchy piles of quartzite. In the soft, green, mossy places were more flowers: always tormentil, thrift, the alpine lady's mantle, bearberry and cow-wheat. At this stage of the day, it was still greyish, and the wind from the southwest was far from being as mild as forecast, but it slowly cleared and I enjoyed the distant views as I gained the summit of Na Tuadhan, with its great folded cliff. I looked across, of course, to the pale summits of Conival and Ben More Assynt, seeing through the binoculars quite a number of folk 'bagging' the coveted summits that Chris and I had climbed during those years in Elphin. The other Sutherland Munros, Hope and Klibreck, and that white range of summits which so nearly makes the 3000-foot mark, Foinaven, were clear in the distance, and were with me all day. I soon left the coldish summit of Na Tuadhan, and set off northwards down a really lovely long alp, oozing with crystal-clear springs which give the hill its name, mournfully musical with the call of golden plover, and amusing with the squeaking of red deer calves. The enriched flushes by the springs had the purple of butterwort in latish bloom, and, at last, the delicate starry saxifrage which my father had found for me on Quinag. There was a tiny mouse-ear and a small, delicate speedwell which loves the damp places. A dipper flew intermittently ahead of me, following the little stream which led gently downhill. I eventually reached the place where an aeroplane crashed in 1941, bits of metal strewn still around the hillside, with two mangled engines. There is, as well, of course, the memorial to the crew, all of whom died; as I studied it, I had the foolish thought that there was no way they could have realised that they had crashed in one of the most beautiful places in the world. I was so glad to be alive.

Then I descended, following the almost circular route of the burn to a small loch, and then a bigger one, where there were some hinds in the slight shelter and a red-throated diver to watch. I kept looking out for ptarmigan, but only saw some droppings. Then I ascended the next hill, Beinn Uidhe, a long grey ridge of the same heart-breaking quartzite; I could follow a few green leads at first, lured on by another eagle. I gained the highest point of the ridge, about halfway along its length, after which it seemed impossible to avoid the grating quartzite, which I took very gently, thinking that a fall could be more than uncomfortable. From above, I spied an attractive loch in the Coire Gorm, and headed for it. For a while I enjoyed its real shelter from the cool wind, and looked at yet more flowers – mostly the same as I had seen earlier. There, in soft sun, I relaxed for an idyllic while, played the fool for a time, before heading up and over the corner of the ridge up to the wide plateau of Glasven. From here, I descended into the next corrie, where, to my surprise, I came across a young couple, with whom I talked for a while. It transpired that they had been camping just between my cottage and Ardvar. They went off on a different route from that which I intended to take, and I had a long path once again to myself, enjoying the views of the steep slope up which I had first climbed that morning. I took my time, splashed around in a waterfall for a bit, and then returned to the car. It had been a wonderful day, although not as warm as I had hoped, and I had climbed that rare thing, a couple of hills in Assynt which I had never been up before.

I knew, of course, that revisiting places which I had known in the past could be very disappointing; sometimes there would be changes, fences perhaps where there used to be none, evidence that far more folk now came that way, that sort of thing; but many days repeated the magic of yesteryear. On such a day, I stopped the car near Oldany and walked down to the Dornie, where there is the narrowest of channels between the mainland and the large island. Violet's husband, Kenny, was working there on his big boat, and he suggested that I should take out the wee dinghy. I rowed it gently up the channel to the first, somewhat sandy bay, where I moored it, crossed the short patch of rocky ground to the evocative, beautiful bay of my youth, where I pottered about, took lots of photographs, swam a bit (but it was cold!), and just relaxed – in seventh heaven. The day was perfect, not too hot, with a slight breeze and no midges. The distant views across Eddrachillis to the hills of the Reay Forest were hazy, but Quinag loomed clear and glorious across the translucent water.

I took my time on the way back. The channel in this enchanted area is very shallow, and the water was totally clear; I could see crabs crossing the lugwormy expanses. There were mergansers, shags, curlews calling, a few gulls, some common seals, and me, messing about in a tiny, stable dinghy, on a flat calm, altogether splendid Assynt afternoon. I had been so lucky; I had returned to one of the places which had stayed forever in my mind, one of the places associated with the happiest days of my youth, and I had had it to myself.

The land in between, the hinterland that lies to the south of the cottage, constantly beckoned. There are some good routes into it, the peat-roads which must have been created to facilitate the movement of peat from the best banks to the various townships. I could never really ascertain when they had been constructed, but it had clearly been a considerable labour. They had obviously been well built, even if now some patches had become boggy. Such peat roads lead into the hinterland at either end of Loch Drumbeg, and further round the coast, from the townships of Stoer and Clachtoll. They make for comparatively rapid access into the maze of hill, water, cliff, bog and woods through which one can wander for days. There is actually not such a decent track into the hill from Glenleraig, but you can leave the tarred road a little way from the cottage, and make an easy way through a narrow, level, boggy flow towards Quinag, and a good path that leads as far as Loch Assynt. I constantly wandered up the glen, and frequently went into the ground above the two lochs below the great line of Quinag's western cliffs. For a while, up there one day, I watched a small herd of red deer, hinds and calves, perhaps fifteen in all, a few of the calves still pale and spotted. Some were lying, like me, in the sun, others rubbing themselves in peat banks (bothered, no doubt like me, by flies), one calf was peacefully suckling. This little group was then suddenly joined in a rush by a mixed group, seventeen stags nearly all now out of velvet, some hinds, calves and yearlings, the calves making a lot of noise, as if frightened. Then three more stags, still in velvet, which, this being the middle of August, seemed surprisingly late in the year. I wondered whether something had spooked this new group, which seemed very restless, but all the action proved again what I had noticed before, which was that in areas like this, where when I was young there had been virtually no deer at all, the groups of 'new' deer were not hefted to any one particular place. Quite often, instead of the very separate groups of stags and hinds with young seen in old, traditional deer forests, these new groups were often mixed and highly mobile, found in one location one day, and several miles away the next. I had observed this very significant difference before, in a similar area of Skye, the Sleat peninsula, where I had lived for a while and where, as in Assynt, deer had not normally been seen in the past.

One consequence of this behaviour difference, in areas newly colonised, is that deer counts must really be much more difficult, and any concept of 'ownership', by individual estates, of the deer that wander through this landscape, even less plausible than normal. The usual notion is that nobody owns the deer, merely the right to shoot them, but in fact you may often hear landowners referring to 'their deer', an idea which to me is as alien as the idea of owning mountains or whole landscapes.

# 19

# Archaeological Riches

One of the already mentioned places in the eastern part of the parish that I was always happy to revisit was normally called the 'Bone Caves', from the quantity of animal and bird bones which had been found in long-ago excavations. The cave entrances are located above a very steep grassy slope up which we had toiled in my youth, under a great boss of limestone, in a narrow glen south of Inchnadamph. It so happened that I made such a return visit one autumn, not long after returning from a wonderful holiday in the Perigord area of France with two dear American friends. We had had a glorious time, during which we explored many of the famous and less well-known prehistoric sites, caves with amazing paintings, and shelters on cliffs above the glinting river. It is true that thoughts of the early inhabitants of these most evocative sites had really seized my imagination, but I was not prepared, when walking up the new and easier path to the Assynt caves, for what I can only describe as a voice in my ear saying simply: 'They were here too'. This was most odd, as I am normally, I think, the most prosaic of people, and not exactly prone to 'hearing voices'. As it happened, no-one else came up the glen that day, and I was able to spend an hour or two in and around the caves, just looking and thinking, and wondering what life in these splendid shelters must have been like. I remembered, too, that when I had been living in Elphin, I had been involved with some filming, in the township itself and also at the caves, during which time we had sheltered in them, watching the softest snowflakes falling densely outside – totally memorable.

Many years later, when I was working with the very energetic local heritage group, Historic Assynt, we had held a one-day mini-conference at Inchnadamph, including a site visit, considering exactly what we knew about the human and other use of the site. To an extent, the day highlighted what we do not yet know about this inspiring place; this is partly because it was excavated a long time ago, and never properly written up, while one or two crucial finds were subsequently lost. While it seems clear that very ancient bones washed somehow into the cave system well before the last Ice-Age, it is the considerable variety of bones, which must belong to the period just after that glaciation, which are of the most immediate interest, as they raise the question of whether there was contemporary human use of the caves. These bones indicate clearly what we would now describe as an arctic fauna: reindeer, arctic fox and lemming, but there are also remains of many other creatures, such as eider and long-tailed duck, and puffin. These are, of course, seabirds, and the only credible way in which they would have been brought into the caves would be by human hunters, which makes me wish that we had reliable dates for these bones. They might, of course, be from the Neolithic or New Stone Age, when a man was buried here, or perhaps from a Viking hunting party camping out in the caves. But there remains also the practical possibility that earlier Mesolithic or Middle Stone Age hunter-gatherers had used these very fine caves as dwellings, probably on a seasonal basis. This is by no means incredible and would give us a very satisfying starting point for the human occupation of the parish, which we otherwise lack!

The area close by, which I tend, rather loosely perhaps, to call 'the limestone corridor', is most easily seen from Loch Assynt down to Knockan, if you head towards Ullapool, or past Altnacealgach if you are aiming for Lairg. It does provide an abundance of evidence for Neolithic occupation; the good land must have been very suitable for the early farmers, especially in the period of climatic optimum, a warm period which prevailed at this time. Despite the lack of later development within this large area, we have remarkably little in the way of remains of either the field systems themselves, key to how the folk of these times lived, or the houses in which they actually resided. Fortunately, their ritual, or religious, life, which centred around care of the dead of their communities, is well attested in around forty chambered tombs. These are not spectacular, as the rough stone with which they were constructed has usually rather collapsed or been robbed, but many of the remaining mounds are substantial and conspicuous. My personal favourite is on the western slopes above Loch Awe and is illustrated in the little booklet I wrote for Historic Assynt, entitled *A Rock and a Hard Place – A Guide to the Archaeology of Assynt's Hidden Lives*, to which the interested reader is referred for a more comprehensive account than will be found here. What can be very clearly stated is that in the Neolithic period, which may have stretched from around 4000 to perhaps 2400 BC, there must have been a significant population living and deriving their sustenance from this inland part of the parish, which is now emphatically depopulated apart from the small settlements at Inchnadamph, Elphin and Knockan. The 'hinterland' and the length of the coast still appear, despite detailed survey and much exploration, to have had little occupation at this time.

In the succeeding period, which we tend still to call 'the Bronze Age', there is good evidence for a climatic downturn, a long period during which the climate would have been colder, wetter and windier, and this would in itself have reduced the area under woodland and promoted the growth of peat. Life, for a predominantly farming community, would have been harder, and it is a fact that throughout the parish we have much less evidence for human habitation and activity. There are some Burnt Mounds, which themselves represent the accumulated debris which grew up around communal cooking places, or (a view now favoured), sauna/sweat lodge type structures where the fuel must have been mostly peat, and some probable roundhouses and a few small cairns. But, overall, the scale of the population at this time must surely have been significantly less than in the Neolithic, a fact which emphasises, at least to me, how far north Assynt actually is, with real implications for the vulnerability of its traditional economy to climatic fluctuations. This must always have been true, and the changing climate, even in my lifetime, is one reason why the haymaking and growing of oats which I saw when I was young, and had helped to harvest, is no longer undertaken.

The succeeding Iron Age seems to have been more prosperous, a fact emphasised by the presence of some imposing monuments, most of which have a rather defensive nature. As far as we can now tell, however, the focus of occupation had changed from the inland limestone corridor to the coast, where headlands and inlets often have contemporary sites. The finest and most elaborate of these is the recently-excavated Broch of Clachtoll; this fine site had really fired my imagination when young – in truth it helped shape my life, as I always brought archaeology into my environmental teaching.

A very different, and inconspicuous, monument from the same period lurks in the woods not far from my cottage. When young I had, strangely, not made much of it, merely trying to avoid falling into one of the holes in the woodland grasses which was about all that could be seen at that time. Once back, I started to clear some of the grass and bracken from around these holes, and then lay down on the damp turf so that I could look inside. I then realised that to do so effectively I needed a good torch and returned at a later date armed with exactly that, as well as my camera. It became obvious that this is one of the slightly enigmatic structures called a souterrain, a long, subterranean chamber, with a strong, stone-lintelled roof. These were most probably storerooms, in whose cool damp recesses dairy produce or meat could be stored; they would have served contemporary structures above ground, making clear that my glen, just like that in neighbouring Ardvar, would have been occupied in the Iron Age. The Glenleraig souterrain is filled to within a few feet of the roof by what I had presumed to be some kind of natural, muddy deposit, but it has been suggested that such strongly built structures might also have served some sort of ritual function and been deliberately filled and sealed at the end of their period of use. Some similar places have been excavated, and the fill turns out to contain a number of very interesting and informative contemporary objects, suggesting that an excavation here might be very productive – and result in a structure roughly contemporary with the broch which could shed a very different perspective on life in the Assynt Iron Age.

The little stream which now seems to flow through the souterrain joins, a few yards downstream, a larger tributary of the Leraig, which soon plunges into its own little gorge. This has sheer sides and has obviously always been inaccessible to the sheep which Dannie and Jockan tended, the cows which the MacAulays farmed, or the deer which, in ever greater numbers, have replaced them. As a result, wildflowers, which they would all have grazed, grow and bloom happily there, unchecked. My botanising in the gorge has been done at a distance, with binoculars, but the two commonest flowers down there are both known for their (very different) scents; the somewhat pungent wild garlic or ramsons, and the aptly-named sweet woodruff.

After this 'busy' period, with lots of monuments to observe, there is, for a long time, a very real gap in the archaeological record; virtually nothing to see. For any insight into the subsequent history, one has to look basically at the place names, and this subject has interested me for some considerable time. By far the majority of local examples are in what can be recognised as modern (Scottish) Gaelic, but will have evolved from the 'ancestral' Gaelic which must have been brought into modern Scotland with the Scots from Ireland, who arrived in Argyll well before St Columba settled in the island of Iona in 563 AD. Certainly, one local name contains the element 'sliabh' which according to the guru of Scottish place names, W.F.H.

Nicolaisen, is an 'early element', indicating that a group of Gaelic-speaking settlers would have arrived here early in the years AD.

The next wave of settlers is perhaps less obvious, but a few local names make it clear that the Vikings or Norsemen (call them what you will) must have settled here, perhaps soon after 800 AD, which is often reckoned to be when they arrived in numbers in Orkney, although I suspect that earlier voyages had ventured further than the turning point of Cape Wrath to the north. The question of 'settlement' is important; it seems to me to be clear that settlement is required for the transmission into common usage of names in a foreign language, and presumably that settlement must be for a couple of generations at least for that usage to hold. The name of the conspicuous coastal feature which we now call 'The Old Man of Stoer' is definitely Norse, although it is not easy to decide whether it derives from 'staur', which means a stake, or something like 'stor mannet', meaning the giant or big man; personally, I favour the latter, but it will be hard to prove it either way. Inland, too, there must have been settlement, as attested by the names 'Traligill' and 'Urigill', 'gil' referring to a ravine. And, presumably, Oldany, the island on whose beach I had been having such fun, represents the 'a', or 'ay' suffix which simply means 'island', as in so many Orcadian examples.

I had long known that the Norse element 'vik' (from which the Vikings are named) was often modified into Gaelic as 'aig' or sometimes 'uig'; this makes it clear that 'Inverkirkaig' comprises both Gaelic and Norse. 'Inver' refers to the mouth of a river, while 'kirk' is the Norse for a church, a church which was possibly standing on that lovely bay when the Norsemen arrived in their longships – such a shame that we have no trace of such a building. But I kept on wondering about my own 'Glenleraig'.

When I was young, I had realised that most of the folk around us spoke Gaelic as well as English; they just did not use it much in front of us. Rhoderick and I had then demanded that we should learn a few words and sentences, with which we then bombarded the patient adults; there is a limit to how often you want to answer the question: 'Ciamar a tha thu?' They were probably glad that I then went on to demand what the local township names meant: 'Drumbeg' we had actually worked out ourselves, the 'Little Ridge'; but Nedd had stumped us. It turned out to be 'An Nead', 'The Nest', which very adequately conveys how the houses sit in the green bowl in the hills. But when I asked about our own glen, I drew a blank. Dannie and Colleen did not know, so when up in Nedd one time, I asked her father. Old Angus was a wonderful and patient old man, with splendid moustaches, who, as I have said, reminded me of a picture I had once seen of Thomas Hardy. He replied that he had no idea, it did not seem to him to be Gaelic, and he had never heard anyone claim to know its origin. He did also confirm that the spelling we knew – Glenleraig – was all that he had ever heard. I later asked his sister, Agnes Stewart, and she said the same thing.

Thinking about this, years later, I remembered a dictum of Raonull MacInnes, father of my university friend Duncan, and a native Sgitheanach. Most of our place-names make sense, he said, if you think of approaching by sea. *That* was how I might work out the name. It did not take long; 'aig' is 'vik', and the 'ler' is 'leir', silt, or sediment, which is exactly what you encounter when first you drop anchor in Loch Nedd, our sea loch. (It is, as I remember very well, extremely smelly!) This is the same name, of course, as 'Lerwick'. The Vikings clearly settled Assynt, both on the coast and inland, exactly as they did elsewhere in the North. Although there are a few sites which might possibly date from this period, there is nothing definite to point to. It is very likely, however, that the design of the numerous local mills, and the nousts, the boat-shaped indentations into which small boats would be placed to escape the fury of the winter gales (like those at the end of the Clashnessie side road), date in type from the arrival of the Vikings, who certainly had a significant role in shaping the economy of our parish, and should be a better-known part of our history.

This pattern of settlement may be found all over the far North; on the coast, but also inland, the Vikings settled for at least a couple of generations. We see this in the middle of the country, where 'Amat', 'Alladale' and 'Diebidale' are found at the head of Strath Carron, and even well up Strathconon where the important place name 'Scatwell' (which effectively means something like the 'field that pays the taxes'), gives an insight into the land-based taxation system which the Vikings introduced. There was much more to these colourful settlers than the rape and pillage which is so often attributed to them.

# 20

# Seasonal Contrast

Life in the far north of Scotland can be full of contradictions; the winter may be bright, full of light, like the months when I began to study the woods in an organised fashion. But the succeeding summer may be damp and drizzly, with almost permanent low cloud hiding not just the mountains but even the lower hills. Often it may be the other way around, of course; during the winters of endless gales, I could feel trapped in the house while the wind roared outside and the rain poured incessantly. If the weather improves, and sometimes the change is as swift as the flicking of a switch, the sense of freedom is intoxicating. And there was always the delight that I could just walk out of the door and head in almost any direction I wanted; there were virtually no obstacles, one road you could follow in either direction, maybe somewhere a fence to cross. The only restriction on where I went, was water; I knew exactly where I could cross my own burn, but otherwise, of course, I had to walk around the many lochs. But they, in any case, added to the beauty of the day. And after a bad winter, I was desperate to get out and walk, and, inevitably, look for signs of the longed-for coming of spring.

One day early on in my time here, around the middle of March, I took the familiar road towards Nedd. I went further than the township, and then took off down to a secluded, relatively low-lying headland, generally just known to me as Duart. This had once been populated, but as it was almost cut off by a long cliff-line and no-one had ever worked out a way to get a road to it, had been at some stage abandoned. It forms the west side of outer Loch Nedd; I had never reached it during my childhood, so it was a new place to explore. I had found the easy ways down to the lower ground, and headed there, going at first right down to the shore. Quinag was shining white with snow, and the waters of the loch were calm, reflecting the grey of the rocks and the purple of the birch. Here I was able to watch some eider duck through my binoculars, enjoying the drake's beautiful soft peach and sage green. Best of all, I could hear the male's call, that slightly surprised, melodic cooing which carried clearly across the still water. If ever there was a sound of the Highland spring, this is it.

Feeling very happy, I went over to a ruined house and some sort of outbuilding, across the little burn where there is a cleared 'dock' or 'noust' to one side. Right down at the shore, the tide was low and the water clear, the bottom sandy; it would have been a good place to have put down our lobster pots! I stopped on a rock, sheltered from the breeze, and sat there, observing the scene. I was idly thinking of all the different beaches in the parish, which led, rather vaguely, to otters; up to this point I had seen rather few. I said to myself: 'I have lately only seen one otter, and that was in Lochinver,' when around the corner and straight at me, there swam a big dog otter. I think it saw me, but I had wonderful views, as, close to me, it fished around the rocks, in and out of the ochre weed.

I then walked round the shallow lagoon into the wood, an incredible tangle of mossy rock and trees, and wandered over the old croft lands; the golden saxifrage had visible buds, and the herb Robert, wood sorrel and celandines were near to blooming in this sheltered spot. In one old garden there is a big elder bush which was growing strongly, with new shoots, and elsewhere there were silver pussy-willows; you could feel the excitement of the new season. I explored the southern edge of this low ground, which faces Loch Nedd and Quinag, where they can be seen through the often impenetrable jungle of hazel (sometimes hazel trees rather than bushes), and groups of fine aspen stems. I noticed one particularly vast hazel above a narrow *sloc* leading to the water: this Gaelic word came to my mind the minute I saw it, and I can think of no neat English equivalent; it means 'throat' and looked like a 'geo' on land.

While I walked around enraptured by this magic place, great and long-tailed tits explored the luxuriant mosses and furry, silver-blue lichens which encrust these old trunks. And then I had to freeze, and remain motionless; ahead of me, on the ground, were no fewer than three woodcock, the complex, scalloped, deep rich browns of their plumage for once standing out well against the green of new grass. I watched for a while, but eventually had to move, when, of course, they flew off at once.

As I was walking around this fascinating area with its abandoned houses and crofts, its shallow lagoon and intricate coast, I was wondering: did the Vikings who named our glen settle here? Did they use the noust that I am sure I see, did they utilise the big hazels and other trees?

Having left Duart, I had to continue up to Drumbeg to collect a few things from the shop; on the dark roadside loch there were two male and two female goldeneye, and against a bank I glimpsed another duck, almost black with dramatic white wing-patches, which might have been a velvet scoter. Clearly, migratory birds were on the move, heading north; soon there might be, as there often are, the whooper swans, brilliant against the peaty water. I frequently marvel at the seasonal contrast which this loch offers the passer-by. In the winter it can appear so bleak and sterile; a few brown leaves move on the sullen surface in the cold wind, under a lowering grey sky. But come back in the summer and the dull waters are transformed; the loch is covered with lily-pads and hundreds of the flowers of the waterlily, exotic, luxuriant, cream-petalled, golden-hearted, unexpected, startling in their richness.

Some summers, certainly, need the brilliance of the waterlily blooms. Later that same year, I was, as ever, recording how I was feeling:

Today, 10th of July, was even worse. I awoke to heavy rain, turned over and went back to sleep. It was very grey and misty all day, regularly damp and always windy. I had plenty to do, cleaned the cottage, etc., but will shortly go mad if this goes on, I must do something outside! This time last year, I was warm and brown, had so many good days to look back on, and now I am caged in the evening, the long days only allowing me longer hours in which to observe the endless rain falling.

11th July. Well, as the weather was just that little bit better, I went out and up the road and took my favourite route up to the lochs under Quinag which at that point I could not see. But there were divers to be watched on the grey water, three red-throats in all, and one incredibly handsome black-throat. Under the low cloud there suddenly appeared a golden eagle, gliding just a bit above my head, silent, immense. There were a couple of greenshank piping in the distance, and sandpipers calling around the lochs (are alarm calls a good idea when there is a large predator overhead?). Suddenly, despite the soft drizzle, it was magic, the enchantment was back.

In this improved mood, I went to the small sand beach from which I have so often swum. I am quite used to swimming in the sea, I reasoned (although this year I had not so far done so), and the lochs are always warmer than the sea . . . but no, it was too cold even to be thought of; my ankles went numb. In order to warm up a bit, I dressed and climbed briskly up to explore the high wood at the back of the loch, which is in a small corrie. The higher section is lovely, with quite a few hollies, and an area of very lush vegetation; is this fed by enriched water from above? Here there

139

are ledges with genuine woodland flowers, which anyone from England would recognise: woodrush, primrose, water avens, woodruff and sanicle, all in bloom. The yellow saxifrage, which grows so luxuriantly beside the road over Knockan, covers quite a large area, and honeysuckle hangs from some of the birches.

Descending again, I did actually try once more to swim but again abandoned the idea, and instead walked up to the very good path which, strangely, slowly disappears as you head back towards the road. Here there were lots of lovely patches of the white lesser butterfly orchid, and in some drier areas, the fragrant orchid, which I always have to smell – such a delightful, strong scent of cloves. Then back through my wee bealach in the low hills, via a reedy lochan where a young greenshank, I think, fluttered about in a hesitating fashion, calling sharply. I watched it briefly, but decided it was distinctly unhappy at my presence, and so wandered on towards the road. There were quite a few birds down there: three strangely silent cuckoos, and a chacking stonechat. But it was the flowers again which attracted my attention, lots of orchids, sundews, butterwort, bell heather on drier outcrops, purging flax, the white bedstraw, lousewort, tormentil, thyme, trefoil; all the little flowers at my feet which the car-borne never stop to see, thinking that it is all 'bare moor', or even, and much worse, the 'wet desert'. The vegetation now all being summer-green, it is *my time*, I feel deeply and truly at home. Quinag now looming through the mist, damp bracken against my knees, the scent of bog myrtle, this is how it was . . . and should always be.

And on 15 July, a brief entry makes very clear how the contrary weather can affect one's mood:

> Had to go to Inverness; heavy and grey, and me not feeling at all well . . . and then the sun came out and everything changed. Came home tired (it is a two-hour drive), but grinning like the Cheshire Cat. A beautiful, calm, sunny evening; strolled by the flats and watched the burn meet the incoming tide . . . there is nothing more peaceful.

# 21

# Ancient Woodland

Once I was firmly established back in Assynt, I did get well and truly involved both with the Field Club and Historic Assynt. This was really at a number of levels; social, recreational and working. I found the combination of exploring our multi-faceted landscape on my own and with others, thinking and talking about it, meeting up with various visiting specialists, all very stimulating, and I tried to adopt a really organised approach to my studies of Assynt through history.

It remains a fact, despite all the work of Historic Assynt, surveys and individual exploration, that there is a huge slice of the history of the parish for which we have almost no archae-ological record. This contrasts strangely with the numerous structures from the Neolithic and Iron Age. As Assynt moves into the period of the clans, the focus of the parish appears to be concentrated on Loch Assynt with a possible, if very small, stronghold on Eilean Assynt at the west end, and the siting of an early parish church at Inchnadamph to the east. It is customary to suggest that, for several hundred years, most of the houses, byres, barns and sheds elsewhere were built either of turf, or of some kind of hazel wattle (the 'creel houses') and have left very little trace. We are very fortunate that the Sutherland Estates commissioned the survey of the parish by John Home of Edinburgh, and this, completed in 1775, provides a clear picture of the settlement and working of the whole region by then.

While earlier prehistory and history can, I know, seem very 'dry', certainly uninformative about the lives of ordinary folk, archaeology has been able to illuminate at least these more recent ages. Historic Assynt excavated three of the ruined houses in Glenleraig, those beside the path (which is now invisible) up to Loch Torr an Lochain and were surprised at some of the details they uncovered. The fires, which would have been of peat, were controlled by air ducts in the floor, which could be closed down, and the inhabitants used fairly up-to-date Staffordshire creamware, and had possessed claret bottles; all, sadly, found in fragments, but certainly not suggesting the squalid poverty that has sometimes been said to prevail at this time.

And Home's survey gives us the names of the people who lived there; by this time, they were using surnames, and some of the rarer (most were Mackenzies), included McLean, Stewart, McCrae, all names which were known in the nearby townships when I was young. (I think the Munros came from Ardvar, which just like Glenleraig had 90 inhabitants.) The miller was Roderick Mackenzie; I cannot help wondering whether he liked his wine . . . Perhaps most interesting of all, the 18 households had 18 'servants': I do not wish to make too much of this, maybe their lives *were* endless drudgery, and they probably slept in the byres, but they had a place in the scheme of things and a roof over their heads, a sense, surely, of security which the Clearances totally destroyed.

While excavations tell us quite a lot about these pre-Clearance houses, we still have no idea when, during the centuries before, these 'farms', found all over the parish, were first settled, and with what sort of building. Strangely, we appear to lack the intimately clustered groups of longhouses which are to be found elsewhere; I saw several of these when living in Skye, for instance, and they are generally believed to predate that more scattered type of settlement where each house sits, separate, in its own ground.

Despite the extent of our ignorance, we can at least assume that earlier settlement, from possibly as early as the Norse period, occupied the same locations as those mapped by

Home, and functioned in the same way, with the in-by, the cultivated land around the houses, and seasonally-used sheilings in the surrounding landscape. These were used principally for grazing, but some, close to the main settlements, functioned as detached portions of the in-by, and grew hay, for example. This very fact must suggest that, in an age without adequate fences, the red deer were at least as limited in their range as they were in my youth; if the crofters I knew wanted to bag some venison, they generally had to go to the corries of Quinag. We did know very well that there was some quiet poaching of deer going on around us and were once given a very nice present of some 'braxy mutton' which was clearly nothing of the kind. It was all on the familiar 'one-for-the-pot' basis, which was then very much a part of the traditional Highland way of life, and had been, no doubt, since time immemorial.

Among the elements which would have been in use since the time of the Vikings are the nousts, already mentioned, and the mills; there is a fine example in Clashnessie. There are also the 'cairidhs' or fish-traps, low circular walls extending out into the tidal areas of various bays. There is a good one at Lochinver, and I think I identified the scanty remains of another where the burn flows into Loch Nedd. With its complex coast, there are (or were) many good fishing grounds offshore; we used to take *Periwinkle* around the Meall Islands in Eddrachillis Bay and did very well there. In those days, there were also legal nets for catching salmon at sea, and one or two we heard about, which were rather less official; they appeared and disappeared at intervals between the little island in Loch Nedd and the shore, for instance! And there are lochs and lochans, as well as burns and small rivers everywhere. Fishing must always have been one of the significant resources of the parish.

Among the other very important resources are the remarkable woods. While we were enjoying our long, happy holidays in the glen, I took the wooded areas rather for granted. I recognised that we were surrounded by trees, but not that it was, in a Highland context, rather remarkable that the view out from the cottage is woodland over 360 degrees. I knew most of the surrounding trees: the birch, the multi-stemmed alders by the burn, the hazel on the hillside in the Back Park and elsewhere. But the woods were the background to our daily activities, and I did not really think much about them.

Having, however, started to study them seriously while living elsewhere, it was inevitable that once I was back in Assynt I would start to take note of the trees and woods encountered on my constant walks. I started photographing trees, something which, in those days of film, resulted in boxes of slides and albums of prints, and I continue to do so in these much more economical digital days. I realised that the woods must always have been an important resource for the local inhabitants, and, from my extensive reading to date, that I should be able to recognise in the field whether individual trees had been managed in the past. Thinking about all this resulted in a project which was supported by the Assynt Crofters' Trust (and funded by the Millennium Forest for Scotland Trust, Caithness and Sutherland Enterprise and the Leader II Programme). I began to take notes and photographs in a much more organised fashion, revisited areas which I thought I knew already, and went to others where I had never been.

I began this work seriously one winter, and I was amazingly lucky in the weather during those months. There must, I suppose, have been high pressure anchored firmly over us; most days began with a light frost, and the sun shone all day. There was some snow on Quinag, the blinding white I glimpsed at times through the black and white of the birch trunks. The colours were superb; the white of the snow and the trunks emphasised the azure of the sky, the twigs of the birch were pink-to-purple, increasingly so as we neared the spring, and the dead bracken – at its best! – was a deep rust-red. The sculptural shapes of the older trees could be seen clearly, the grasses between them, close-cropped by deer, were a vivid green, like the mosses which clothed many of the rocks.

While walking quietly around, I did see some deer; strangely they seemed more nervous in the woods than when sauntering past the cottage. The level sweeps of grass had been ploughed by battalions of badgers (who needs wild boar?) which now slept in the extensive setts, themselves more visible now that the ferns and bracken had subsided. Occasionally I spied a quick, dark-brown movement which was a pine marten, but it was the birds, the mixed flocks of tits, who enlivened my days, twittering among the lichen-draped branches while I ate my sandwiches and drank tomato soup from my thermos. I was completely alone for days and could not have been happier.

Once I started doing this, I very rapidly decided that I needed expert comment on the validity of the conclusions I was reaching. I contacted the ever-helpful Chris Smout, and he gave me the name of Scotland's equivalent of the famed Oliver Rackham, the 'guru' of ancient woodland studies, Peter Quelch. The latter, too, was most helpful and enthusiastic, and very soon I was taking him round some of my favourite places within the substantial area of woodland in reach of my home. To my delight he confirmed my conclusions; within a matrix of younger birch regeneration are older, veteran trees, which show proof of long management, coppicing and pollarding, which allowed the harvesting of wood from these deciduous trees, effectively prolonging their lives. This is the traditional woodland management found all over Britain; what made it important was that it proved that this area, which tended in the past to be dismissed as birch 'scrub', contained a variety of veteran trees dating from an era when woodland was valued as a resource, like any other in Britain. Assynt has a history of woodland management in common, for instance, with that of Hatfield Forest in Hertfordshire. It is, sadly, undocumented; only the trees prove the historical facts.

It is of course only common sense that in an area which was well populated in the past as the home survey shows, any neighbouring woods would have been exploited in many ways.

Some of the trees which prove this are quite near the places I had lived. I had spent some time in a cottage in Drumbeg, and after a while had found an amazing area just over the ridge behind the house; it is densely wooded, much of it thick with complex, often collapsed willows growing in the wettest ooze, which makes exploration quite tricky. One day, hidden in all this, but growing on rather drier ground, I stumbled upon one which is hugely larger in the trunk. It looks as if it had once been a substantial coppice stool, cut many times at ground level to encourage regrowth; subsequently two stems had been promoted, or had simply got away, but in their turn they had both been pollarded, in other words cut at a higher level, again to facilitate regrowth. The resulting shape is, although not very tall in this windy coastal location, massive and impressive. I found another old tree in a similar sodden jungle in my glen, not far from the cottage; this was an alder, rather columnar in its broad lower trunk, which had obviously been cut at two levels, giving it a two-layer 'wedding-cake' sort of appearance, its symmetry only disturbed by one large side limb which had somehow escaped harvesting.

It would be a brave individual who would confidently date such trees, but they are growing very far north, and in generally poor soil, so it is permissible to assume slow rates of growth. Accordingly, it might be fair to assume that both trees are around, or over, three hundred years old, an age which puts them back well before the Clearances occurred in this area of Assynt: Glenleraig was cleared in 1812, just over two hundred years ago.

My interest in these trees was far from merely academic; I thought they were beautiful things which united my love for nature and history, and this place, and I felt that they linked me to earlier inhabitants. I had harvested some wood from the sycamores the MacAulays had planted close to the cottage, and these ancient trees I had discovered had been used in the same way by some of the folk whose names I read in the Survey of Assynt.

There are places nearby with a considerable number of oaks, and many of these have been coppiced over generations; Peter reckoned that a number might easily be around three hundred and fifty to four hundred years in age. Down in an area of low, coastal ground, in what seems poor soil, we found a circle of apparently youngish oak stems, each of which looks rather J-shaped, which very much aroused our interest. I came back to this specimen several times over the succeeding years; it is frequently grazed, but once I found that it had, for a while, escaped the teeth of sheep and deer, and the whole of the space between the stems was covered with oak leaves, growing up from the ground. The inescapable conclusion is that these stems are growing from an old coppice stool, and we put a speculative date on it of about 1000 AD, making it older than Ardvreck Castle or Calda House on Loch Assynt, which are recognised as the principal historic monuments of the parish, passed on every trip to Ullapool or Inverness.

While involved in these explorations, a group of us found what we think represents a charcoal-burning platform, which was no doubt fuelled with the wood cut from the neighbouring oaks. Like so many other parts of the Highlands, our parish probably had an industrial past, on however small a scale, powered by the local resources of woodland. It cannot too often be said that woodland survives because it has value, and often will die of neglect if it is seen to have none. The sheep farm in Glenleraig, and the crofting townships of Nedd, Drumbeg and Culkein, are well-provided still with woodland, which clearly had a real value for their inhabitants; there are great concentrations of managed trees of almost all species around their crofts. Sadly, these trees have effectively no protection or statutory recognition. They are not well known – my report on them and many of the photographs were pre-digital, with only a few examples printed.

While I was working on this woodland project, I chatted to some of the older local inhabitants, trying to ascertain how some of the different tree species were used. The wood of alder, for instance, which will rot in air but not in water, was often used for fencing and structural posts in wet ground – although it might then once more start to grow! Alder, hazel spars of which the bark is waterproof, and flexible willow might be used for creels, holly where truly hard wood was required, as, perhaps, in boatbuilding where the curved boughs would come in handy. Adie, who lived on one of the wooded crofts, told me that holly could be so hard that it was often not possible to shape it with an adze. Frank Ross, who used to come up from Edinburgh to spend the summers here, now retired and back living in Nedd, told me that rowan – surprisingly perhaps, because you will often be told that it is a sacred tree – was used for the shafts of carts. (It also is a hard wood.) Looking around the crofts, I could see several rowans which had been repeatedly cut and had grown some splendid shapes. Perhaps the final and most significant comment was that folk from townships where there were no trees growing had a right to take suitable wood from the more favoured places; while this list may not seem to amount to very much, it proves the rather obvious fact: trees were valued.

It is easy, I know, to think that all this information about old trees is rather academic, just a piece of history. But when I was working on this project, these were not simply 'pollards' or 'coppices'. With an interested friend, I spent a little time one day coring a few healthy-looking trees to see if we could establish their ages. There were some fine willows in Drumbeg, just above the little Port na Ba; we decided to core one pollard above and below the point of cutting, and our estimate was that the tree itself was around 120 years old, and that it had been pollarded some 60 years ago. That meant that I had probably known the crofter who had been cutting the willow branches for some special purpose. He likely came from the nearest cottage, and I suddenly could see his face; I remembered chatting to him in Kitty's shop one day, when I had given Joey a lift up from the glen. *People* made these trees the shape they are, and the trees helped the people to live in this place.

It would be nice to produce a modern map of the parish, with all the farms and the sheilings along with the neighbouring woods. These would cover a substantial part of the area, and it is important to remember that, apart from the mountainous areas and the wet ground (large areas of which were cut for peat), all the rest was labelled by Home often as 'rocky, muirish pasture'. Assynt was, to a surprisingly large extent, both inhabited and used; it was a worked landscape, which is why the present inhabitants often react rather strongly to any suggestion that it is 'wild' or, even worse, 'wilderness'. Assynt is a cultural landscape which, despite its rocky nature, hard climate and northern location, sustained a population for thousands of years.

One of the most useful trees in sustaining that human population must always have been the hazel, and the single-stemmed, pollarded hazels I had discovered were just one proof of that; they must belong to a group of managed trees, remnants of which may be seen in Scandinavia, the 'fodder-pollards'. Clearly, the massive stems result from the maintenance of a single stem through decades, probably centuries, the others being used at intervals as hazel still is, for poles and sticks. Once a good thick stem was established, it was cut at a height above the reach of grazing animals, and regrew from there, reaching up to the light as hazel will often do. In years when the hill grass came late and animals faced starvation, the young branches were cut as the fresh leaves came in the spring, and the foliage fed to the needy stock.

In general, there is a tendency, as trees were repeatedly coppiced, for the new growth to be on the outer, lighter side of the old trunk, which means that, in time, coppice stools might achieve significant size. I found coppiced alders, ashes, hollies and birches of considerable girth, all over Assynt. With the hazels, it is perhaps a little more difficult to be sure that they have been coppiced, but I found at least one where I had no doubts at all. It is in another well-wooded location, on the side-road out towards the sea at Achmelvich, where more recent regeneration of birch surrounds some older trees. One glorious hazel there looked, when I saw it last, remarkably healthy, but it was effectively hollow, with space within the surrounding stems for perhaps three or four folk to stand. I can see no reason to question why it has taken this form. It must have been coppiced over a few centuries at least, and takes its own, unheralded place among Assynt's fine veteran trees. Its diameter is about six feet, which, according to Oliver Rackham, would give it an age of at least three hundred years (in England, so probably more this much further north).

Some of today's Assynt crofters are fortunate enough to possess true woodland crofts, but not all are likely to be aware that they are, for a start, following in a long and very distinct tradition which is much older than crofting itself. Many of them cut the birch for firewood; perhaps not so many, sadly, are aware that if they protect the inevitable new growth which will follow, they could prolong the lives of those trees far into the future, creating a perpetually renewable resource, and preserving the precious scenic diversity of the parish.

# 22

# Hurricane

During my exploration of the many wooded places, I had been struck by several areas which had obviously experienced really severe weather, with lots of trees smashed, and many that were effectively upended, the flat root-plate now vertical. Most of these deciduous trees were in fact still living, vigorous in new growth which might be at right-angles to their old trunks; the shapes which result from this are extraordinary, a real testament to the life-force of nature. Although I had, inevitably, experienced plenty of gales, I had never seen one which caused this sort of damage. That was to change; in January 2005, we had a hurricane.

The New Year had come in with storms, and a lot of thunder and lightning; I had come home after celebrating my father's birthday at Drumrunie, when the cottage or a pole nearby was struck by lightning. I was actually on the phone at the moment of the strike; the connection was severed with a fearful noise in my ear, and then the power went off, leaving me in the dark. Because my cottage was on the very floor of the glen, at its very lowest point, I was not used to there being strikes close by, so there was the inevitable feeling around in the dark to find the nearest torch before I could begin to marshal the candles and camping gaslight. The next day, both power and telephone were restored but the weather forecast warned of a much more serious storm to come. The gale duly arrived after dark, and the phone promptly went off again. I had everything organised this time, lighting all ready, torches strategically placed, the wood-burning stove going well with lots of dry fuel inside the house. I had power through the evening, and kept listening to the radio, but slowly I had to turn it up as the noise of the wind grew in strength. By bedtime, it was stronger than I had ever heard inside a building since a hundred-mile-an-hour gale in Orkney, where our solid stone house was very exposed, in contrast to my current situation. At bedtime, I opened the door and stood outside, in the shelter, for a while. The gusts around the building were astonishing, but more impressive and ominous was the wild screaming of the wind in the trees on the high sides of the glen. I went to bed with an extra-large dram, and actually slept quite soundly; probably the only person for miles to do so.

I was woken early by the roaring of the burn and first light showed me that its water had been held back by the high tide; looking out of the door showed that the water was now higher than I had ever seen it, lapping at the stone slab at my feet. I could see that the far section of the track up to the road was also underwater. I dressed quickly and walked the short distance to a point from which I could see the causeway across the flats; this was also covered, to quite a depth, something up to now unheard of. The phone and power were off again, so it was much later that I heard of the tragedy in the Western Isles caused by this ferocious weather and incredible high tides.

Washing and breakfast took longer than usual; I had to get the stove burning well before I could even boil a kettle, let alone make some porridge. Then I went out outside to have a good look around. The gale had swept down the glen, and from this direction the cottage was particularly sheltered, being rather hunkered down against a low bank. There was no damage to the building, no slates lying on the grass, which was a blessing, but the wind had left confusion in its wake; one big, carefully-stacked woodpile had fallen all over the place, and part, even, of the rather decrepit stone dyke had collapsed in a heap. There seemed to be twigs and branches everywhere, and even down here, the damage to the woods was considerable.

I did part of my familiar walk up the burn, noticing that some of the ancient hazels, which Peter had pointed out below the mill, had now been smashed out of all recognition; only the photographs I had taken earlier showed what they had been. I then headed out into the open, towards the road; there was an open timber and corrugated-iron shed up there; it had lost its roof in the storm. I found large sections, a few iron sheets each, screwed on to heavy beams, which had taken off and blown hundreds of yards. If you had been hit by one of these flying wings in the dark, you would almost certainly have been killed.

Later that day, with the causeway now dry apart from the seaweed, I took the car quickly up to Nedd, just to see how things were in the outside world. Here I was told that the road beyond was still blocked by all the fallen trees; I could hear chainsaws going, so retreated home, in order to prepare for another night without power or phone. (Mobiles were not working either, of course, as all the masts and relay stations were without electricity, too.)

The main problem with the long dark evening was the boredom. There was so little one could really do. I did read for a while by the camping gas light, but I did not like to have it on all the time from four, by which time it was really getting dark in the cottage, until ten or eleven when I would head for bed. I was partly unsure how long it was going to be necessary to live like this, how long my supply of gas would last, and whether it was wise to breathe in its fumes for so many hours. That left the candles, which smelt different, at least, but it was hard to arrange enough of them to read by. Tending the stove took some time, and so, of course, did making my evening meal on it, but I could not listen to music, nor have the nice, long, hot bath of which I dreamed. It did strike me as rather ironic that if I had been in the unimproved cottage of my youth, the old Nurex would have had the tank clearly bubbling away and I could easily have had that bath.

Rather too obviously all that was left was drinking; and I had quite a lot of wine in the house, having been given some at Christmas. I was very conscious of this temptation, allowed myself only a bit more than usual, but it took a real effort . . .

The next day I was able to go up to Drumbeg, in order to find out how they had fared, and whether there was any news from anywhere, any idea as to when we might be re-connected with the outside world. The short answer to *that* question was: 'Not a clue . . .', but the story of the night of the hurricane (which is what it turned out to be) was much longer, and very much more dramatic. Of course, they, too, had lost their connections, but found it much harder than I had to settle for sleep, being in a much more open situation. During the night, Violet, with her son and daughter, heard the most appalling crash outside. John was all for going out to see what had happened, but Vi would not let him on the very sensible grounds that it was obviously far too dangerous. It was only at first light that they could assess the astonishing truth.

Vi lived in one of a group of houses, pleasantly laid out on a level site, looking over Loch Drumbeg to Quinag. Each house has a small back garden, behind which is a wall, and a small hill. It so happened at this time that a house over the top of the hill had renewed its oil tank, and the discarded old metal oil tank was left sitting on the top of the rise. At the height of the storm, this oil tank took flight; it flattened a fence, then flew down the hill, over the wall and part of Vi's back garden, and landed on top of John's car. The noise on landing can be imagined, and John's car was very thoroughly written off, but had the wind direction been somewhat different, the oil tank might well have crashed into the back of one of the houses, and goodness knows what damage might have ensued.

We remained without information, without power or phones for the rest of the week, a period of considerable frustration for most of us. When Friday came without any progress, I made my decision and headed for Ullapool, arriving without prior warning at the house of a friend, in order to stay the weekend. Ullapool and area were back to normal; never did the services we are used to seem more wonderful.

Winter weather can really impinge very seriously on us here, and living on a long loop of single-track road only makes it worse. By this time, the prolonged spells of frost or snow had largely gone, and with them, the seriously cold temperatures of my youth. Now, some winters, the night-time temperatures hover around zero, and you never know what will happen. Light snow may fall and then melt a bit; the sky will clear, the temperature will drop below zero, you have one of those nights with an apple-green sky, and in the morning there will be ice. Or another day, rain will fall on a road whose surface is below freezing, and again you will have ice. Often it is black ice; invisible, frequently, but, equally often, lethal – 'like a bottle' is the constant local phrase. Sometimes, deep snow falls on the ice, and when the snow plough arrives, it fails to take a corner and ends up with its nose in the ditch, its tail still blocking the narrow road. It stays blocked until another vehicle is found which can pull the plough out of the ditch. This quite often happened between, say, Drumbeg and Lochinver; if you happened to be following the plough home, you might wait for hours in the car until the road ahead was cleared, or you could reverse until you found somewhere to turn, and take the long way home . . . but this was risking the steeper hills and tighter bends from near Kylesku.

And there lurked everywhere, but particularly on that longer route home, the added danger of the deer. I doubt if folk living outwith the Highlands have any idea of the havoc these 'iconic' (heavy irony!) animals cause. Most of my friends have had very near misses or have actually hit – or been hit by – deer on the road; cars have been badly damaged, sometimes written off, and drivers on occasion are badly hurt. One Sunday I had been having lunch with my recently-widowed mother, and saw as the evening fell, that the sky was clearing and the temperature dropping. The road had been wet as I drove down, water easing from the snowbanks on the verges, and I knew we were in for more black ice. I left my own car there and borrowed my mother's old Land Rover Freelander, which had, of course, four-wheel drive. I set off home, driving gently but securely through Elphin and Inchnadamph, turning up beside Loch

Assynt to cross over Skiag. There is careful judgement required for making the ascent of a hill on ice; you need to maintain some speed in order to have the momentum to get up the hill – if you come to a halt you may have real problems in setting off again – but if there is a badly-cambered bend near the summit around which you cannot see, that necessary judgement must be very finely-tuned. By now it was, inevitably, dark, so at least if a car was coming the other way, I should see its lights . . . and there were none in evidence. So I rounded the bend, still very much on black ice – you know it in the very lack of feeling through the steering. Instead of a car, there was a herd of red deer, right across the road. I dared not brake on the ice, knowing I would skid totally out of control if I did; fortunately I was still ascending, so I could let the hill reduce my speed. It *just* worked; I had just slowed enough as I reached the milling deer, who were slithering around all over the road, a few still trying to lick the road for salt, despite the vehicle which came within inches of them.

Leaving this main road a bit before Unapool, I ventured on the single-track towards home, and when I reached a level stretch, I stopped to check the road surface. My feet almost went from under me the second I cautiously left the vehicle; yes, the road was like the proverbial bottle, and I had to navigate steep hills and serious hairpins to get to the cottage. The only answer was to use, as far as possible, the very edge of the road, or the verge itself, where there was always some grit or gravel. I knew the road like the back of my hand and could pretty well always see headlights in the distance, so meeting an unexpected vehicle was unlikely, but I still had to get up the hills (1 in 5 and 1 in 4 in a few places); back to maintaining momentum on the way up. But there were also some steep downhills where momentum was the last thing I wanted. Suffice it to say that the Land Rover and I managed it, although I was very tense on the descents.

I was just getting near to my destination, and beginning to relax, when I became aware of a stag approaching on my left, coming up to the road at an angle, on a definite slope. Fortunately, I was still going quite slowly, but I did think that, seeing and hearing me approaching, he might hold back; there was nothing pursuing him, and he was alone, not the last of a group crossing the road. But it was clear that he was determined to cross ahead of me; he redoubled his speed. By this time we were very close. On this level, the road was as icy as anywhere, and, once more, I needed to use the verge to find enough grip to enable me to brake. But taking to the verge would bring me even closer to the accelerating stag . . . a few panicky seconds later, he had leapt into the road in front of me. I must have missed him by an inch. I was still shaking when I got in my door; another night when a dram came in more than handy.

# 23

# Sporting Estate

My constant walk was up the glen, in the shelter of the deep valley and the trees; I could enjoy this under most weather conditions. Eventually the wood thins out, especially on the eastern side, and you are in more open country, heading towards the rampart of Quinag's great western cliffs. This section of the burn is gentler, shallower, a contrast to the falls and rocky pools you have just passed. Then you reach another zone, level, peaty, an old loch-basin, where the burn loops slowly around, shallow gravel sections intervening between deep, dark, almost sinister holes. Here there are hints of an old channel, and an obvious ox-bow lake, which is the scene of splendid orgies in the spring – involving toads, it should perhaps be explained!

On the eastern side of this very different zone is a significant area of green, an obvious and important sheiling, bounded by a high bank, and contrasting at almost any time of the year with the much damper moorland all around. In the summer, bracken has taken over much of this good ground, and it is best visited in the spring, when the dippers may be singing from the stones in the burn, and the cuckoo calling among the soft-green birches. On a slight rise, some distance above the burn, may be seen low walls, roughly circular in plan; a very small drystone cell has been built into these, and belongs to a later time. The main structure might be the low walls of a Bronze or Iron Age farmhouse, of the type which is often (and to my mind rather misleadingly) referred to as a 'Hut Circle', and, if so, would be proof of perhaps the earliest occupation of the glen. Subsequently, we have proof of occupation during the succeeding Iron Age, in the form of the souterrain, and the Vikings have at least left the definitive place name from their own period. No doubt this sheiling, the 'Ruigh Dorcha', being such good land, would have been utilised all through this and subsequent periods, right up until the Clearances in 1812.

The Clearances did have an enormous impact on Assynt, both socially and in terms of the use of the land. This is not a book, nor even a chapter, about the Clearances; other writers have written much on the subject, and I contributed a little in my book *Castles in the Mist*. The point most pertinent to this chapter is the huge depopulation of this part of the parish. In 1775, it so happens that there were ninety inhabitants of Ardvar, and the same number in Glenleraig. After the evictions, I think it is likely that one dwelling, possibly only used seasonally, was inhabited at Ardvar (the basis of the Lodge to which we walked when I was young, and which I wrote about in *North and West*). Some time after 1812 our cottage was built, housing the shepherd of this new sheep farm, his family, and, often, a 'boy' or shepherd lad. Jockan had, in his youth, been the 'boy', sleeping in the little room at the back, where my father much later built the bunks. There were times during my own occupation of it when I was the only inhabitant of this glen, where there had once been ninety people living, working the land, and needing a mill to process the oats and barley they had grown.

Their use of the numerous sheilings, which may often still be easily identified, was an efficient way of utilising the resources of the landscape on a seasonal basis, the practice of transhumance which continues today, for instance in the Pyrenees. It is ecologically beneficial in varying the impact of grazing livestock through the year; to an extent, it was mimicked after the Clearances, in the efficient and constant shepherding of the sheep on the hill, but that practice, too, has long since discontinued, and the impact of any grazing animals is more intense as a result.

After the sheep farm was established, and some of the former residents of the glen had settled in Nedd, which became in course of time a crofting township, the sporting potential of the whole area began to assume some importance. There were some grouse on the moorland, trout in the numerous lochs and streams, runs of sea trout in the small rivers like the Leraig and the Oldany, and even a few salmon. There were certainly some roe around all the woods, while the red deer must have remained restricted to the much higher hills.

The sporting potential of the Highlands was clearly recognised quite early on. A drawing in the pages of the Home Survey shows a man fishing with a rod, as opposed to the rather less sporting but much more effective practice of netting, and the arrival of Queen Victoria and Prince Albert in Deeside only confirmed the fashion (which already had been established) for enjoying the landscape in this way. It is often thought that this involved only the grand sporting estates, with important salmon rivers, grouse moors and deer forests, but the general interest in, and practice of, field sports went much further than that. In Assynt there were, ultimately, the big lodges like Loch Assynt and Glencanisp, but there were much smaller lodges, too, let out with rough shooting and the right to fish many of the lochs and larger burns. One such lodge was Oldany, and it so happens that through a friend (the son of the Mandlebergs who lived there in our day), I acquired a copy of their Game Book for the years in the run up to the outbreak of the Second World War. This was fascinating to me, because it involved a number of people whom we had known, and places which we had known intimately and I was constantly exploring. It emphasised, too, a number of things; one was how much things had changed in under fifty years.

The Oldany Game Book is very much an informal document, kept by one of the sporting party and annotated helpfully by our friend who had often been part of the whole scene. What is not entirely clear is the extent of the area over which they held the sporting rights. It seems to have reached as far as Ardvar in the east; they went down to the house there once or twice, but there is no reference to anyone living in it at the time, nor how it functioned. Their rights seem to have stretched as far as Stoer Head, although they did not spend much time out there. Inland, into the magical hinterland of lochs and abrupt hills, their boundary is again unclear, but they spent a great deal of time around and on the lochs from Clashnessie to Drumbeg, as is only to be expected. Apart from collecting one or two visitors, and trips for provisions, the sport was the main preoccupation of everyone there; if there was nothing else obvious to do, they fished the burn, and recorded everything that they caught or shot.

From the Glorious Twelfth, of course, they were after grouse, and walking the rough moors found significantly more than I ever saw, also walking considerable distances there in the 1990s and later. I certainly made a note if ever I saw any and cannot find reference to anything that could be called a covey; a brace was the most I ever recorded. Once or twice, they did comparatively well; the Glorious Twelfth itself in 1936 produced 13, they bagged four on the 14th, two on the 15th, seven on the 17th, and so on. The total for their 1936 season was no fewer than 108 grouse, and 173 the following year, a number which would be astonishing today.

They were shooting duck, too, on many of the lochs, again far more than I ever met inland; the winter population of Loch Nedd, with a number of mallard, was the greatest concentration that I ever saw. They got a few mallard and teal at regular intervals, as well as the occasional widgeon. Interestingly, there were, even then, greylag geese out on the small island of Chrona, which we could see, markedly green, in our views from the Clashnessie shore. For this activity, they arranged a complicated process, with guns in boats out on the sea, and on adjacent headlands in case the geese left the island and headed for the mainland.

Boats and boatmen were relevant, too, when they went, as we did later, sea-fishing. They caught the same sort of species, of course, and one of their number added to the range by becoming fascinated by his attempts to spear flounders at the mouth of the Oldany. Like us, too, they tended lobster pots on a regular basis; their meals, rather late in the evening to us at around eight-thirty or nine, were fairly splendid, starting often with the crab or lobster of the day, and progressing through the duck or grouse which had been hanging for the prescribed time – someone must have had a good system for remembering what had been shot on what day!

Of considerable interest is that they saw and shot some black grouse (four in 1936), especially around Loch Poll, which we had fished constantly in youth, and which I regularly walked to in later life. Neither in the 1960s or 70s, nor in the 90s or the first decade of the third millennium, did I ever see or hear any black grouse. The relevance of all this is that nowadays most ornithologists would tell you that black game needs some pine, and around Loch Poll there is absolutely none. As I have mentioned, there are some old pines on a headland, An Abha, which almost cuts Loch Drumbeg in two, but they simply cannot be enough to alter the habitat. In any case, the Game Book makes no mention of shooting there; it is around Loch Poll that the black grouse are found. I suspect that at this period, they were sustained in the autumn by going into the strips of oats, hay, potatoes and maybe turnips which would have been growing on the Drumbeg crofts. The sportsmen from Oldany were similarly after the partridges which haunted the Clashnessie crofts; another species which has long disappeared from the parish. They shot 13 in 1936. And, although there are certainly still snipe in Assynt, they were being shot in some numbers in the run up to 1939. They are hard to get, of course, with their erratic flight, but five were shot in Strathcroy on 27 August 1936, four near Culkein on 4 September, with a total of 27 that season. The lack, by the time I was there as a child, and certainly nowadays, of small-scale cultivation, has to be one of the reasons for the disappearance of the black game and the grey partridges since the 1930s. There is likely, however, to be another, much more insidious reason for their absence; ever since the Industrial Revolution got underway, our landscapes, already acid, will have been made more so by the fallout from such processes, circulating in the atmosphere and falling as rain. All over Britain, moorlands are much poorer in species than they used to be; while some causes of such decline may be relatively easily addressed, the impact of the industrial age is a challenge which we have hardly yet assessed, let alone dealt with.

There was another factor in the comparative richness of the sporting quarry revealed in these pages; with game, there went, of course, gamekeepers, and they spent the year pursuing that class of creature they called 'vermin'. Anything that might affect the sporting 'bag' would be trapped or shot, with the inevitable result that foxes or pine martens, for instance, were rarely seen by these hardy walkers of the hills. The writer of the Game Book was told of an otter which had been trapped and killed during the preceding winter, and he, seeing a diver (he does not specify whether it was black- or red-throated), takes a shot at it, an act which would horrify us now. The logic of the day was simple: the diver eats small fish, the fish are ours to catch, therefore we have the right to shoot anything which interferes with our sport.

And some magnificent creatures were disposed of in this way; the writer also tells that he was informed that during another winter, a golden eagle which had got into the habit of taking young lambs was similarly shot. Francis, the writer, went to look at the site of the eyrie used by that dead eagle, and, again, this is of interest to the local, contemporary naturalist. As far as I can tell, that eyrie was not very far from the Oldany–Drumbeg area; it does not seem to have involved a really long trek into the hills. I deduce, cautiously, that the ill-fated eagle had been nesting in that same hinterland. No eagle nests there now, a fact that is perhaps explained by the fate of this particular bird in 1930.

The richness of the visible animal life around my cottage, the sightings of marten, badger and otter which so delighted me, would have been unknown and anathema to the Oldany sportsmen and women of those days. They had, however, far more to shoot – and eat – than anyone would now manage – except for one species. It is more than ironic to record that they wished they possessed a good herd of red deer; they certainly remarked on the few they did see. Now, of course, an evening stroll in the long daylight of the Assynt summer would witness dozens grazing openly on the fertile fields in front of their comfortable lodge.

# 24

# Heading North

The whole of this section of coast from Ardvar to Stoer Head is basically north-facing, and in reasonable weather, every road trip and many walks give splendid views to the north. The view of the sea is terminated by the smooth shape and vertical cliffs of the Isle of Handa, around which we had once taken *Periwinkle* in a spell of very calm weather. We did, occasionally, take the road up to Scourie and the tiny port of Tarbet in order to cross to the island, but there were often queues for Kylesku ferry, and as we had other reasons to head in this direction, we, in those days, only once or twice made this trip. Once the elegant bridge and fast new road were completed, the lure of points further north was considerable, and latterly I found plenty of reasons to head for Handa. As if its natural attractions were not enough, I had past links with Dr Jean Balfour of Scourie Estate (of which the island is part), and she asked me to chair meetings of the management committee, which I gladly did for some years. We often met elsewhere, of course, but we did meet there as well, which made for a fascinating day out.

The island is, like Stoer Head, composed of Torridonian sandstone, which, for almost half of its circumference, makes very fine cliffs, with one massive stack. Unlike Stoer, however, these cliffs hold a major seabird colony, which is the great attraction of the island. The south and eastern aspect is much more gentle, with some lovely sand, which gives the island its Viking name. The whole place makes a strong contrast with the incredibly contorted, bare and colourful gneiss of the near mainland.

You land on one of the beautiful sand beaches, and head past the ruins of the deserted village. Much of the walking is on wooden boardwalk, and sometimes, if the day is warm, you may catch quick glimpses of the numerous common lizards which live, presumably, underneath it. There should be red grouse lurking somewhere near in the heather, but this thins out as you reach the gentle, boggier heights of the island. By now, there is almost certainly a constant fly-past of one of the most spectacular inhabitants, the often aggressive great skua or bonxie, a bird which we never saw when I was young but which has spread around the West Coast since. The last time I went there, despite the bonxies, there were still divers on the lochans close to the cliffs, but they must have had a worrying life. By now, the island is full of noises; you are near the great cliffs and almost countless seabirds; this is one of the great sights of the far north-west. After a number of visits, I was watching puffins on the top of the Great Stack one day, when I realised that there had been a wall around its perimeter. Presumably you could once reach this flat, naturally-defended area across an arch, a dizzyingly high version of that which still survives on the much lower reaches of the Stoer cliffs. We are sure that this is another mad, improbable fort, presumably from the Iron Age but, for various obvious reasons, no archaeological investigations have yet taken place there, as far as I know; in any case, I think the puffins would resent the disturbance!

I have always walked in this direction, subsequently heading down the gradually declining western side of the island. As you do so, there are splendid views south to Assynt; Stoer Head is conspicuous, its own stack looking slender and top-heavy. Quinag, which changes dramatically in aspect from every direction, is here seen sort of 'end on', with Canisp a gentle cone, and the ridge of Suilven, terminating in that abrupt drum, profiled beyond.

The good road can whisk you through Scourie and past the turn-off for Tarbet; soon you get some views of the complex pattern of water, islands and rocky headlands that is the extensive Loch Laxford, another place well-known to the Vikings. The road takes you inland, towards those hills which are so clearly visible from around Drumbeg, the abrupt, craggy grey summit of Stack, the strongly-angled screes of Arkle, and the long white ridge of its close neighbour, Foinaven, Soon, however, the road swings over an arched bridge across a dark pool; this is the salmon river which leads into that complex sea-loch, flowing from Loch Stack where we had watched my grandfather fishing. His constant ghillie there was Felix MacLeod, Jockan's brother (and, I suppose, brother-in-law, as the two brothers had married two sisters).

As mentioned earlier, my grandfather, Jock Menzies, used to stay in the Garbet Hotel in Kinlochbervie, which is reached across another boggy, rocky, lochan-filled moor before you take the narrower road beside the next sea-loch, the more fjord-like Inchard. We often went this way, either to have a meal with him, or to head for the further township of Oldshoremore, where our cousins still go for holidays. Their cottage has a splendid view along the sweeping beach, backed by genuinely green croft land, naturally sweetened by blown sand and full of wildflowers.

There was, however, always a temptation to head that little bit further north, towards Cape Wrath, the most northwesterly point of the Scottish mainland. If I really did want a total change from my cottage in its deep, wooded glen, I would head in this direction for just a few days, staying in the friendly little Youth Hostel at Durness. I enjoyed this place very much; the wardens were always fun to talk to, generally local and full of useful information as well as humour, and it offered all I needed for just two or three nights. I always ate pretty simply, being in awe of the industrious folk, so often from right across Europe, who took about an hour to produce some incredibly healthy, largely vegetarian meal, by which time I had long finished my simple repast. For such a short stay, the lack of a shower (in those days) did not really bother me, I had normally been for a swim in loch or sea at some stage during the day and felt adequately clean.

The road from Rhiconich, at the head of Inchard, heads up on to another soggy moor, and then makes a long, gentle descent through the bare glen of the River Dionard which issues from the crags and mists between the foothills of Foinaven and Cranstackie. As I drive down this so-familiar road, one particular memory always comes back clearly. The road crosses the dark river just where it goes through a little gorge; the deep pool would invite any fisher to try his or her luck there. And once we were driving down the road, when we slowed to watch an elderly couple who were doing just that. In fact, it was clear that the fisherman had connected with a fish and was playing it. The roads were very quiet in those days, and we simply stopped to watch, to see whether he would succeed in landing it. But as we looked on, we became rather concerned; he was standing above the river, on the little cliff, and his equally elderly wife, armed with the landing-net, was now hovering uncertainly on the brink, wobbling back and forward. My father, then a strong, vigorous forty-something, ran over, took hold of the net, found a safe foothold lower down, and landed the quite big fish, all in a matter of moments. There was a round of applause which surprised us; watching Dad, we had failed to hear that another car had arrived quietly, stopped, and was enjoying the show.

As the road descends, there is a brief view, a dazzling vignette of pink sand, blue sea, and real green grass. Ahead is a complex area of remarkable beauty, bounded to the west by the great empty headland of Cape Wrath, and to the east by the long, dark loch of Eriboll. In between, there is sand everywhere; the complex swirling of the sandbanks in the shallow Kyle of Durness, the long crescent beaches and dunes of Faraid Head, the many strands, some obvious from the road, some hidden, bounded by cliffs of the most extraordinary colour, strewn with stacks, as the road turns the corner and heads east. It is an area of complex geology, and among the many rocks to be found, there is an area of the same limestone that appears in Assynt, in Elphin and Knockan. With some damp areas, and some dry places, part sweetened again by blown sand, this is a paradise of wild flowers. Leaving the main road in Durness village, heading past the old M.O.D. buildings of the Balnakiel Craft Village where once I thought to live, I would arrive and park below the strong, high house (mostly built in the 1720s but almost certainly incorporating much older work), where the burn flows across the beach into the bay. Here it is hard to know where to head.

One possibility is to follow the little road to its end, past the ruined church, and through the golf course, which must be one of the most beautiful in the world. Its greens and fairways are mowed, but there are large areas, particularly down towards the path by the turquoise sea, which are not, and which are covered in flowers. Some in this windswept location are tiny, but I always look for them: the minute, vivid Scottish primrose, which is of a colour I hesitate to name; people seem to have very different ideas. I have heard it described as purple, crimson or deep pink, but it is certainly very special, only growing here and in the far archipelago of Orkney. But, on a similar scale, there are exquisite eyebrights, and many other, larger species. Further on, there is a nice little bay, and then the great sandbanks where I have played happily in the waves. Wandering back on the low hinterland, on one occasion I encountered a flock of golden plover in their breeding plumage, which is remarkably complex, edged with deepest brown and washed with gold. My favourite bird book says that the bird has 'a recognisably gentle expression', and their call is rather mournful, evocative of some wonderful days in the wilds. Heading back down towards the golf course, I encountered some greylags, contrasting rather with the delicate plovers, and pondered over some archaeological features, a crazy dyke which meanders across the slope without ever seeming actually to enclose anything, and traces of possible habitation.

But most people, I think, will miss all this, and leaving their cars, will follow the long beach under the dunes of Faraid Head, which reaches quite some distance out into the great ocean. At first, it is not a great area for swimming; the water is very shallow, and the tide goes out for miles; you can find yourself walking for ages before there is enough depth. Better to continue, over the little rise or around the foot of the rocks if the tide is out, and along the next long, and equally beautiful beach. It is well worth spending most of the day just exploring this wonderful headland. The dunes are, again, full of wild-flowers; once I was fortunate enough to visit when the delicate, pale, grass of Parnassus coincided with the blue-purple of selfheal in lovely expanses, a tapestry of flowers. And, as I wandered happily through all this beauty, I met a fox, dark red and handsome.

One day in early May I was there with a small group of folk; there were swallows around the old house, dunlin skittering along the edge of the limpid water, groups of eider further out, and the unmistakeable, magnificent great northern divers, dramatic with their black-and-white backs. Further out on the headland, we had views of a number of diving gannets; perhaps these were non-breeding birds, bachelors seeing the world. The nearest breeding colony of which I am aware would be in Westray, in Orkney, a significant distance perhaps even for these wonderful birds, unless food was limited back in the Islands. The divers have occasionally bred somewhere here in the far north; one July day, I watched entranced as an adult and juvenile fished repeatedly in the shallow, translucent water. The young bird was learning how to fish, did dive itself, (and I could follow it under the water as it pursued the small shoals); when it came to the surface, the adult called to it in what I can only call reassuring, solicitous tones.

# 25

# Transformation

We had arrived in Glenleraig in 1959, and left, reluctantly, in early 1972. When I returned in 1995, the place was quite different. I have already outlined the changes in the cottage; there were significant changes, too, outside. The floor of the glen is flat, and the side of the glen, up which the road travels at an angle, rises fairly steeply from that floor. This whole bank was later fenced against deer, and quite closely planted with a number of species, bushes like blackthorn as well as birch, rowan and some non-native species like sycamore, a few of which were also placed close to the gable of the cottage. This bank had never been thinned and had become an almost impenetrable jungle of interlocked trees and bushes, all reaching for the sky. Part of the adjoining valley floor had also been fenced, and within it, there remained a chaos of old fruit bushes, interwoven with brambles and thickly edged with nettles. This was all that remained of a market garden started by the last farmers in the glen.

Apart from that, the proportions of the view from the front of our cottage had changed. The trees along the burn, particularly on the little island and on the far bank were significantly taller, so the area of open ground appeared reduced. A small willow between us and the byre had grown tall and shapely, beautiful and symmetrical – until it was cut in part to clear the power lines which now reached towards my home; again a change from our early days. All around us, trees had been springing up and growing.

Exploring other areas many years later, I realised that this period of regeneration during the 1950s had been experienced in other areas further down the West Coast. I did try to work out why it might have happened and established at least some of the factors which could have been involved. It was possible that there might have been a reduction in sheep numbers over the period of the Second World War, with some men going to fight, and overall crofting activity being reduced. There might also have been some propitious climatic circumstances leading to some good seed years; I did notice significant variation in seed production in the local birches over the period I lived there but could never work out how long a period of weather would actually influence the volume of seed produced. Does it include the weather during the last summer, autumn and winter, or is it simply the spring itself which makes any one year a better seed year than another?

I was never sure about this (still am not), but there were another two matters which could also have clearly been relevant. Asking around in Nedd produced the information that 'the electric' arrived there in about 1952. In the early years, I think that electricity was relatively cheap, and this may have caused the older crofters to cut less wood for their fires; coal deliveries started to be more regular, too. And the horses were put off the Nedd grazings. Horses are notoriously heavy grazers, and when we arrived in Assynt we had seen the last of the herds of ponies which each township had possessed – they still frequented the Stoer Green in those days. The cessation of, or reduction in, cutting might have caused an increase in seeding, and the reduction in grazing allowed the regeneration to occur. This is, of course, speculation; the belt of regenerating birch from those days is not. Others have followed, mostly, as one might expect, downwind, out towards the mouth of Loch Nedd.

This pattern of movement on the part of a woodland which was natural in being not limited by towns, cultivated fields, or coniferous plantations – only Loch Nedd itself really got in the way – was one significant change within the overall surroundings of the glen. Other changes were even closer to home.

I have described how that walk around the Back Park was the 'daily minimum' walk for our two dogs. I at least always went in the same direction, along the flat fertile floor to the Holly Pool and the little footbridge, beyond that to the enclosing, fine dyke which we followed uphill until it curved back parallel, almost, to the road, then following it down in a series of little steps, fertile, flower-covered 'alps' which led down again to the cottage. These had changed completely; in their place, as I have said, was a sea of tall bracken.

The explanation for some of this transformation is easy enough to find. There were some small patches of bracken beginning to encroach on the meadows in 1962, but after we had left the glen the farmer had cut quite a lot of the neighbouring hazels which had been suppressing the bracken growing underneath. This, once freed of the covering hazels, had exploded into vigorous growth across the fertile soil of the meadows, slowly eliminating the flowers. And then the farm had been given up, and the cows and sheep of the mixed enterprise were no more; there were no animals to trample the soft growth of spring bracken, and it romped everywhere unchecked.

The removal of so much hazel had revealed, to one side of the Back Park, a slightly elevated platform which had presumably once been a garden; there were a few lovely double narcissi blooming in the spring, and one young birch cherry had managed to establish there, despite the overwhelming bracken. Before the bracken grew up to smother everything, the little tree was covered with dense, white-to-cream blossom, and there was good grass around it, studded with the brilliants of lesser celandines. One soft morning, a roe doe was quietly grazing there, beautiful in her summer coat of rich red. She watched me calmly, unworried by my presence at the back of the cottage. The glen's pair of swallows, which nested in the old byre, swooped around above our heads, and a lone greenshank piped as it headed for its feeding grounds on the flats.

I started at intervals to cut the bracken back, beginning with the steep bank where I remembered the constant sound of grasshoppers. I tried to spend a while every evening, until the midges made that impossible, swiping at the emerging stems; slowly, in theory at least, reducing the energy of this pernicious plant. The trouble was that in the early summer I was often away working, and might come back after a month, at which point it was impossible to tell that I had ever done anything. The increase, overall, in the amount of bracken around the glen has been astonishing; from the Park dyke to the road, and up the hill to beyond the ruins of the pre-Clearance village, is now simply a sea of bracken.

Trying to fight my way around the Back Park one day, following the walking route described, I discovered, on the ascent to the high point of the route, that some of the lovely globeflowers were blooming, though often hard to see amid the encroaching bracken. It was interesting that I had no memory of seeing this flower in bloom in the past, and so I worked some more at keeping back the bracken, as ever with rather limited success. One significance of the presence of this plant, which I had also seen in wetter, rougher ground up beyond the mill, is that it needs quite fertile soil, suggesting the underlying presence of a richer volcanic dyke in the surrounding gneiss.

The above describes what has happened to the drier ground. On the wetter, the rushes which had always been there in front of the house, and become almost as dense as the bracken, have spread, like the bracken, into what had been the best ground in the glen, the level part of the Back Park which I had once seen grow a good crop of oats. Looking at that space now, part occupied by rushes and bracken, it is hard to imagine that it was ever productive land. These monocultures, dense expanses of rushes and bracken, are in fact of little benefit in ecological terms; they are not particularly good for anything and possess dramatically less biodiversity than the rich meadows they replace. There is nothing singular in this transformation; huge areas of the Highlands and Islands have changed similarly over my lifetime. Even well-known places like the Lake District have gone the same way. This is truly a disaster for biodiversity, but it is also, potentially, a real problem. It is hard, writing during the whole sorry saga of Brexit, to know how self-sufficient in food production Britain will have to be at any future stage, and that future may be much more problematic as Global Warming gathers momentum, but it can be clearly said at this point that such seas of bracken will be very hard, if not impossible, to return to food production, even at the level it was in 1962.

In those early days, I saw the glen mostly as the most wonderful playground imaginable. I had no thought then of habitats, no real recognition of the true diversity around us. The cottage is surrounded by natural woodland, parts of which are ancient, with veteran trees, rich with lichens, mosses and liverworts. Within that woodland lies the sheltered, enclosed, marine environment of Loch Nedd and the tidal flats, over-grazed though they are. And a walk up through the woods takes you on to the open hill, that complex mix of rock, flow, bog and loch which is the Assynt hinterland.

One day in early April, after a week away, I awoke to a glorious morning, and decided I must get out. Initially I was rather tired, and just wandered about. I went first to the bridge and the road, where the tide was advancing over the flats, and some sheep were standing patiently on a tiny island of green, reflected in the smooth waters. Better by far than that, two greenshank, slender, long-billed and long-legged, were also posed and reflected, close to me; very soon I would be hearing their lovely piping as they flew over the cottage on their way to the flow where they breed. Full of delight, I went up the road to Nedd, where three bullfinches, two colourful males and one drabber female, were happily feeding on the new pussy-willows, silver in the brilliant sun. I carried on through the township, looking down on the mirror-perfect waters of the loch, up to the corner in the road above a friend's house, where a couple of stonechat, just going into full breeding plumage, were flit-ting happily among the massed hazel. I then strolled around the wooded Nedd crofts, where primroses and celandines were vivid in the sweet grass, and buzzards soared overhead, mewing as they flew. Next, up to Lochan Dubh, where a male goldeneye flew off, and something, totally invisible to me, made the most extraordinary noise; it remained a mystery to me for the rest of this wonderful day. There were signs of otters, and I found an obvious badger sett in the nearby woods; spring-cleaning had begun in earnest, there was a good heap of old grass, the winter's bedding, rolled some distance from the entrance.

I then walked across a patch of open hill, damp and rough going, with no visible sign of spring at all, but Quinag, bold and clear, reared up ahead of me, and, like the buzzards, my spirits soared. I had my own old route down through the glen woods; as I walked, tits and wrens flew about and called, I caught sight of the rich browns of a woodcock's back, and deer were lying in the heather, enjoying the sun. There was a pied wagtail, cheeky and cheerful, in the Front Park. I felt tired when I reached home for a leisurely lunch, but I was elated. Life was good, and my home beautiful and rich in natural beauty. And, perhaps most important of all, after a long northern winter, spring was actually here; summer would, inevitably, follow.

# 26

# Understanding the Peatlands

I have, at the time of writing, known Assynt for sixty years. During this considerable time, I have walked across its broad landscapes, struggled up its steep mountainsides, sauntered along its airy ridges, trudged across miles of loch-studded moor, squelched through bogs, fought my way through its dense woods, leaped across its narrower burns, swum in the larger pools and countless lochs, scrambled up and down its rocky crags, gingerly worked through complex rockfalls, walked the rugged shores and even tested the water in its bracing bays. All this I have recorded in many ways.

For long periods, I noted on the Ordnance Survey map every walk that I took, except the ones which I did almost every week. Most of those walks I wrote up the same evening or very shortly after; I have many such notebooks and journals, reread during the writing of this book – I just wish I had been more organised in my approach to writing them! I have at times gained part of my rather erratic living from the sale of paintings, which were nearly all Assynt landscapes, captured in oil, watercolour and pastel. I have always taken photographs, and have uncounted thousands: slides, prints and in recent years, digital images. I think anyone would have to admit that I know the parish reasonably well.

To me, being so familiar with the land, its most evident characteristic is the sheer variety of scene; it is a most intricate landscape. But I know, from the reactions of many more casual visitors, that they see far less of the variety than do I. Perhaps they are transfixed by the madness of the road (once at least fairly peaceful, now, alas, at times really dangerous), or by the drama of the rearing mountain outlines: the great buttresses of Sail Garbh of Quinag, or the bold drum of Caisteal Liath of Suilven. Or perhaps it is just the rockiness that they see, the endless jumble of crags, rather than the subtleties of the vegetation between them.

All this is understandable, but that subtle variation exists. The *Flora of Assynt*, which I have already mentioned, is not only magisterial and beautiful (which is quite an achievement!), but it is also comprehensive, and lists the habitat-types which may be found in the parish: they are Rocky Shores, Dunes and Machair, Saltmarsh, Islands, Woodland and Scrub (Canopy and Ground Layer), Heath, Mire and Crags, Freshwater (Lochs and Lochans, Burns and Rivers), Upland, Man-made or influenced Habitats. In addition, because of the complex geology, there are often significant divisions within such categories, caused by the rocks beneath. If ever anyone knew Assynt better than I, it was Ian and Pat Evans, and this wonderful book is testament to that.

Apart from knowing Assynt through my own time of sixty years, and seeing many changes within that relatively short interlude, I have tried, as an amateur archaeologist and then on a more organised basis with Historic Assynt, to learn about the parish through a much longer period. The reality that neither a landscape, nor the human population within it, is in the least bit static, came quite early to me, and for many years I studied (and later taught, on courses at universities in Stirling and Glasgow), environmental history, a logical development for someone with my background and interests.

What that lifetime's study of Assynt has made entirely clear to me is that ecology cannot be understood without a background knowledge of the relevant geology (what the land is actually made of), geomorphology (the influences which shaped that basic structure), and their interaction with the prevailing climate. 'Climate', too, is not a constant; there is the fact of climate change, and there always has been. Otherwise,

179

we might be stuck in endless Ice Ages. Soils derive from the interaction between the geology, geomorphology and climate, but they, too, are nothing like static. They may develop depending on the vegetation which subsequently grows on them, but they will certainly also be modified by the episodes of climate change, the upturns and the downturns which are a regular feature of the history of the planet.

I have said a little about the climate of the parish; suffice it to say that we are very far north, and although the famous Gulf Stream clearly does modify the temperatures which would otherwise be experienced, they tend to be rather low, and the prevailing weather for weeks may involve low cloud, rain and driving wind. This is a *very* oceanic place, but that does not mean that it is without warmth or drought, either. Constant change would be a fair description.

I have made some references to the underlying and complex geology. I have in other places provided my own, simplified accounts of that geology, and will not repeat the exercise here. If the reader wishes to examine the world-famous geology of our parish in detail, there are now some splendid accounts, both beautifully illustrated and explained, produced by the British Geological Survey, for example *Exploring the Landscape of Assynt: A Walkers' Guide to the Rocks and Landscapes of Assynt and Inverpolly*. Suffice it here to say that this is an area of great geological diversity, both of types of rock, and in their inter-relationships; in other words, the way they are found together, and the 'experiences' they have been through in the course of the three thousand million years they have seen. This is one of the ancient landscapes of our planet, subject to every Ice Age there has been, and it looks it.

Many of those rocks are very hard, in one way or another impermeable; as an illustration of what I mean, take the hard sandstone which forms the dramatic peaks of Quinag and Suilven. If you have a house built of its purple, gritty rock (like the Primary School in Drumbeg where Colleen used to teach) you will know that it is actually rather porous; it will absorb rain, especially if it is constantly driving from the west. But that same rock is also laid down in the landscape in thick beds, which are comparatively undisturbed in how they lie. Rain falling on the flat surface of the beds in which the sandstone was laid down will not sink far into the rock, let alone through it; it lies on the surface, causing large, waterlogged expanses.

Such entirely natural conditions, experienced over a wide area and a very long time, have led, equally naturally, to the formation of peat. Again, I have written elsewhere about the formation of peat, so will not reiterate that detail, which should, in any case, be widely known. 'Peat' really was a problem, it appears, for many of the early, 'eco-warrior' type of ecologist; they didn't like it, and didn't try to understand it. I have tried to work out exactly why, and think that I have made a little headway. Part of the problem lies in the inadequacy of common, vaguely scientific, vocabulary. I remember when I first came face to face with the results of this not very scientific attitude. It was at a conference at Battleby, where an individual who had been employed by the Nature Conservancy in the early years of the Ben Eighe National Nature Reserve (the oldest in the country) briefly addressed us. He actually said: 'When we took over Ben Eighe, we found that the soil was so poor, it really did not matter what we did with it, so we planted it up with blocks of lodgepole pine.' (You may still work out, if you have sharp eyes, where those plantations were – they have since been felled, thank goodness.) It is the problem of this imprecise, old-fashioned vocabulary: a 'good soil' or a 'bad soil', these are human-centric, non-scientific terms which should never be used. Even 'nutrient-rich' or 'nutrient-poor' suggests the old ideas, which are really more to do with agriculture, how useful a soil could be towards maintaining a human being, than a neutral account of its composition. Soils, or anything like soils, are not 'bad' or 'good', they are simply different.

In any case, the emergence of newer information has significantly improved our understanding, and should transform the way we all view peat and peaty soils in general. All my long summer walks over the peaty moors of Assynt were beguiled in many places by the great numbers of the delicate heath-spotted orchid, as well as the more occasional butterfly and lesser butterfly orchids. Orchids are rather special plants, in that they produce tiny seeds which have no accompanying nutrient source; once they land on these peaty soils, they are dependent on a complex network of mycorrhizal fungi for their nourishment. The mycorrhizae in fact apparently 'colonise the seeds and supply them with food'.

We are learning now about the important role of such mycorrhizal fungi in woodlands, how they effectively help to maintain a wood, even help the trees to 'communicate'. All this is fairly new to me, and fortunately there is one modern writer who makes these new discoveries very easy to understand. She is Isabella Tree, and with her husband she has watched the transformation of the former farmland of their Knepp Castle Estate in Sussex. Since the abandonment of their agricultural practices, the fields have been left to their own devices, and among many changes has been the appearance of orchids. Isabella has researched and written up the role and import-ance of the mycorrhizae, and I can do no better than to quote from the relevant chapter in her excellent and important book *Wilding*, published by Picador.

She writes: 'The appearance of orchids is visible evidence that creeping underground mycorrhizae . . . are spreading their web beneath our fields. Like soil bacteria, the mycorrhizae are freeing up essential elements in the soil, phosphorus, copper, calcium, magnesium, zinc and iron, making them available in a form that plants can absorb.'

How many of those minerals are actually present in our northern peaty soils I have no idea, but the only conclusion must be that the comparative luxuriance of the orchids I have referred to, is supported by those same mycorrhizal fungi. But there is significantly more: 'Mycorrhizae also contribute a final, compelling argument to the value of rewilding the soil, that of carbon sequestration.' While the peaty soils of the north require no 'rewilding', they, in which so many lovely orchids grow, must contain the complex webs of mycorrhizal fungi referred to in Isabella Tree's account, and probably too the substance she describes, called glomalin, which aids carbon sequestration. This must put our denigrated peaty soils (sometimes, in the old days, referred to as 'devastated and degraded'), into a much more objective, modern, scientific context. They are specialist environments, and apart from their own intrinsic interest, of immense importance to the future of the planet on account of the amount of carbon they keep locked up, and, even more significantly, the amount they are still locking up as their covering of healthy sphagnum mosses grows.

Of course, there are places where the covering of peat, the complex carpet of mosses, is eroded or otherwise unhealthy. A particular cause of this is trampling from great numbers of cloven hooves; the old school of ecologists will immediately flag up sheep as among the main culprits here, but in Assynt the hill ground has long been virtually devoid of sheep; they are nearly all on the road or in the enclosed parks. The horses have gone, but it has to be said that in the damp ground which characterises much of Assynt, cattle are also something of a problem as their weight and fairly sharp hooves do poach the ground pretty badly. Active management, i.e. constant movement of the hill cattle, is a necessary part of keeping them on this sort of ground.

Which brings us to the deer. Again, I have written in *Castles in the Mist* really quite a lot about the problem of our much increased deer numbers, and will not repeat much of that. And previous chapters highlight the huge change in numbers in Assynt during my lifetime. Suffice it simply to say that trying to establish what numbers of deer are really sustainable here, and achieving that target by culling, is an urgent task. The numbers we have limit very seriously the possibility of natural regeneration of our precious woodlands, and by trampling and cutting into the mosses which are the living surface of our peats, they cause drying and oxidisation of the peat, releasing carbon dioxide and methane into the atmosphere.

It must be added here that precisely the same process occurs when attempts are made to plant any trees on the peat – or, critically, on the peaty soil. This should simply not be done. It is irresponsible, in that it will add to the greenhouse gases in the atmosphere, and lock up far less carbon, in particular, than is already firmly embedded in the existing peat. Such planting only differs in degree from the planting by forestry companies of the Flow Country, of which everyone now would disapprove. It is, sadly, all part of the human attitude expressed by that employee of the Nature Conservancy to whom I have already referred; the unspoken subtext is that we humans are so clever that we can improve on nature.

Assynt, being the contorted rocky landscape that it is, has little of the vast expanses of deep peat which may be found in the Flow Country, further east in Sutherland and Caithness. Peat, despite being fairly solid when you come to cut it, as I did all those years ago in Elphin, can seem like a liquid; it will grow to fill the small rocky basins with which Assynt abounds, like the old 'loch-bed' through which a section of the Leraig burn loops and which my father roughly estimated to have a depth of twenty-four feet in the dark pools. The River Inver also cuts through a peaty expanse, just a little way downstream from Little Assynt; on its northern side is the bigger expanse of the Blar nam Fear Mora which is a good example of a raised bog, where the continued upward growth of mosses has raised the water-table and encouraged the growth of peat, creating a gentle dome. And if, when driving to Lochinver, you look quickly across the river, you may spot a small section of real patterned bog, such as is found in the Flow Country; a system of long pools descending the gentle slope.

I found another of these remarkable pool systems one late afternoon, when I was making my way home after a very long stravaig over the moors. It had not been a wonderful day, but it had strayed dry, and I had been feeling fit and happy, rejoicing in a whole day simply spent out in the open, watched by the great hills. It was autumn, and the only sound had been the occasional distant roar of a stag; the hill ground now was quite a deep brown, and I would probably not ever have noticed this piece of patterned bog unless it had been against the declining sun, its almost parallel pools lit by the evening glow, a ladder of light on the dark, against building black clouds. It was a new element in a landscape I thought I by then knew well, another of the little surprises which Assynt can provide.

# 27

# Subtleties

There were some interesting aspects to being back in the area where I had spent so much time in the past; every now and again I might bump into someone I had known so many years ago, but had not seen since, something familiar to everyone over a certain age, perhaps. But the same would happen with houses, or places; I would remember that I had been there before, when, perhaps, different people lived there, or, when arriving somewhere I did not visit very often, how it had looked when I had last done so. It happened to me one day when looking over our bridge in what is now the vain hope of seeing sea trout in the pool; I realised that the foot of the pool was not as I remembered it, not as defined. I then took a longer look at the final section of my burn, from the Holly Pool, past the cottage, and down to the sea.

The Oldany Game Book had made it clear that the house party there had occasionally fished the Leraig Burn, and I knew fine that they would not have resorted to using a worm; they must therefore have been casting a fly, which would have been easier before the burnside alders grew up – perhaps that was one reason why they had been repeatedly coppiced and are now so multi-trunked? I knew that these people tended to make changes to their environment if they felt that it would improve their sport (although, interestingly, there were few, if any, references to the heather having been burnt where they were after grouse). I knew that the small lochs and burns were often altered, the lochs dammed so that a small spate might be released through a sluice in order to encourage a run of sea trout in the appropriate season. The little dams remained, two on lochans towards Ardvar, and, by coincidence, one on the lochan nearest to my parents' new place at Drumrunie. The sluices themselves have all gone, but the little dams remain perfectly visible. In light of this, I felt that it was more than likely that there would have been a little tinkering with the Leraig itself. In fact, the Holly Pool still showed signs of this; it is one of the longest in the burn, and in our day there was an open, grassy space on the far bank, which allowed a fisher to stand well back, in order not to throw a shadow over the pool, and to cast over the shallower water towards its foot, a tranquil, clear amber here, with long, trailing, furry weed. The pool had effectively been lengthened and deepened by the placing of several large square stones across the flow; we called them the 'Stepping Stones' but never used them that way, being inclined to take the rather more secure footbridge further upstream. And then I had another memory.

My grandmother had done a lot of river fishing with her fisherman husband, Jock, and she was familiar with the traditional alterations which people made to improve the sport on fast West Coast rivers. She could see the 'ghost' of croys, stone piers, in the section beside the cottage where there was still quite a good pool. There is a tendency for these rivers to develop into simply a series of rapids, as so much stone is brought down in violent spates, and these rapids are not exactly easy to fish. So existing pools were often enhanced with the short piers called croys, built out from either side; these deepen the water-level, while providing tranquil zones beside the banks. There is still a good flow between the croys, even when the river is quite low, which helps prevent migrating fish being trapped by shallow rapids right across the burn, as happened above the bridge. And, with the croys in place, you have a greater area of calm water over which to cast your fly, while the shallows make a good nursery areas for tiddlers; we often saw them jumping under the alders.

So, one summer when my grandmother was looking after us at the cottage, our mother having gone south with father, she put Rhoderick and me to the task of restoring the short croys which she could see had once retained the water of the pool by the cottage. It was not at all cold, and providing you were careful not to drop stones on your fingers (or your brother's!) it was a pleasant task for a summer day. (It did need to be a day with a nice, bouncy breeze or the dreaded midges would emerge from the undergrowth and fasten themselves on bare legs and arms.) I now decided to restore the croys which had again pretty well disappeared in the intervening years.

So, at intervals, in the appropriate weather conditions, I had a glorious time, diving back into childhood, not damming a wee burn as we had so often done, but, effectively, playing in the water, enhancing the pools in the section of stream which I regarded as my own. I was screened from the road by the young alders on the island, so could not be seen; I felt that a grey-haired figure in the middle of the burn might be that little bit conspicuous . . .

It was around this time that I happened to look out of the kitchen window to see two young men walking through the Back Park one evening, heading for a corner in the burn where it shallows over a ridge of obviously very hard rock. I knew one of them, and wondering what they were up to, I went out and asked. It transpired that they were intending to catch some eels; I was interested, as this was below the gentle rapid where I had, by accident, caught those eels in the past. While they were getting set up, one of them asked whether I had any wine in the house, which I did, so I brought out a bottle and some robust glasses. There, sitting on a rather cold rock, we had an impromptu ceilidh; fortunately it was not a midgey night! And they caught no eels . . .

Sometime later, I restored another element of the past: *Periwinkle* came back to Loch Nedd. When my parents had moved down to Coigach, they had put her on Lurgainn, that long and beautiful loch which the road to Achiltibuie follows through the wonderfully grouped Coigach Hills. Through the years, my father had almost given up fishing, and the boat was lying there beside the water, rather old and neglected. We decided to move her, and it took the help of a friend to winch her up the steep slope to the road, in real contrast to the ease with which, decades before, she had slipped down it! There followed a period of restoration, of boat and trailer, before she was towed back up to her home of all those years before. In fact, the weather that summer was disappointing, and the old engine was reluctant to start, so my enjoyment of her was more limited than I had hoped. But one afternoon, I simply rowed her around the dark green, secret shores of the loch, some thirty-five years since we had last done so. There were no seals, no porpoises, and for some reason a herring gull decided to attack a young heron, which resulted in the peace being completely shattered. But a young guillemot suddenly surfaced right beside the boat, which restored my good mood. Typical of that summer, only a few days later, in weather that was more like November, cold with gales and rain, a very high tide meant that I could move her up to a more secure location below the road, but, in doing so, I ended up in the waves, soaked to my waist, trying to heave her around against the strong northerly wind.

I had meantime noticed another subtle change around me. When we were young, and Ardvar was a sheep farm, it did not matter in which direction you went; in the summer, perched on nearly every rock it seemed, there would be a wheatear. These are attractive little birds, migrants that arrive in the spring. As some readers probably know, their name is supposed to be a polite variation of the vernacular 'white-arse'; they have a conspicuously white rump above a bar of black on the tail. They are pretty birds, the male coloured with black, grey, a peachy brown throat and breast, and a dark facemask with a white eye-stripe; the female is rather softer in shade. We always looked for them, and were seldom disappointed. But when I returned some decades later, they were much less in evidence overall, and there were none in the Ardvar direction.

One day, I was in Drumbeg, where there were still plenty of sheep, and they had been hanging around the viewpoint above the nearby small islands. There were, inevitably, droppings everywhere, and on the droppings were buff-coloured dung flies ... and going after the dung flies with real enthusiasm were some wheatears. It seems that if you lose the sheep, you first lose the dung flies, then you eventually lose the wheatears; Ardvar had long since seen the last of its sheep.

In time, deer had arrived and taken the place of the sheep. As I have said, there were plenty of *them* all around me, and I had seen how in a hungry winter they could be desperate for food, and would try almost anything. I had seen that they chewed the hollies into extraordinary shapes, and browsed happily on seedling birches, especially when the first, brilliant spring leaves showed above the dark heather and dead grasses. It is particularly this springtime pressure which means that the existing woods need protection, and that protection, given the existing population of deer, must include room for natural regeneration. New planting schemes have been fenced against deer, but in a countryside as complex as ours, it is often difficult to establish a fence-line which will deny them any chance of breaking in. And, of course, once you have deer in the wooded security of a plantation, it can be very difficult to remove them.

In general, at that stage, I did not feel that they had overgrazed the hill-ground, the hinterland over which I roamed constantly. One year, however, I really saw what damage unchecked numbers of deer can do. I had decided to go back into the past, to climb again one of the grey hills of Eastern Assynt (aptly named 'Creag Liath'), rising up behind the cottage of Lyne where Bill and Ingrid Ritchie had lived when we first arrived in Elphin. That was many years ago, and I decided, when the 29th of June actually looked like a real summer day, that I would head back up there.

It was coolish up high, slightly breezy, but very pleasant, and the walking was easy if you avoided the bare expanses of rough quartzite. The views over the eastern corries of the hill, towards the headwaters of the Oykell and the linked summits of Conival and Ben More, were wonderful. There were lots of golden plover, to my great delight, and there were mountain hares, bluish now having lost their winter white, which I did not see so often; distant views of golden eagles, too. But there were deer everywhere I looked, and what should have been arctic-alpine meadows, bright with tiny wildflowers, were grazed down almost to nothing. Sharp hooves had trampled the thin peaty soil, and erosion was setting in; if left unchecked, all this grazing would eventually, but inevitably, destroy the mossy grasses, and the hares and golden plover would move elsewhere . . . like the wheatears.

But some small, vulnerable, almost ephemeral things, can survive. One day I met the friend of our childhood, Colleen, by chance; we were at the cattle-grid on the hill between Nedd and Drumbeg, and we were both looking for the same thing. When I was young, and we walked at times to Drumbeg for the mail, or something light from the shop, we always used to look for the tiny gentians, purple and white, which grew up by the grid, on the broad verge. On this occasion we found them again: Colleen must have been in her seventies, and I nearly fifty; we had both known them throughout most of our lives.

# 28

# Changes through Time

Assynt is full of surprises; I cannot remember the first time I walked up the Leraig burn, but I have, since, taken a few new visitors that way. Having swung round the end of the Back Park dyke, and into the wood proper, most of them, walking through the birches with the occasional hazel and rowan, enjoying the falls and rapids beside them, believe that they are in a natural woodland. It is very easy to miss the footings of a narrow bridge which once crossed the burn, or the lynchet – a ridge formed by ancient ploughing across the slope – above them, and the strange hazels above the dark water always pass unnoticed. But just a little further on is a very obvious field wall, one side sloped for stability, the other steep to keep animals out. Up to this point, we have been walking through what was once the in-bye land, the productive ground of the community whose houses are above, on the hill beside the road. And, within sight at this point are the visible remains of the little mill which used to process the cereals grown on exactly that land; it all stopped with the Clearances in 1812, just a little over two hundred years ago. Assynt, which many folk want to be a 'wilderness', has been inhabited and worked for thousands of years.

To understand how this and any landscape has evolved, it is important to have a clear idea of the presence (or otherwise) of a human population, and what they were doing at any time throughout its history and prehistory. In the past it was all too common for an ecologist to blame human activity for any changes in the landscape which he or she could not otherwise understand. I have read old research papers which established that the far north-west of Scotland was the first area in Britain to be substantially 'deforested', and that this must be due to human activity. This could only make sense if you ignore totally the geology, which is one, largely, of ancient and impermeable rock, and the climate with low summer temperatures, high winds and high rainfall – all of which impact on the vegetation. And, if the archaeology and common sense suggest that this area was sparsely inhabited, probably among the last in Britain to be settled, then the conclusion of these studies becomes very difficult to support.

It used to be thought that sometime after the last Ice Age had scraped the Highlands bare, and the late, cold period called the Loch Lomond Readvance had caused peat to form in many locations, as the climate recovered an army of bushes and trees advanced northwards. It was then often suggested that the result was a primeval forest that stretched even in the Highlands from coast to coast. This was often summed up in the airy assertion: 'The Highlands were covered in trees, and we cut them all down.' For many of us this received opinion seemed too simplistic, somewhat improbable and maintained in ignorance of the fluctuations in climate which archaeology has made quite clear. The New Stone Age, when all those chambered tombs in the 'limestone corridor' of Assynt testify to a flourishing agriculture, was followed by a prolonged climatic downturn. This lasted perhaps for several hundred years, led to the formation of widespread blanket bog, and is likely to have fragmented any existing woodland. Other discoveries slowly ate away at the simplistic view, amongst which was proof that some exposed areas began to lose their woodland before there was any evidence of human agricultural activity. And, again through archaeology, it became clear that continuing and regular volcanic activity in Iceland has deposited microscopic glass shards, coated in toxic chemicals, over our area. It is impossible that this can have been repeated without having impact on the vegetation; I have heard it suggested that the disappearance of the existing, and apparently poor, stressed pine in Caithness, followed exactly such a major eruption of Hekla.

Also, in recent years, Frans Vera has set out a strong case that the 'Wildwood' of the popular imagination was far from the reality. It is his view that large herbivores worked their way northwards with the advancing trees and bushes, and maintained a complex, mobile and dynamic mosaic of woodland, scrub and open spaces. (Again, the interested reader is referred to Isabella Tree and her *Wilding*, a useful and very clear account of this important theory.) To many of us, this makes a lot of sense, and it is an argument which is supported by the natural processes which are being worked out at Knepp. The lack of big herbivores, or of active management of the trees, may go far to explain the rather uniform, dense, and somewhat moribund appearance of some of our much-vaunted woodland nature reserves. All too often, these are hemmed in by agricultural land, managed moorland, or human infrastructure, with the result that the woods have, to use a simple but critical phrase: 'nowhere to go'. It is often forgotten that many of our tree species regenerate best in open ground, so woods in a natural situation move around the landscape, ebb and flow up and down the hillsides. So often this is impossible; whatever their problems, this is far less true of the Assynt woods than of some others.

In our parish, it seems entirely fair to suggest that after the Ice Ages and the Loch Lomond Readvance, there would be many lochs and lochans, some or many basins of peat, and quite a lot of bare rock; this inevitably means that the native woodland would be fairly fragmented, whether you wish to invoke Frans Vera's ideas or not. As I have indicated, the first significant human population of which we have any proof is in the Neolithic, when farming communities worked the limestone land. These farmers did what all farmers do; they grew crops and kept stock. In any Highland or Island location they would have continued at least some of the hunting and gathering activities of any people they found already living in the area; the game and fish, for instance, must have been irresistible. Sadly, there really seems to be nowhere in Assynt with well-preserved field systems from this period, so trying to assess the extent of worked, as opposed to grazing, land at this time is rather difficult. It may be fair to suggest that the 'good' land, so much of which remains visible in Knockan, Elphin, Stronchrubie and Inchnadamph, would have provided room for both the required cultivation and herded grazing.

As areas of this good land, listed above, are bordered to the west by bog or the inhospitable slopes of quartzite which lead up to Cul Mor, Canisp and Quinag, it again seems most unlikely that herded animals from the limestone corridor would have had any impact at all on the Lewisian hinterland beyond the mountains. We also have virtually nothing which might prove contemporary occupation of the coastal strip, despite the patches of good land which do exist there. I therefore incline to the view that the area west of the mountains remained largely unaffected by human activity throughout the Neolithic. And, judging by the relative scarcity of remains from the subsequent Bronze Age, one might argue that human impact on the natural vegetation was still low. The prolonged climatic downturn from perhaps around 2000 BC will probably have had a much more significant effect in increasing the fragmentation of the existing woodland. There certainly seems to be evidence of considerable change around this time; particularly in Coigach to the south, as in many other places in the Highlands, there will often be found in eroding peat the well-preserved stumps of pine. The first of these which I really noticed is on the margin of one of the small lochs near Drumrunie which my father fished after moving from Glenleraig. They look very fresh, they sometimes even still smell of resin, and it is quite difficult to credit that many of them have been found to be around four thousand years old.

As I have said, the succeeding Iron Age population would appear to be mostly settled on the coast, where the bulk of the sites are concentrated. In trying to assess their impact on the hinterland, it is presumably to the many sheilings that we should look for evidence. From my own rather superficial visits to many over the years, I can only suggest that few contain structures which look as old as the putative roundhouse in Glenleraig. None that I have seen have the very obvious sheiling-mounds which I have observed several times in Skye, and which might suggest long periods of occupation and use. It would be very nice to have more evidence, but at this stage of our knowledge it is probably not permissible to assume continuity of use of these important sites from the Iron Age to 1775, when they were mapped by John Home.

But the sheilings themselves are also very significant in considering another of the popular theories which have unfortunately influenced how people look at the Highland landscape. This theory has been described by one of the greatest ecologists of whom I have ever heard, someone whose wider work should be read as much as his magisterial studies of the native woodland of England. This, of course, is Oliver Rackham, and the theory is one which he has called a 'factoid' – something which is said so often that no-one can recall who said it first and whether it has ever been checked. The factoid in this case is what he calls the 'Ruined Landscape Theory', and he discusses it at length in the context of another area in which I am passionately interested, the Mediterranean. In two rather eclectic but very detailed books, written with Jennifer Moody, after wide-ranging and exhaustive work he has concluded that the 'Ruined Landscape Theory', so often applied to the vegetation of the land around the great Mediterranean Sea, has no basis in fact. This theory, that human activity has led to the degradation and desertification of the natural landscape, is certainly still alive and kicking in the context of the Scottish Highlands and Islands, but the Assynt sheilings do emphasise that it may be as inappropriate here as in the Mediterranean.

John Home's Survey has remarkably detailed maps; considering the nature of the landscape with which he was dealing, it has to be said that he and his helpers did a wonderful job. The map is well annotated, and the accompanying text has a number of useful passing comments. Among the most interesting to me are two that are relevant to Glenleraig. One is the mapping of the Ruigh Dorcha sheiling which is still green, well-drained and obviously fertile. It has stayed so since 1775. Not far away, behind Nedd, Home describes one of the eminences, Gorm Cnoc, as a beautiful green hill. It is now anything but green; as the seasons pass, its vegetation remains undifferentiated from all the other humps and bumps on the lower Assynt skyline; there is nothing anyone would call grass. Since 1775, this part of the landscape has become 'ruined', if that is how you wish to describe it; but the Ruigh Dorcha, under the same management (or lack of it), and pretty well the same climate, has remained triumphantly 'unruined'. Gorm Cnoc is higher and more exposed (and in Assynt subtle differences are critical); if anything has 'ruined' its landscape, it is not human activity, nor even a lack of it; it has to be some interaction between the geology and the climate.

I sometimes took only a copy of part of the Home maps with me when I went for a walk, rather than relying on the Ordnance Survey. This was partly in order to assess exactly how accurate he had been in this complex landscape, partly because I wanted to see if I could locate his old tracks and sheilings, and partly for fun. I should mention, perhaps, that I mostly did this when there was really no chance of getting lost, or when the weather was so settled that it would not matter if I did. I went, one such day, to explore the headland which reaches out into Eddrachillis Bay between Lochs Nedd and Ardvar. The quickest way to get out there was to avoid the near steep shore of Loch Nedd, and, instead, follow the road for maybe a half-mile, before striking off along an obvious ridge of rock which runs towards the north. It gave me superb views before I had to descend to Loch Torr an Lochain, to which we had so often walked in my youth (memories of the dogs and Kandi the cat!). A bealach leads from here through to another, smaller lochan, from where a gentle descent heads for a more open area. Here there was a magnificent and very isolated old aspen growing and I always used to go over to it, almost to 'pay my respects', certainly to have a good look around. Aspens grow in groups as clones, but this individual was far from any other, and had presumably actually grown from seed. Unusually, there never seemed to be many suckers springing up around it; presumably the deer were grazing them all off. Soon after, I found a youngish wych elm which made me wonder whether I was seeing casual regeneration from seed, or whether these isolated trees were remnants of an old wood. Home certainly marked sheilings in this area with woods alongside, so the latter view might be correct.

As I was not far from the shore of the sea-loch, I wandered down there and looked about; in some of the little damp gullies, I noticed a tiny flower growing which I did not think I had seen before, so I crouched down on the damp peat to get a better look. I could see at once that it was a butterwort, one of the family of small insectivorous plants with which I had been familiar all my life. This one, however, had leaves with tiny reddish veins, and the flower was pale pink, as opposed to the darker violet-blue which I knew. I had to wait till I got home, of course, to look it up in 'the book' (normally Francis Rose's *Wild Flower Key*), when I discovered that it is *Pinguicula lusitanica*, or pale butterwort. The following Sunday I was having lunch with my parents and told my father about it; he was a keen botanist, and slightly miffed that he had never seen it – out 'the book' had to come while he checked whether I was right!

I watched a couple of curlews and a family of mergansers, before heading back inland for a while, walking through Strath Mor and down to the very point, Rubha na Maoile, where I sat for a good while, simply enjoying the view over the scattered islands as far as Handa, and waiting to see if any creatures would pass by. It was calm, greyish; being out on this headland felt very oceanic, and things did begin to appear. First of all, a few gannets, very black-and-white in the monochrome distance, then a bull Atlantic seal, swimming tranquilly along; I am sure he saw me, but he was quite unconcerned, and went quietly on his way. Then – the thrill of the day – three porpoises, quite close in, quiet, rather solid citizens of the sea. After that, more gannets, and then silence . . .

East of the headland is quite a deep bay, Camas nam Bad, the Bay of the Grove, the name probably referring to the pronounced point between here and Loch Ardvar, which is still quite well wooded. I strolled along, through a flat, peaty area with quite a lot of prostrate juniper, which rather intrigued me. Growing in such an exposed location, right beside the sea, I was not at all surprised that it grew so flat, but rather that I had found some growing here, far removed from the nearest other examples. Juniper burns very well, but dies when it does, and so its presence might be taken as indicating an area which had escaped being burnt through the many centuries of muirburn. Just inland, behind a flat, peaty zone, is Loch a' Mheallard, which must have been an arm of the sea in times past; it is just possible that the tides once flowed over the flat expanse of peat to its east, entering Loch Ardvar from this side. That would effectively have made Meallard itself an island. I had a good look around this wooded ridge, which I had never explored properly before; again, there is quite a mix of trees here, oak, aspen, wych elm, hazel, a very big old birch growing in a rockfall, a significant number of hollies, some cut low down as stub-pollards, and one multi-stemmed coppice. (Holly is so hard that it is almost inconceivable that grazing by any stock could create a tree with so many stems.)

While I was wandering around like this, I was encountering many deer; some groups were simply hinds with yearlings, but others included stags, some still in velvet, which, this being the very end of August, surprised me very much. I came to the conclusion that there must now be between 100 and 150 red deer between Lochs Nedd and Ardvar. When I had first walked that way, there were none. I had a clear memory of gathering sheep here with Johnnie Kerr, one fine day in my youth. We had walked all around the ground, collecting noisy ewes and lambs as we did so; roe deer bounced away out of the heather above the woods as we went, but not one red deer did we see. Now there were red all over the place, but apparently no roe.

It will be obvious that I am totally an 'outdoor person', and these days walking were important in getting me outside after being confined indoors by the spells of poor weather. They were useful, too, in that for about ten years I wrote a monthly column for the Sutherland paper the *Northern Times*, entitled 'Country Commentary', through which I tried to interest people in the landscapes around them, while also dealing with major country issues. Inevitably there would be a seasonal element in this writing, so getting out and looking around at all times of the year would help provide material for the next issue. But it did go beyond that; my well-being *depended* on being out in the surrounding landscape, quietly watching the lives around me. This was where and when I was happiest, where I felt most alive.

# 29

# Wild Encounters and the Changing Landscape

Living on my own (and being, mostly, quite a quiet individual!), and having no pets, I would obviously be seeing more wildlife than we had, as a family, in my childhood. The increase, though, was mostly in the mammals which I saw as I wandered, or worked, throughout Assynt. It was still quite unusual to meet a fox out on the hill, or even at night, on my drives home after regular meetings in Lochinver. Badgers could often be seen around the houses in Drumbeg at night, but they were active during the daytime as well. I had one or two quite surprising encounters; one day I was exploring the old in-bye land at the head of Loch Ardvar, which is now mostly a birch woodland. I was walking downhill, when I saw, coming up towards me, the very obvious black-and-white of a badger. There was no cover available, so I froze, stood stock-still, hoping that the animal might not have seen me; I have read some accounts which suggest that their sight is not that good. I was as ever clad in old green outdoor clothing, which I hoped might help. I was on a slight eminence, and felt rather obvious, but the badger kept on coming; by the time it was within about ten feet of me, I knew full well that it was aware of me, and got something of a shock when it grunted, and, darting towards me, disappeared . . . what I had not realised was that I was standing immediately above the entrance to its sett!

Driving at night, perhaps back from the East Coast in winter, was often a nervous business, as you could spend a lot of time dodging deer. But other creatures could also give you a terrible shock; during the brief period when I was actually living in Drumbeg, I had survived the long journey from Inverness, and was heading up the hill to Nedd. I was feeling that all was well and I would soon be home, when an animal leapt from the high bank, on to the road, and then stopped right in the middle of it. If, as so often, the road had been icy, I would not have dared to brake, but as it was, I did an emergency stop, and just missed it. It was an otter, and it looked somewhat irritatedly at me, before calmly leaving the road and heading downhill towards the loch.

In the strange way that things can happen, a few days later I saw another otter, under very different circumstances. This was early March, and on a calm sunny day, the sort of day that makes you feel that spring will come soon, and life is worth living. I had done some survey work in the nearby woods, and as the day was improving further, decided that I would take the track to the Dornie, and see whether Violet's husband Kenny might be taking the opportunity to work on his big boat. In fact, he was there, and once again, he offered me the little dinghy. I could not resist the chance to do some more exploration of this unusually sheltered part of the Assynt coastline, with its quiet inlets and rocky islets, and duly set off. I pretty well repeated what I had done the last time, except that the tide was lower and some channels were almost dry. I landed at the first beach and crossed to the main sands, the scene of so many happy childhood days, and just drank in the view. In the hazy sun, it was idyllic and calm there, but I could hear, from the other side of the nearest headland, that there was a noisy heave on the open sea, a really big swell crashing against the rocks in a way that reminded me of a spring day in Orkney.

When I returned to the dinghy, the tide was even lower, and it was really quite tricky to find water deep enough to allow me to row, but, in compensation, there were quite a lot of birds around: several gulls, a few shags and mergansers, several curlews, to my delight, reminding me again of Orkney, two ring plovers scuttling on a beach, and two greylag on one of the wee green islets. And as I rowed silently around a big rock, an otter, almost the colour of the weed, leapt from it into the sea; it was only about six feet from me, and I had not seen it until it moved. I could see the seabed clearly here; it is sandy, with patches of gravel and weed. There were several sea urchins, one large starfish, and a number of fish flickering away. I wondered what the otter had been doing on the rock; probably eating – there was clearly plenty of food in the immediate area.

One-off views of animals seen on such days did give me reason to wonder what exactly was going on. As a look at the map will show, the Assynt hinterland is seamed with narrow routes through its bumpy skyline. One wild autumn day, I was sheltering in a long, narrow bealach, eating my sandwiches, when I heard a stag roaring not far away. That, of course, was not exactly unusual, but, as far as I could tell, the animal was roaring on its own; I never heard a reply. I stayed still, waiting, in case it was coming my way. It was; it duly appeared, and I watched for several minutes. Slowly making its way up the slope across from me, looking very thin and tired, it was grazing in fits and starts. At regular intervals, it lifted its head and roared, somehow as if it knew that this was what was expected, even though there never came a reply. Apart from me, the silent watcher, he was quite alone and unaware; of course it is tempting to suggest that the only thing on his mind was sex, but, in truth, he looked far too knackered for that.

The intricate landscape of this hinterland has many natural routes through it; the countless lochs and lochans are linked by burns and tiny streamlets, up which the trout swim to spawn, and the otters move. Bogs and flows weave their way between ridges of bare rock, providing habitat routes for frogs, toads and the herons that pursue them. The woods, too, follow these natural routes through the landscape, whether from Loch an Tuirc via the Manse Loch and Loch Roe down towards Achmelvich, or from Gleannan Salach via Loch Poll down to Oldany. These linear woods have a few gaps, but in general they amount to woodland routes through the craggy landscape.

Linking up these woodland corridors would make much more sense than the rather arbitrary imposing of blocks of new planting across the map, which has happened in a number of places; planting on the exposed ridges simply makes no sense. And, looking at where trees actually grow in Assynt in relation to the complex geological map of the parish, it seems that these linear woods often follow the line of the many volcanic dykes which criss-cross our hinterland, where the soil chemistry will have been made less acid.

The idea of creating a habitat network of woodland, just as there is of freshwater and moorland, is an attractive one, but, once again, the number of deer presents a real problem. In order to fill the gaps in these linear woods, deer-fences would have to be used, which would further reduce the open, natural quality of Assynt, and cause, inevitably, eroding lines of trampling as the deer follow the new fences. It is hard to see that there is any solution to this; the deer population is an established fact, and the estates, whether 'new' like the Assynt Crofters' Trust and Assynt Foundation, or the 'old' ones like Ardvar and the Assynt Estate, all need to earn income from the sporting opportunities offered.

I have seen not only the spell of regeneration which was underway when we arrived in Assynt, but a significant amount since. This is mostly of birch, waves of which have overtaken a headland behind Drumbeg, and parts of crofts near Culkein Drumbeg. Here again, Assynt is demolishing myths; these are exactly the areas where the sheep have most been hanging around since active shepherding on the hinterland largely ceased. And part of that area was managed by a crofter, a very pleasant man whom I knew, one of whose main hobbies might best be described as pyromania. He regularly burnt his ground, and was annoyed that his croft was disappearing under trees; he often complained to me about it. He was most amazed by the aspen, which seemed 'just to have appeared' and grew, it seems, fast enough to outpace the grazing by his sheep and the deer. His ground was growing splendid straight stems of aspen, and I found others in Glen Ardvar, which I estimated were, very roughly, up to forty feet in height. Despite the burning and the sheep, on these coastal areas there has been significant regeneration of the woodland.

This regeneration is mostly of birch, with some rowan and willow. There are young alders, too, as in my glen, but it seems that their seeds are mostly water-borne and the trees are mostly moving down the burn, heading for the sea. Willows, too, are much in evidence in these coastal places; there are some splendid hybrids which should be more studied and used in new plantings. In other places, of course, the birch is thinning out and becoming moribund; here, so often, the bracken is ready to take over.

The first-time visitor, simply following the coast road and being impressed, as they nearly always are, by the overwhelming rockiness of parts of the parish, might be surprised to learn how much the new plantings, with their inevitable fences, have changed the hinterland. Where they see a few sheep in the small parks, mostly with encroaching rushes and bracken (or new houses), they can have no notion of the hay-meadows or the patches of oats and potatoes which we knew over fifty years ago. And the idea that John Home, surveying in 1775, could be impressed by the luxuriance of the barley he saw at Oldany ('growing to the height of an ordinary man'), would surely be incredible. For me, perhaps inevitably, there is much that is somewhat negative in these changes on the land, but there are one or two places where things have changed for the better.

I recently found, and digitised, two old slides which were taken in 1959, the first summer we spent in Assynt. They show my brother and me enjoying a sunny day at Clachtoll; both there and at Achmelvich I remember extensive areas of erosion, gullies forming in the 'blowing sand' – this phrase was used by John Home in his description of the farm at 'Auchmelvich', so the problem was obviously of long-standing. These areas were stabilised fairly successfully a good many years ago now, and the campsites, which are understandably very popular, were pushed back somewhat from the areas at risk. But down on Stoer Head, at Balchladdich, when I last passed that way, sand from the beach had blown right over the little coast road. As global warming seems to be bringing increased windiness to the north, such problems will presumably only increase. And, along with the wind will come ever greater downpours; we know, too, that sea levels are rising. What effects continuing climate change will impose on the natural vegetation of Assynt, and the wildlife that depends on it, we cannot be sure, but I do think that if I were still living in the cottage by the burn, I would certainly be checking my stock of sandbags!

Although nearly everyone knows that global warming means, for instance, that spring flowers are appearing earlier than before over most of Britain, the picture is not nearly as simple as those words suggest. Spring always was regarded as a rather 'fickle' season, but what was most noticeable, during the years when I lived in Assynt, was the constant fluctuation in the weather; one day almost of summer, the next almost back to winter. I often wondered how the newly-arrived migratory birds coped with this constantly varying picture, which must have affected the ease with which they could catch the insects on which so many depend. Sometimes I would see insects either remarkably early in the year, after perhaps a few very mild days, or having appeared when the climate was pretty well doing its worst. One year, at the very beginning of May, I saw a newly-emerged emperor moth, a creature which looks so spectacular in its colouring that it seemed totally out of place on the drab, wind-blasted heather where I found it. Its wings were not yet dry, but it must already have been sending out the pheromones which attract the males; a few had arrived and were trying to mate with her. I was wondering what they were all eating – the only nectar-providing flowers I had seen all day, and several miles away, were some sheltered primroses.

The next day dawned grey and cold, with an easterly gale. It ended up, as I noted in my journal 'as awful a day as you can get', sleet blasting past the windows. What had become of my sex-mad moths? Were they cowering somewhere in the flattened vegetation? Or were they already dead? What did a day like this do to the new lambs, the birds, the flowers, the trees with their first, fresh, brilliant leaves? How did they all survive in this climate?

# 30

# Community

If our glen has changed significantly, so, too, has much of the rest of the parish. Some changes are very obvious, like the number of new houses, especially on the coast. Most of these are holiday-homes; I remember that the postman, who was quite a friend of mine, once said that around Stoer at least fifty per cent of the houses were not in full-time occupation – by now it may be more. Some of these holiday homes are extremely large, and prominent in the landscape; the planners seem rather relaxed, considering that the scenic beauty of the area is officially recognised. The situation has been made rather worse by a proliferation of fences. Assynt was, in my childhood, quite an open landscape, with just a few fences; some of these are now irrelevant, relics of an older agriculture, and collapsing. There are quite a few new ones, in areas where there are still sheep, as active shepherding is now much reduced, and many sheep are simply moved from one park to another.

It is the deer-fences which inevitably create the greater visual impact. Of course, I understand why people have erected them. If they want to grow anything at all, even at times within the village of Lochinver, it is necessary to erect real barriers against the ever-present deer. I faced this problem when I returned to Glenleraig. I did want to tidy up the surroundings, which were rather messy by then, and this I did, removing bits of old rotting posts, and cutting a couple of patches of grass, one in front, the other behind. They soon began to look reasonably presentable, and I also cut a walk along the level, above the riverbank at the back of the cottage, which was really attractive.

But the trouble was that I wanted to grow things, and the deer effectively made that impossible; in the early spring, after a hard winter and before any grass had come, I saw them eating everything: they tried the rushes, the small patch of Japanese knotweed which grew beside the shed, and a few rhododendrons that people had planted around the place, as well as the first shoots from a young alder beside the burn. None of these things are supposed to be at all palatable to the deer, but they were eaten down. I could have put up a deer-fence around the cottage, but it would have been tantamount to living within a cage, necessitating posts and wire close to the front windows, and between the house and its greatest attraction which was, and is (and ever shall be, I hope) the dark pools and rippling shallows of the burn. I could not face that, and created small, temporary protections for a few small beds of flowers, which I would then liberate if I were spending time outside in the sun and could enjoy their appearance. Eventually, I did build a small cage to one side, where I could grow some herbs, fruit and vegetables.

Apart from the fact that whenever I was out on the hill, I might well meet up with many of these deer (which had not been the case up until 1980, when I had moved to Orkney), it was possible to see evidence of their presence from high on the glorious ridges of Quinag. From this elevated viewpoint, where on some special days I would sit, enjoying my lunch and the views over Assynt, you could see many deer trails, routes repeatedly taken by the animals as they moved around the landscape.

Much of this view from Quinag, by far the greater part of the area of the parish and beyond, had belonged when I was a child to the Vestey family. Although that family still owns part of that former area, the overall picture of landownership has changed significantly. Their policy of retaining ownership of virtually everything in the area had changed while I was living elsewhere, and part of the estate had been offered for sale, divided into a rather surprising number of lots. The story of this part, called now the North Assynt Estate, is well-known, and of enormous significance in the recent story of land ownership in the Highlands and Islands. The group of which I had been Honorary Secretary while living in Elphin, the Assynt Crofters' Union (and which I could at least feel that I had helped to keep alive and kicking), had campaigned vigorously to acquire the rights of ownership of the land under their feet, and eventually, as the Assynt Crofters' Trust, succeeded in doing so. This remains little short of revolutionary, and a great testimony to the vision and energy of the three men who had led the campaign, Bill Ritchie, John MacKenzie and Allan MacRae (all of whom I had known to some extent or other), and all those who had worked so enthusiastically to further the dream of owning what was, in effect if not in law, their own land. This was a great catalyst for change within the Highlands and Islands; much boosted subsequently by Tony Blair's New Labour Government which created the Scottish Parliament, and *its* subsequent support for the Community Land Unit. This gave encouragement, advice and funding to help many other communities follow the trail blazed by the Assynt Crofters, exemplified, for me, by the transformation achieved in the beautiful island of Eigg, which I visited over many years.

By the time I returned in 1995, this Highland-wide process had inspired other projects within the parish. A rather neglected and dilapidated conifer plantation to the south of Lochinver Bay had been acquired by a community group and was slowly being transformed into an asset for the locality – a place of activity, natural history interest, and recreation for the nearby village. The group then went on to purchase a part of the hinterland, an area north of the river Inver, which had been acquired, fenced, planted and then put up for sale, under the title of the Little Assynt Estate. This has been, again, transformed with great effort into a community asset, with local people involved in many aspects of its management and practical work. This included the first all-abilities path within the Highlands, making the delightful landscape and fishing opportunities available to those whose age or disability would before have made it all completely inaccessible. In the most recent of these community purchases, the Assynt Foundation took over what had been almost the core of the Vestey Estate, including the deer-forests of Glencanisp and Drumrunie; it was on the edge of the latter that my parents were living at the time, over the 'border' in Coigach.

While there were many differences between their home there, and mine in what had been formerly our holiday-home, there was one key similarity; both were relatively isolated, and you could walk out from each into the 'wide blue yonder', heading for the lochs or the peaks, or wherever you wished. A brisk walk would soon take me far from the road and the occasional houses, and it was often tempting to make for one of the many 'bumps' on the skyline and enjoy the views in all directions. One August day, a warm and breezy afternoon tempted me out, and I quickly headed into the hill. I was going 'nowhere in particular', as so often, and thoroughly enjoyed getting there; I rapidly became rather sweaty and swam in a lochan to cool off – pretty well the first time that year that it had actually been an enjoyable thing to do! As I pottered around to dry off, there was a guttural call above me, and I looked up to see that a kestrel had decided to attack, repeatedly, a raven which looked much bigger; the kestrel must have been a male. The raven landed three or four times on a prominent rock, which simply seemed to enrage the kestrel all the more; I wondered whether it might have a nest nearby, although it struck me as unlikely that there might still be young in the nest at this time of the year. Perhaps the kestrel was simply in a bad mood?

I certainly was *not*, and I slowly climbed up to the skyline and there sat on some nice dry moss, looking all around me. The view from this point was familiar, and, looking all around, I thought there was something *different*, something strange silhouetted on a ridge across the loch below. I put the binoculars on it, and, sure enough, it was not a new rock, but a young golden eagle, just sitting there, looking all around. I sat on my vantage-point, watching it for ages as it sat on its own, rubber-necking all the time. It was somewhat against the light, and I could not see the tell-tale white patches, but its posture, something in the 'vibes' it was giving off, made me sure it was young. Young eagles spend a surprising amount of time just sitting around like this, reminding me rather of sulky teenagers, and I lost track of time as I waited, in vain, for it to fly from its rock.

We seemed, the young eagle and I, to be alone in this magical land, the famous 'cnoc-and-lochan' landscape of Assynt, watched over by the eternal hills. I had my own little 'rosary' ritual, naming the peaks from Ben More Coigach in the south, up to the great ridge of Quinag beside me, remembering a day spent on each, whether with a companion or on my own. This quiet early evening *belonged* to me and the young eagle alone, in a way that seemed far more real at that moment than could have been possible through the mundane processes of sale and purchase.

But, of course, that was fantasy; every mountain in that panorama, every loch around me, actually has an owner, and now there are more of them. The Vesteys as I have mentioned still own land here; they retained the Kirkaig and Inver Rivers, with their good fishing, and much of the ground behind Inchnadamph, as well as the crofting townships around Lochinver. There are other private estates, too. Ardvar, no longer a sheep or mixed farm, nor simply a sanctuary for nature, is one such, while Quinag itself was acquired by another class of landowner, the John Muir Trust, an environmental charity. So our parish now has a great mix of landownership, and with that goes, inevitably, a whole range of interests and intentions, some of which at times collide. During my time there, I worked with or for most of these concerns; some engaged local interest most effectively, and I was always impressed by the considerable amount of time which individuals devoted to the various projects. There were other community bodies, too, increasingly involved in running premises, if not land. During my time, the community created and ran Assynt Leisure, part at least of the local Visitor Centre, and the Assynt Centre itself, which was a base for the elderly. Historic Assynt I have already mentioned; in addition to the extensive work of surveying and recording, excavation and stabilisation, some of which I have already described, it also looked after the old church at Inchnadamph, and the ruins of Ardvreck Castle and Calda House. There are other active groups also, like the Assynt Field Club, again mentioned earlier. For a small community of about one thousand folk when I last heard, this is an extraordinary level of achievement. I think it is fair to say that some of this activity derives from the encouragement and initiative shown over many years by the Assynt Community Council; this was thriving when I took over as Chairman, and remained so over my ten years in office. The members were keen, deeply interested in the community, and fun to be with; most of them I counted as friends – several I had known for decades. It was, however, a shame that we could not spend all our time in encouraging new local projects – we had, sadly, to work very hard to resist the downgrading or disappearance of local facilities and services, a constant process which was well underway before the financial crisis of 2007 led to yet more years of government austerity and regular cuts. Despite the appearance of prosperity lent by all the prominent new houses, the reality was always that of a 'fragile community', words which we came to detest, but which did convey an uncomfortable reality.

The truth is certainly that community ownership of itself has not brought real prosperity, nor transformed the economy which struggles to support the people on the land. It is still, sadly, an ageing population; more so, in fact, than when I was a child in the glen. Primary schools have been closing throughout the years I have known the parish, and when new secondary schools were established on the West Coast, Assynt missed out. For their secondary education, children from all over the parish have to make the trek to Ullapool, which in wintry conditions can be difficult and hazardous (there is, of course, less gritting and ploughing of the roads than there used to be). Ullapool and Gairloch have benefited significantly from the establishment there of secondary schools; they have been a considerable catalyst for development and growth. Lochinver has not had this stimulus, and the fishing, which was once thought to have such enormous potential, has also experienced this long-term tendency to decline. Against this generally unpropitious background, the community and its many activities have struggled on through good times and bad; they deserve applause at least for that – and much more.

While I have seen all this effort (and been a small part of it) at close hand, I have to say that there exists at least one real problem: the community is just not large enough to support consistently and through time all the ambitions it has or has had in the past. In the light of this experience, I think I would suggest that while the idea, and often the experience, of community ownership in the Highlands and Islands is both logical, praiseworthy and at times astonishingly effective, there are perhaps times when it should be made more difficult, rather than easier, to attract the necessary support, financial and otherwise. There is one real, and enormous benefit which the traditional type of Highland estate owner has nearly always over the community trusts: they are often very wealthy individuals with access to considerable reserves of capital, which some of them (not all!) use at times to invest in projects which offer significant employment to a community in real need of it. A good example of this is the small estate on which I lived, the privately-owned Ardvar Estate. The family owning it invested very substantially in the creation of a salmon farm which was based at their beautiful, almost-enclosed sea-loch just along the coast from my cottage. Of course, they were business people, and set out with the intention of running a profitable enterprise, which for many years it was, but it was also a significant employer in a location where jobs have long been scarce. The pragmatic conclusion has to be that a *mix* of landowning interests is what the Highlands and Islands still needs.

It would be nice to think that attitudes towards the newer landowners are now improving. A while after I arrived back in 1995, the Assynt Crofters' Trust, in search, understandably, of a reliable source of income, began to work on a small-scale hydro scheme, utilising some of the lochs in the Oldany system, including Loch Poll which had meant so much to my family in its fishing days. The overall disturbance caused by small dams and raising the water level a bit in a few of the lochs was inconvenient at times, but there seemed to be a surprising amount of negative public comment about it. I thought about it carefully for a while. Instinctively and emotionally, I did not really care for the idea. It would affect, to some extent, the natural beauty of places which I loved. But I recognised that it was an entirely logical development, one that should meet various long-term needs, both ecological and financial, which I totally understood and supported. And, looked at objectively, in harnessing one of the rather few obvious natural resources of the Assynt hinterland, it would disturb only a small portion of it. I therefore resolved to support it, and duly wrote to the local paper saying pretty well exactly that. After some thought, I added a rider: this was to the effect that when I was young, many of the Assynt crofters, most of whom were actually well past retirement age, were constantly criticised in some quarters, for 'doing nothing'. Now, it seemed, from the same quarters, they were constantly getting criticism for 'doing too much'. Progress . . . of a sort?

Some time later, I was driving along the single-track road approaching Oldany, when I stopped in a passing place at the approach of another local, a very active crofter from the Stoer area, whom I did not know well. He wound down his window, indicating that he wanted to talk, and so in the relaxed fashion of those days, we did; actually only briefly. He wanted to say that my letter to the paper had been read and thoroughly approved of by 'the people of the place'. This was totally unexpected, and equally unexpectedly, tears came to my eyes. This, if ever it existed, was acceptance; I belonged.

In some way, my comment above, that the existence of the community-owned estates, like the Assynt Crofters' land, has not really transformed these places, might be read as exactly the same sort of criticism. But these bodies have no need to justify themselves to anyone other than their own members. At the time of that initial, mould-breaking purchase of the North Assynt Estate in 1993, I remember well that it was constantly being said that such enterprises would certainly fail, and soon. I doubt whether anyone would claim that their progress since has exactly all been plain sailing, but the very fact that now, some thirty years later, ACT still exists and functions, and that it has been the inspiration for many other localities all over the Highlands and Islands, is justification enough.

I have always felt that all landowners need to be aware that the privilege they have, of holding hundreds or thousands, or tens of thousands of acres of land, does bring with it a real responsibility towards the communities on, or beside, those extensive holdings. This hit me powerfully one day when I was out on the hill, working on a woodland project for the Assynt Foundation. I had left my car where walkers are asked to park, and crossed the emerging river below a truly lovely loch by the obvious bridge, following the track along the shore and up into the wooded area. At that point, I could not really remember whether I had been this way before. It is most attractive, the side of a wooded glen, with open grassland, no doubt cut out of the wood, on each side of the track which wends its way gently uphill. As it all opened out, views to the south beginning to show, I could see that there was a house ahead, and suddenly I remembered; I had been here before, a long time ago. This had been the route we had taken when climbing Suilven for the first time; my father had stopped at the house to chat to the keeper's wife who lived there, and whom he knew. But then it hit me like a blow; the house above the attractive wooded glen was empty, slates coming off the roof, windows broken. No-one lived here, and the place had obviously been empty for some years. I could not believe it; this was within perhaps three miles from the parish centre at Lochinver, an area where there was a shortage of housing. Here there had been a solid estate house, set above a fertile valley, and now it was being allowed to fall down. I did not know its story then and do not now; I simply knew, and maintain now that it should not have been allowed to happen. Someone could have been found who would have loved and tended that beautiful place. The crime may simply have been one of neglect, but it was a crime nonetheless.

# 31

# A Complex Coast

Assynt's great mountains command the views of the parish and attract many visitors. As I have indicated, there are some, Quinag, Suilven and the Munros, Conival and Ben More Assynt, which lure many walkers and climbers, but there are also rather less frequented hills where I have often wandered alone. The hinterland, which is for me such a special place, is also fairly quiet, although there are fishermen who explore, just as my father did, its innumerable lochs. The little coast road, now featuring on the over-publicised North Coast 500 route, is far busier than it used to be; this is a great shame, as it means that visitors now have a much less relaxed drive around the long Assynt coastline. This in itself has a great deal of variety and interest; at least you can stop in numerous places and look around. But for a proper exploration of the frontier where land meets sea, you really need a boat.

We had used *Periwinkle*, our family-sized fibreglass dinghy, to explore the magnificent fjord country, the broad reaches of Loch a' Chairn Bhain running inland under the bold peaks of Quinag to the narrows and islands of Kylesku, where the ferry used to run, and the curving concrete of the bold new bridge takes traffic northwards. Inland from here, the sea broadens out below Unapool, before dividing, two narrower lochs reaching even further inland between higher, wilder hills. As we did in my childhood, you may take a boat to the inner reaches of the two lochs, land, and explore the deep, quiet glens, listening to the almost perpetual sound of water cascading down their steep sides. The only alternative is a long and rough walk;

when I did it, I started from close by the sandy loch above the gorge near the road over Skiag, the high ground which leads over to Loch Assynt. Eventually you find yourself at the top of the escarpment over which a medium-sized burn falls to create the highest waterfall in Britain, Eas a' Chuil Aluinn, wild and impressive after heavy rain. (Be careful, this ground is eroded, rough, very slippy and vertiginous if you go too close to the edge.) From here, I would have to head further inland in order to be able to make a safe descent to the floor of the glen; I did some great, long and wild walks over this country, but there was always that steep ascent to be tackled again before taking the rough path back to the road and the car. This used to be sheep-farm country; there are houses down at the shore from which the shepherds ranged over this imposing territory.

I had discovered that Jockan had worked here in his long life as a shepherd, and here he had been hit by appendicitis; in great pain he was carried on a door to the boat, which took him slowly down the loch to Kylesku, and an ambulance which then tackled the long road – all slow and single-track in those days – to the nearest hospital which was on the far east coast. (I had some inkling of what that journey must have been like, as I had developed appendicitis myself and been taken by a more modern ambulance along the faster roads to Inverness; despite probably more effective painkillers, that two-hour journey was more than just uncomfortable.) Since the sheep went, this now depopulated area has been deer forest; in the days when I was walking here, there had certainly been far too many beasts in the recent past. The peat hags, lots of them, were all still eroding, their steep edges cut by sharp cloven hooves.

The relatively sheltered shore from Kylesku north-westwards, via Torgawn, Reintraid and Kerracher (which lonely location had in my time an extraordinary and glorious garden) is, in many places, wooded down to the water's edge. There are wet areas, too, of course, but much of the remainder is bracken-infested; it would make a natural area for the further regeneration of the nearby woods, if only the bracken could easily be controlled. One day as I explored it, I remembered old Angus telling me that he had been close to that shore one day during the Second World War, when a naval ship had come slowly in and anchored. A small boat put out, heading for the nearest beach, and Angus had walked to meet it. As he did so, he was greeted very carefully in halting Norwegian; the sailors on board had no clue where they actually were, and had assumed from the spectacular scenery that it must be Norway.

This section of the road is rather exciting, even when devoid of other traffic. There are steep hills and hairpin bends; it is true that some of it is a little bit wider than it was in the days when I learnt to drive here, and there are several more passing places, but it is still quite an experience. As you turn the corner, beginning to head along the southern shore of the wide Eddrachillis Bay, the ground is more open and there are fine views over the lovely enclosed bay of Ardvar, with its islet dun and fine lodge, northwards towards the many islands by Badcall. Then you proceed over open heights, through wooded glens, beside lochs and lochans; this is my home ground, from Glenleraig through Nedd and Drumbeg, via Culkein and Oldany. From this direction, you arrive rather suddenly at a little bridge over the mouth of the Oldany burn, where there is a hint of some rather nice territory, and not much space to park in, out of the way of other traffic, in order to explore. This is a shame, as it is well worth it. A track takes you down to the Dornie, the narrows between the mainland and Oldany Island, the place where Kenny had kept his big boat and lent me the dinghy to explore the various channels in this unusually shallow and sheltered section of the Assynt coastline. There are salt flats, like the ones in Glenleraig, but these seem less grazed most years, and at times are covered with the pink blossom of thrift. There will be seals, far more than we ever saw in my youth, perhaps a few seabirds, maybe mergansers and some herons, all backed by a lovely mixed woodland of birch and oak, threaded by the lines of aspen, their round, loose leaves shimmering in the breeze.

As you head westwards, this outer section of the coast experiences more wind, and is progressively less wooded; the wide bay of Clashnessie, with its background waterfall and shifting pink sands, is in some contrast to the wooded setting of Nedd, and the new houses stand out rather clearly. Across the neck of land to Stoer, you enter what has always been for me a very different and special section of the coast. Stop somewhere if you can in the township of Stoer and look southwards. The houses behind you are mostly traditional Highland – white, and nicely grouped. Real sweet grass falls away before you to a low green between an attractive loch and the wide sweep of Stoer Bay, backed, beyond a chaos of sandstone boulders, by the tower of the broch. From the village, the view includes the sparkling sea and headlands further south, with a splendid backdrop, the well-spaced 'signature' mountains of Assynt and Coigach. Although the skyline is without parallel anywhere, the foreground view reminds me always of the Hebrides; there is a genuine island feel to this part of the coast.

It is a very popular area, with good campsites; lots of people are attracted to the fine beaches. The sand at Stoer Bay can come and go – there one year, gone the next – but, so far anyway, the main beach at Clachtoll has never disappointed. When we were young, we had simple names for these beaches; there was Big Clachtoll, and just around a rocky corner to the south, Little Clachtoll. Then, ranging further one fine day, we found the next, south-facing and smaller; this had to be, and has stayed for me, Baby Clachtoll. The views south from here are glorious, and the gneiss shore rocky and contorted as it descends to the ever-inviting, shallow, turquoise water. I thought of this area as being the 'Assynt Mediterranean', and here I would often come in July and August, longing for silken sand and warm water. I completely love swimming, and often was deeply frustrated that the water off the Assynt coast could be so alluring in summer, but frequently turns out to be freezing. You could often only make quick sorties, immerse yourself briefly, and then retreat to the land, which was never exactly what I had in mind.

Given the chance, and a fair degree of privacy, I had always preferred to swim naked, and the two main beaches at Clachtoll were obviously too busy for me to try there. I did discover that if you swam around six o'clock, when most folk had left the area, it was often at least possible to have a quick skinny-dip in Baby Clachtoll (although since those days someone has built a house rather close by), and this I did. There is a wonderful, rocky coastal path from around here to Achmelvich, and walking it one day, I realised that below, in one place, at a particular stage of the tide, there is actually another even smaller beach. This could only be reached by quite a scramble down the wonderful rocks, which rather reduced the likelihood of finding it busy, and so I began, when conditions permitted, to use this as my 'Mediterranean break in the sun', during which I could wander happily around the sands, or lie peacefully, clad or unclad, really not worried whether I was seen from a distance. These days I remember very well; I took photographs to remind myself that I was actually doing it, splashing in the water, resting on the sand, trying to convince myself that I was warm, truly relaxed and happy. Only occasionally did I coincide with days of real heat; after a long afternoon spent joyfully in the water and on the sand, I would drive slowly home, salty and relaxed, admiring the soft colours and hazy prospects, arriving at my little white cottage in the verdant glen. If, best of all, there was a bouncy warm breeze, I could spend a midge-free evening outside, comfortable in a deck-chair beside the murmuring burn, listening to the birds, watching the darting dragon- and damselflies, writing in my journal and sipping a long gin and tonic, the sort my father had dreamed of on the endless walk back from a full day climbing Quinag.

Along the coast south of Clachtoll, the beauty and diversity continue; you wend past long lochs and innumerable rocky hills, climb over a height commanding classic views of Canisp and Suilven, before entering another zone of long wooded glens. These run down to attractive bays: the dark, shaded waters of the mysterious Loch Roe on the way out to the sands of Achmelvich, the wide bay between two river mouths of Lochinver, very much the 'capital' of Assynt, and even further south, the stonier beach of Inverkirkaig where another dark, fast river runs into the sea. A bridge over it takes you on an even madder, smaller, twistier road, our 'Lost Road of Ross-shire'. This is Coigach, similar in many ways to Assynt, but a separate parish, another place.

But, in this coastal round, I have missed out yet another, totally different, place: the long headland of Stoer Point. It is of Torridonian sandstone, the hard rock that makes the mountains and the smooth island of Handa, and, bounded by significant cliffs, is a flowing, peaty landscape with one broad valley running down via a loch to the sea at Balchladdich. The headland, like Coigach and others further south, reaches out into the Minch, and as you take the narrow road towards the fine lighthouse, there are huge open views across to the Hebrides. Beyond the scattered township of Raffin, which always seemed rather bleak to me even though kind friends came to live there, there is not much to see apart from the bare hill, the great expanse of sea and the enormous sky. Two little bothies lie down a track towards the shore. We used to know a sweet Swiss couple who came to one for their holidays, and once met their neighbours, fine artists from Edinburgh who also visited regularly, drawing inspiration from this peaceful, oceanic landscape. The walk around the headland, above the sandstone cliffs and top-heavy stack of the Old Man, has been a favourite throughout my entire life.

Because the route via the lighthouse towards the Old Man of Stoer is so popular, I preferred often to approach the great cliffs from the other side, the east coast of the peninsula where there is another township called Culkein, 'the back of the headland'. This, in our day, was I think mostly called Culkein Achnacarnin, from the next township, but it tends nowadays to be referred to as Culkein Stoer. There is a long beach of sandstone boulders, a little pink sand, and a low shore which leads out to a headland of low cliffs with a natural arch. This is the site, wild and exposed, of another of the Iron-Age forts, the point of the headland being blocked off by that wall of massive boulders. Across the narrow neck of the arch, there is the top of a broad stack around which are traces of much neater walling, which, as I have said, may be the base of a small Viking tower, similar to others in Orkney.

From here, you head westwards towards the fine, higher cliffs, which lead to the ultimate point of the headland. There are shags and fulmars, maybe some gannets, and often a lobster-boat at the creels. I liked going out to the furthest point, really just for the feeling of reaching right out into the great ocean, and then would pass above the Old Man itself to the trig point on the top of the highest hill. Here I would sit, as so often before. We had come here with the dogs in the Glenleraig days, Angus and Niall and I as teenagers had looked from here one winter day, and I came here several times when there were sightings of a sea eagle flying around the Assynt coast. (Interestingly, on these occasions, I saw the golden eagles flying above Glen Ardvar; were they patrolling the boundaries of their territory?) It is, always was, just a great place to sit and look over the wide expanses; these are often the subtlest shades of blue and grey, the wide Minch on one side, the jumble of the Assynt foreground now distant and muted, the hills, perfectly spaced and individual, stand as sentinels watching the silent land.

When I was young, armed with the gift of my fine new camera, I had come to photograph the curious, dark-eyed fulmars as they flew past on stiff, motionless wings. Later, I came regularly to see whether we had, any given year, still got a few puffins on the dark-red cliffs; here I had heard the unmistakeable clear piping call of the whimbrels, north-bound in the spring; and on autumn days the skeins of geese, heading south, called loudly as they flew low above me. One amazing day, as I stopped to photograph the light over the sea, an engaging little bird hopped cheerfully around my rucksack. I could see clearly that it was a wader, small to medium-sized, but unlike anything I had seen before. I took a couple of pictures of it, scribbled a few notes so that I could recall its distinguishing features, and on returning home notified a couple of my most appropriate friends – Ian Evans, previously referred to in his botanical role, and Andy Summers, the Highland Council Head Ranger. They were both intrigued, and when they went to investigate, the friendly little bird was still in the same area, and as co-operative as before. My little friend was then authoritatively identified as a buff-breasted sandpiper, a native of North America, a real coup considering that I am the most unlikely twitcher ever! In fact, it spends the non-breeding season in South America, heading to the open tundra of Canada and Alaska to breed, but apparently often crosses the Atlantic, ending up on our shores; truly a well-travelled bird before it hopped around my feet!

# 32

# Time for Change?

Living in Glenleraig meant that I spent a small fortune on motoring; I was constantly getting into the car to go somewhere. If I went east, past Ardvar and under the two great northern peaks of Quinag, that was generally because I was leaving Assynt, whether to go north, east or south. The road west, via Nedd and Drumbeg, was the one I took constantly, often to go as far as Lochinver, because that was where virtually everything was, or happened. It was seventeen miles of single-track road, but it normally took at least forty minutes, often more. Like everyone else, I drove it in torrential rain and wind, through sleet, snow or on black ice, but there were some days which were so bad that I actually did just stay at home in the depths of my sheltered glen.

The reasons for all this travelling were, of course, the usual: seeing friends, going shopping, going to work, going to the doctor, going to the bank when we had one; but apart from all that, it was going to meetings. As I have made clear, Assynt, despite its small population, has a number of very active community groups, and it seemed that if you started getting involved with one, you would end up being asked to join another. In the end, I think that most of us felt that we were significantly over-extended, but as we believed in what was being done, we just stuck with it and did our best to help. My main priority was the Community Council, which only met every month, but even so there were times when I was working away from home for several weeks and could not manage to be there. In the summer, community activities tended to take a break, but the local population most certainly did not; most of the active ones were involved one way or another in work that had to cope, somehow, with the annual influx of visitors, or directly served them.

There were plenty of social gatherings, too, and the usual one-off events. The village halls around the parish were well-used and I went to lively ceilidhs in most of them, Stoer Hall especially, where I passed some very energetic evenings; vigorous dancing seemed the best way to cope with too much good food and drink! Despite the small size of the community, and its overall age, community life in Assynt flourished, and no doubt still does.

My mother had been the first of the family to sample that community life. It was early in our time in the Glen, when our new neighbours Dannie and Colleen came to the cottage to ask her whether she might take them to the Assynt Games' Dance; my father was away south at the time. At that time they did not have a vehicle, which was making life, three miles from the nearest shop, rather hard. Thinking it might a be somewhat rowdy affair, my grandmother was not keen for her to do it, but my mother pointed out that she had been in the WRNS during the war and had coped with dozens of drunken sailors and airmen; a few fishermen and crofters, some of whom she would know anyway, would not bother her. She, like Dannie and Colleen, loved dancing, and, predictably, she had a wonderful time. By the time she got home, she had several potential boyfriends . . .

When I moved back in 1995, there were still quite a number of people I had known well and who remembered me, and from time to time, I reinstated the old custom of visiting them as we had done so many years before. At the same time, I met a whole lot of new folk, made new friends and wanted to enjoy their company, too. But I was also working away for quite long periods, and had family and friends to see as well. True, my parents were just 'over the border' at Drumrunie, and Sunday lunch there became quite a routine fixture, but I had to take some tough decisions in order to ensure that I could live my own life. I did feel guilty that I did not visit all the old folk I remembered as often as perhaps I should but had to maintain some sort of balance between past, present and future.

Living in the Highlands imposes yet another problem. The weather can be bad for long stretches, and when the good weather actually returns, there is suddenly a real pressure on time. There will be countless chores outside to finish while the weather is good, the garden to tidy, a spot of painting to do, wood for the stove to chop and stack, the car to clean or its paintwork to repair. But equally, it would be lovely to get out in the boat, to climb Quinag with an increasingly important friend, or to do a new walk through a recently discovered group of old trees lurking up till now out of the way, and unseen . . . Sadly, often enough there was a meeting to go to, or the 'joy' of a dental appointment in Inverness.

I had, as I have said, arrived at a time when many of the folk I had known previously were still around, but advanced in age. Jockan of course had died when we were in Elphin, but Johan, his wife, was still living in Drumbeg, although she soon had to go into a home in Ullapool. Slowly most of that generation died while I was there, each departure awakening memories of my own past in that place. And then, of course, our own generation started to pass on; Violet's husband Kenny died, and, several years later, so did she. Inevitably, there were tragedies – people killed in dreadful accidents, children orphaned, all the difficult events which overtake us at some time or other, but which a small community does feel very deeply; all the funerals to attend, new graves to stand by.

Although my life continued to be as active as before, and Assynt was as absorbing and interesting as ever, I started to become aware that the nature of its climate was beginning at times to affect me. Some winters were without any clear, frosty or snowy spells to enliven them. Grey, windy, wet day followed grey, windy, wet day in an interminable succession. A real gale, the hurricane of January 2005 for instance, was actually exciting, but low cloud and drizzle, week after week, simply wore you down, and even the old locals started to complain about the unending gloom.

One morning I got into the car, and went up to see Violet in Drumbeg, where she had been living for some years, and said to her that I now felt that to wake up, get out of bed, open a bottle of whisky, get back into bed and watch TV all day seemed an entirely reasonable way to organise one's life ... and she agreed. That year, as I remember, summer fell on May the 13th; the trouble was, of course, that when May the 13th dawned a lovely day, I had no idea that it would be the last decent one until September. I spent it doing chores, outside in the fresh air at least, followed by a quick walk along the road in the late afternoon, admiring the yellow irises between the road and the river. It was good, but not enough; the next day the rain started again, and so it continued. Eventually, when August came, I was so desperate to see the sun that I went to Inverness, straight into the travel agent and said: 'I don't really care where it is, and I can't really afford even one week, but for goodness' sake get me to the sun!' I duly went to Corfu for one marvellous, if really quite limited, week, and when I returned to Assynt in late September there was a better spell, the best in fact of the year, which set me up for the next winter.

Some winters were obligingly snowy, and therefore quite bright; however much disruption the snow might cause to our lives, it was not depressing. Even if I could only walk along the road, once it had been ploughed, because of the depth which blanketed the land, the glacial views were magnificent, the landscape a blinding white, the shadows deepest blue like the sea, the sky a duck-egg green that trailed red streamers as the frigid evening came on.

Within a few years, my symptoms worsened with the weather. I was at the time working much of the time in a rather grim little office, with a 'view', if it could so be called, into a neglected and lifeless courtyard. Quite often, I might see no-one during the day, and I drove back home in the dark. Actually, that is a totally inadequate description; I scuttled home like a rabbit to its burrow, wanting to talk to no-one, simply to get back to base. I was not sleeping well, which is unusual for me, and felt generally unhappy and slightly unwell. I coped really badly, too, with the vicissitudes of life, the people being difficult, the trials and tribulations we all face. And then there came the defining moment, the occasion when the reason became obvious. One evening, not feeling too bad, I switched on the television to watch a David Attenborough wildlife documentary. The familiar face appeared, backed by a blazing blue sky, and I promptly burst into tears. There was no mistaking the message; I had clearly got the famous S.A.D., Seasonal Affective Disorder; the climate had finally got me down.

For a while I tried various ways of ameliorating the situation. A friend gave me a lamp to have on while I ate my solitary meals, I took St John's wort, I went for counselling, and I talked to anyone who would listen – suffering in a very British silence was never my thing! Some friends, it turned out, suffered from it too, and they were very helpful. One other friend, quite kindly I think, said something to the effect that there was still a certain stigma about depression or any other kind of mental trouble. This rather narked me; as I was writing my newspaper column at the time about countryside matters, I took the opportunity to devote an entire issue to my attempts to recognise and then deal with S.A.D. That at least brought me some letters, grateful that I had decided to publicise a very common condition.

These measures, however, were not enough; my symptoms remained, so I went and saw the very helpful local doctor,and ended up on anti-depressants. I was very lucky with these. I had virtually no side-effects, and I did not feel particularly 'out of it' or strange. What I did achieve was a dose of clarity.

I could suddenly see that while I loved Assynt, the climate which I had endured reasonably easily in the years in Elphin, now, some twenty years later, really got me down. And the cottage I loved in the glen which was truly 'home', had been built, rather inexplicably, down on the floor of the glen, quite unlike the houses of the farm which John Home had mapped. It was not even in the sunniest position on that glen floor, which would have been slightly further into the Back Park. In fact, the sun did not touch the cottage from the beginning of November until well into February, almost four really dark months. I could see, quite clearly, that I needed to move, or to spend the rest of my life taking pills, an alternative which hardly appealed. It was a surprise, even to me, that when I reached the conclusion that I should move, it did not hit me with a wave of emotion. I was a very emotional teenager and young man, that I well remember, but time and, perhaps, the beastly things which some people will do to you over the course of the years, had made me fairly pragmatic; it was, simply, time to move.

I was, however, not sure whether I would keep to this resolution; I did decide that I needed to find out whether I could actually leave Assynt. And, fortunately, I saw a way to do this without entirely burning my boats. It so happened that my brother was then living in a tied house, connected with his work, away south in Laggan, and the old cottage which had been his home before then had been empty for several years, something which does most Highland properties no good. That cottage was situated near Spinningdale, on the east coast of Sutherland, where the climate would be brighter and drier than in Assynt. But the trip across Sutherland via the Oykell which we had followed when first we came to Assynt, took, at the most, an hour and a half. If I wanted to get back to Assynt, I would be able to.

And so, slowly, I laid my plans, deciding when to move, and how, and trying to reduce the clutter which I seemed to be so good at collecting (and still am!). In the meantime, of course, I carried on enjoying as much as possible the wonderful parish in which I lived. A favourite, and regular, destination over the years has been Inverkirkaig, an attractive coastal settlement with which my family had quite long connections. We loved its dark river, and often, throughout the years, walked the track beside it, up to the hill loch under Suilven. I remember how my father could stand on the edge of the small viewing place above the dark pool under the fine waterfall, apparently unaffected by either the height or the dizzying roar of the falls when in spate.

If walking the path, it is best to park down beside the river, close to the bridge, and go up past Achins; when we first went there, this was a wonderful bookshop and the family who owned it also wove; my mother bought several moorland-coloured bothy blankets, which I still use, from the friendly Bangor-Joneses. It was also a great pleasure, in my later working life, to bump into Malcolm, their young son; his historical researches have added enormously to our knowledge of Assynt. When I returned in 1995, Achins was still a wonderful bookshop, run by another friendly family I had known for years; there was also by now a tearoom, and at times I exhibited some of my Assynt pictures there. So it was always difficult to walk straight past the buildings, but the lovely walk ahead beckons, leading you at first through woods close to the riverside.

The Kirkaig has all the attractions of my own Leraig burn, but on a significantly larger scale, and with the added lure of a run of salmon. I had joined the Assynt Angling Club, through which I got the occasional day on the river. The one I remember best was in some ways totally unlike the day my family had once had on the Inver, when we fished all day in brilliant sunshine. On this occasion, it poured with rain all day; the river was black, foam-flecked, running fast and high. Half the best stances were under water, the riverside path flowing as well, and I had to be very careful not to fall into the torrent. I tried to fish, and all the time the rain continued to fall; I was soaked to the skin within a few hours, and at length gave up. There in the deserted car park, I had to strip and wring out my sodden clothing before even getting into the car. There was, however, one similarity with that long-ago day on the Inver: I caught no fish!

I have followed the Kirkaig path so often, and many times with very special folk; my family, of course, and on another occasion with our best friends from Orkney. After several months living amid the smooth-flowing lands of the gentle archipelago, Assynt seemed huge, wild, tempest-tossed. On another lovely day, a dear friend, Fiona, whom I knew from youthful days in the Glen, walked the track with me; the path begins to climb, avoiding the deep ravine occupied by the river, and then the astonishing profile of Suilven rears up in front of you, close, intimidating, like no other hill. We had our picnic lunch above the loch, admiring the mountain and the beginning of the long watery way east towards Loch Veyatie and the limestone lands of Elphin. This is the southern limit of the parish, and apart from Suilven, the views are of the neighbouring hills of Coigach, Cul Mor and Cul Beag. That day, we took another route back towards the coast, following a lovely parallel glen, threading its woods and lochs, before cutting across towards Achins and the road. On yet another day, this time in autumn when the bright aspens quivered by the plunging falls, I meant to lead some other friends the same way. But the water level was much higher, and the obvious way down blocked, so we had to take to the heights and clamber over some crags. I was worried that the girls might find it difficult, but I need not have worried, and the views we had were extraordinary. This was Assynt at its most magnificent, a view to recall for all time.

# Envoi

The Highlands and Islands have inspired a considerable literature; in the Introduction I quoted from one of those books
– Gavin Maxwell's *Ring of Bright Water*. There is a very different book from which one might quote with equal validity; this
is written by Alasdair Maclean, native of a peninsula which
reaches far out towards the Hebrides. His book is *Night Falls
on Ardnamurchan*, and is subtitled *The Twilight of a Crofting
Family*, and, as you might expect from those words, it bids
farewell to a way of life which has really gone. The exact mathematics do not matter, but I suppose that Alasdair's parents,
whose death is the turning point in the book, would be the
same generation as the inhabitants of Nedd and other townships whom I first met in 1959.

Most of them must have been in their seventies, the sort of
age when you begin to look for easier ways to do things, for that
little bit of ease. Nowadays, their lives would seem significantly
devoid of comfort and very restricted. Few of the households
had a car; they depended on mobile shops, which still went
round, and the mobile bank for access to money. Kitty Ross'
shop was over a mile distant, and the road had a couple of
significant hills, up which one or two of them still carried their
shopping. Their houses all had radios, I think, but there were
no televisions at all; everyone read a lot, and the mobile library
was an important meeting place.

I think often of our neighbours Johnnie Kerr and Hughac,
who lived out of the main group of houses, up a significant hill.
They had no telephone, and as Hughac became ill, Johnnie

must have gone up and down that hill in all weathers. I did once learn how restricted their diet was; before the winter came on, they got in a barrel of salt herring and a sack of oatmeal. They had a vegetable garden, which provided them with greens and potatoes, and that was the basis of their winter diet, eked out with occasional little luxuries from the shop, and lots of tea. Hughac, of course, was always baking, like all the women in Nedd, Drumbeg, Clashnessie and elsewhere.

Despite what does seem to have been a life of limitation, they always showed us a welcoming and dignified courtesy. Somehow, they coped with the privations inflicted by the weather, the long winter days when the wind howls around the houses, the rain is endless, and you need the lights on from dawn till dusk. That generation were, I suppose, survivors; few, as far as I heard, succumbed to alcoholism, which is, as I have hinted, where depression can all too easily take you under such conditions. I was always conscious of their strength and steadfastness, qualities which I felt I lacked when the long dark days got to me so many years later. And their humour was quick, spontaneous, frequently quite 'robust'; you would never call these folk 'narrow Calvinists', although many did go to the kirk regularly, and the Sabbath was definitely a very quiet day.

Many of these households were childless, so the next generation was reduced in number, and some of those few moved – perhaps east, to the Inverness area, or south, probably to Glasgow. It sometimes seemed to me that those who remained in Assynt found life rather more difficult than their parents had. Empty houses were now being sold, mostly to folk from outwith the area, and prices began to rise so that locals might now be trying to bring up children in caravans, scarcely habitable in bitter winters, while good houses lay empty for much of the year. And as school rolls started to decline, the schools began to close; often the teachers and their families would move away . . .

If that simply sounds like a slide into despair, it has not turned out quite like that. Some of those who moved into the parish, lured indeed by its beauty and interest, found that there was still a strong sense of identity and community, and many strong characters. Together they set out to stop the rot and develop projects to improve the quality of life for all. Some of these projects have indeed been mould-breaking, above all the long and successful campaign which became the Assynt Crofters' 'buy-out'. The pattern of landholding in the parish and all over the Highlands and Islands has changed, but so has what Alasdair Maclean's family would recognise as 'crofting'; then again, so, largely, has that life's privations. But the stark facts of remoteness, allied to the harshness of the climate, mean that anyone who lives there has, at times, much to cope with.

As a result of all this, Assynt cannot really be considered as 'just another Highland parish' (although I do recognise, of course, that every parish or island has its own special features). Assynt's major claim to fame is that it led the process of Land Reform in Scotland, but it has also been studied in real depth. Its remarkable geology, archaeology, history, wildlife (especially its botany), and native woodlands have all received detailed attention. And this is now more important than ever; in the wake of acceptance of the dangers of Climate Change are coming waves of 'instant' solutions, the most repeated of which is the call to plant trees almost anywhere. Understanding the land you are managing is more important than ever, if serious and expensive mistakes are not to be made; we all need to know, and appreciate, 'our patch'.

And Assynt has been 'my patch'. Since I left, I have returned at least twice every year, even if only on the shortest of visits. I lived in Spinningdale in eastern Sutherland for a couple of years, before venturing further afield. But having spent so much of my life in the far north, I am constantly reminded of it, and try to maintain contact with the friends and family members who still live there. On one such recent trip, I spent a night near Dornoch with a friend, setting off the next day to drive across Sutherland. It was a fine day, right across the empty interior of the great county, and I took my time, stopping regularly to get out of the car, look around, scan the hills and breathe deeply of the clean, moist air. I went first past the cottage in the glen which runs down to the Dornoch Firth at Spinningdale, where I had spent two happy and fulfilled years, descending then through the pleasant mix of wood and farmland to Bonar Bridge. From here I followed the so-familiar route along the slow-winding Kyle of Sutherland to Rosehall, and thence via the Oykell over the moors to Assynt, where the wild profile of Suilven beckoned me on. I turned north at Ledmore, and took the road, as countless times before, up to Inchnadamph and over Skiag, almost to Kylesku, before following that glorious little road round the coast under Quinag, stopping to admire the view painted by Sir Winston Churchill, then past Ardvar, descending slowly into the glen to see if anyone still lived in 'my' cottage.

A plume of wood smoke from the chimney confirmed that this was so, and I halted in a passing place by the Point where folk used to camp; the remains of a fire made it clear they still do. The dark river still ran calmly through the tidal flats and down past the black and ochre rocks of the Loch Nedd shore. Of course there were changes along the way; Nedd was disturbingly different, but the house of old Angus Munro was cleanly-painted and well cared for, the grass of his croft still clear of either bracken or rushes.

In a rather quiet Drumbeg, I stopped to have a snack with two of Violet's children, still living in the same house, and then on I continued right round as far as Lochinver, where I managed to see her second son. After this, I took the return road along the shore of Loch Assynt, heading back south towards Ullapool, my destination for the coming evening. But on the way, I halted in Elphin, and was fortunate enough to meet up with the couple who had bought the little roadside house from me, when we moved to Orkney. The croft beside it, which they do not own, has changed almost totally. The byre-cum-barn has collapsed totally, now just a pile of stones and rusty corrugated sheets, and the meadow where we gathered the sweet blue hay now only grows rushes, dark and rank. There was no sign of the waxy orchids or golden globe-flowers which made it so beautiful all those years ago. And the little new house we had built on the gentle ridge above, surrounded by tall, dark conifers we had not planted, was significantly larger, but was looking rather empty. (On a subsequent visit, we made friends with the new owner, an inspiring artist, who is tackling the effects of some years of neglect.)

From here, I continued on over Knockan, down to Drumrunie where I made a detour to look over the house to which my parents had moved after Glenleraig, and where they had lived in their retirement. Here, it is hard to get a good view of the place; the geans and conifers my parents had planted between them and the busy road to Achiltibuie have grown well, perhaps too well, and I could only catch glimpses of the garden they had created there. The back of the house, sheds and garage which are about all you can see down the short, steep drive, looked well-tended, and the place had that happy air of being lived in by folk who care. So, feeling pleased, I went on down the road to Ullapool, where I stayed with my brother, who has taken over the neat house bought for my mother when eventually she decided to leave Drumrunie after the death of my father.

It had been a good day, a wonderful drive across the beautiful North of Scotland. But it had been much more than that: almost a pilgrimage, a tracing of landscapes which for us are historic, deep with meaning. I had seen many changes during the course of the day, some good, some bad, which is exactly what you learn to expect in life. But that procession of six family houses, seen in one day, made one thing sharply clear. This is where we come from, this is where the Nobles belong, and it all started in Glenleraig, the cottage which nurtured us, and shaped our subsequent lives. That little white cottage, in the wooded glen, under the radiant hill, where the murmuring burn runs to the dark sea-loch, is my eternal home, whether I am there or not.